# MODERN SCOTLAND

# Modern Scotland

*Second Edition*

JAMES G. KELLAS

London
GEORGE ALLEN & UNWIN
Boston          Sydney

This edition first published in 1980

An earlier version of *Modern Scotland*, of which this is
an updated and revised edition, was published by
Pall Mall Press in 1968

GEORGE ALLEN & UNWIN LTD
40 Museum Street, London WC1A 1LU

**British Library Cataloguing in Publication Data**

Kellas, James Grant
  Modern Scotland. – Revised ed.
  1. Scotland – History – 19th century
  2. Scotland – History – 20th century
  I. Title
  941.1081        DA815        79–41693


  ISBN 0–04–941008–3
  ISBN 0–04–941009–1 Pbk

Typeset in 10 on 11 point Plantin by Trade Linotype Ltd, Birmingham
and printed in Great Britain
by A. Wheaton & Co. Ltd., Exeter

# Contents

SHETLAND

ORKNEY

SUTHERLAND

CAITHNESS

ROSS

AND

CROMARTY

NAIRN

MORAY

BANFF

Inverness

ABERDEEN

INVERNESS

Aberdeen □

KINCAR-DINE

ANGUS

ARGYLL

PERTH

Arbroath △

Dundee □

Perth

FIFE

Glenrothes △

KINROSS

CLACKMANNAN

Dunfermline

Kirkcaldy

STIRLING

Stirling

12

15 △13

8 9

WEST LOTHIAN

Edinburgh □

EAST LOTHIAN

DUNBARTON

2

3 4

7 ● Glasgow

10 11

14

BERWICK

BUTE

RENFREW

6

MIDLOTHIAN

PEEBLES

SELKIRK

ROXBURGH

Irvine △

Kilmarnock

LANARK

Ayr

AYR

DUMFRIES

Dumfries

KIRKCUDBRIGHT

WIGTOWN

Index
1 Dumbarton
2 Clydebank
3 Greenock
4 Port Glasgow
5 Paisley
6 East Kilbride
7 Rutherglen

8 Coatbridge
9 Airdrie
10 Hamilton
11 Motherwell & Wishaw
12 Falkirk
13 Cumbernauld
14 Livingston
15 DUNBARTONSHIRE (part of)

□ Cities
● Large Burghs
△ New Towns

Miles
0  10  20  30  40  50
0  10 20 30 40 50 60 70 80
Kilometres

Map 1  *Counties, Cities, Large Burghs and New Towns of Scotland*
(1930–75)

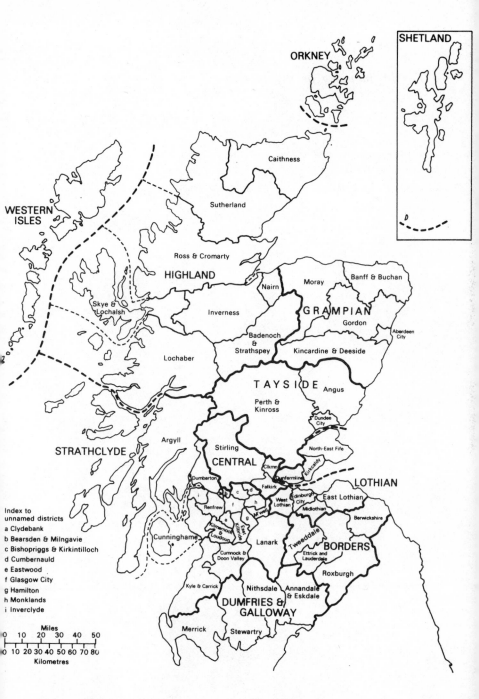

SHETLAND

ORKNEY

WESTERN
ISLES

Caithness

Sutherland

Ross & Cromarty

HIGHLAND

Nairn

Moray

Banff & Buchan

GRAMPIAN

Skye &
Lochalsh

Inverness

Gordon

Aberdeen
City

Badenoch
&
Strathspey

Kincardine & Deeside

Lochaber

TAYSIDE

Angus

Perth &
Kinross

Dundee
City

Argyll

STRATHCLYDE

Stirling

North-East Fife

CENTRAL

Clkmn

Dunfermline

Kirkcaldy

LOTHIAN

Dumbarton

Falkirk

West
Lothian

Edinburgh
City

East Lothian

Index to
unnamed districts
a Clydebank
b Bearsden & Milngavie
c Bishopriggs & Kirkintilloch
d Cumbernauld
e Eastwood
f Glasgow City
g Hamilton
h Monklands
i Inverclyde

Renfrew

Midlothian

Berwickshire

Cunninghame

Kilmarnock
&
Loudoun

Lanark

Tweeddale

BORDERS

Ettrick and
Lauderdale

Cumnock &
Doon Valley

Roxburgh

Kyle & Carrick

Nithsdale

Annandale
& Eskdale

DUMFRIES &
GALLOWAY

Miles

0   10   20   30   40   50

0 10 20 30 40 50 60 70 80

Kilometres

Merrick

Stewartry

**Map 2** *Regions and Districts of Scotland (1975–   )*

*To the memory of my mother*

# Preface

This book is a contribution to the somewhat scant literature dealing with the history and institutions of Scotland since 1870. This is the period during which most of the institutions in Scotland as they are today were established: the modern educational system, the reunited Presbyterian Established Church, the political and administrative organs and the economic enterprises. That most of these can be described as peculiarly Scottish is evidence of the continuity of Scottish history and the strength of Scottish national differences. But it is essential to relate the development of Scotland to that of England and Wales, and extensive cross-national comparisons will be made.

Too often in the past, British history has meant English history and Scottish history has meant parochial history. This has contributed to much ignorance of both British and Scottish history. In this work, an attempt is made to look at the variations between Scottish and English society, and to provide some of the groundwork for further research. It is only from such research that a truly British history can be written.

I must thank colleagues and others for their help and advice, especially Mr Archie Brown, Mr John Haughney, Dr John Highet, Mr Donald MacKay, Professor W. J. M. Mackenzie, Mr Andrew McPherson, Mr George Murray, Mr Peter Smith and Professor David M. Walker.

*Glasgow,*                                                                J.G.K.
*1968*

# Preface to Revised Edition

In the eleven years since the publication of the first edition, much has changed in the social and political life of Scotland. Thus, while the historical sections of the book remain the same in the new edition, the contemporary aspects have had to be rewritten, with much new statistical information. It is perhaps an indication of how much Scotland is 'on the move' that so many changes have been necessary. Yet many of the basic continuities remain, or return in cycles.

*Glasgow,*                                                          J.G.K.
*1979*

# Chapter 1

# The Meaning of Scotland

There is always argument about the meaning of Scotland. Is it a nation? a sort of state? a region? or what? No one argues about the meaning of England, although exactly the same difficulties of definition occur there too. This is because Englishmen seem equally happy to use England in place of Britain or the United Kingdom when they are talking about a *state*, as they are to confine the term to the England of the atlases when dealing with a *nation*. In most cases, they are unaware of any difference between these 'two Englands'.

One might expect the Scots (or anyone else) to have no problem in identifying Scotland. And this is the case. There is only one possible location of Scotland: to the north of England. As the term is never used as a synonym for the British state, it lacks the double meaning which is ever-present in the word England. However, this does not tell us the meaning of Scotland. If Scotland were merely a geographical expression, its usage could be resolved by cartographers. But Scotland was once a state, with a developed nationality of its own which it has retained even though its statehood is no more. Yet, while it is not a state, even in the sense used in federal systems, it is more than just a unit of local government. It has preserved important institutions from its period of independence: its own law, religious Establishment and educational system; and it has political institutions not enjoyed by any mere region of England: the Scottish Office and the Scottish Committees of the House of Commons.

These are all facts which can be discovered easily by the most casual observer. They are paralleled by the cases of Wales and Northern Ireland within the United Kingdom – but not exactly. Wales made no Treaty of Union with England: it was conquered. Memories of independent statehood are dim indeed in Wales, and Welsh institutions were not maintained under the British constitution as were those of Scotland. Even today there is no Welsh law, no independent Welsh educational system, and no Welsh religious

Establishment. The political institutions which have so recently been granted to Wales (Welsh Grand Committee, 1960, and Welsh Office, 1964) have functions covering only a small area of Welsh life. While national sentiment may be more powerful in Wales than in Scotland, with a stronger linguistic basis, continuous administration from England has erased most of the specifically Welsh social institutions.

Northern Ireland is different again. Ulster was granted autonomy only because Catholic Ireland demanded independence from Britain. In 1920, the British government hoped to include both Southern and Northern Ireland within the United Kingdom by giving each Home Rule in the shape of a government and parliament. These were to have jurisdiction over domestic affairs, leaving imperial matters to London. Only the Ulstermen accepted this scheme, although they would have been just as glad to have remained firmly within the old unitary system. The south threw it out and fought its way to separation and statehood. Thus arose the paradox of Ulster, with its political status close to independence but its loyalty and national sentiment closer to union with England. It is even questionable whether a national consciousness exists in Ulster: British patriotism and the Union Jack predominate.

Clearly Wales and Northern Ireland cannot help to explain the case of Scotland. The Scots united with England in 1707 on a voluntary basis, and nothing that has happened since has changed their overwhelming consent to the Union. They were not conquered, nor were they set up in business by mistake. They knew that, on balance, it was better to 'come in', with safeguards, than to 'stay out'; and as they had been 'half in' since the Union of the Crowns of Scotland and England in 1603, government from London was not a great novelty.

However, this was not the only sense in which Scotland was close to England. And here is the 'Scottish dilemma'. For centuries the social and cultural development of Scotland had been linked with that of England, but the English influence was probably the least important of three competing cultures which dominated Scottish history. The first may be described as native. Separate statehood created the Scottish nation out of the ethnic confusion of Picts, Britons, Scots, Norsemen and Angles who inhabited northern Britain. By force of arms the Scottish Crown established itself in stages over more and more of the country, until present-day Scotland was its domain. Only then could the Scottish nation emerge, for the Scottish state preceded the nation. The same process took place in England, in France, in Spain and in Portugal.

The Scottish nation-state was bound to react negatively to England, its 'bad neighbour'. Out of the dynastic struggles of the Scottish wars of independence came the first anti-English feelings in Scotland, the essential precondition for its nationalism. The English were foreign, hostile and strange. All Scots could unite against them, if for no other purpose.

Peace hardened the division between the nations. At the Reformation, England chose an Episcopalian Reformed Church, Scotland a Presbyterian one. The laws, educational institutions and literature of each grew apart: England developing its own in virtual isolation, Scotland looking to the rest of Europe for part of its inspiration. This was the second cultural influence on Scotland, and it became natural, indeed necessary, for its people to leapfrog over England to the Continent for political allies, for trade and for cultural stimulus. Scotland took Calvinism, Roman law, its architecture and much of its outlook on life from Europe, especially France, the standby of the 'Auld Alliance'. Scots travelled freely in Europe, as soldiers of fortune and as students at the universities. There they found a culture (or cultures) that was more appealing than that of England, in which country, if they were allowed to enter at all, they were frequently treated wtih ridicule or hostility. For many years after the Union of 1707, Scots were looked on as foreigners in England, and it was probably Queen Victoria who finally brought harmony to the nations. She lived in Balmoral for much of the year, preferred the Presbyterian Church service to that of the Anglicans, and surrounded herself with kilted servants, even in London. To her is due the fact that the Victorian age is the first truly *British* age.

Try as he might, no Scot could turn his back on England in any age, and the third direction of Scotland's cultural development has always been the much-feared process of anglicisation. Anglicisation means becoming English, and it has been in progress ever since Queen Margaret (Saint Margaret) set foot on Scottish soil from England in the eleventh century – most noticeably, of course, in the language.

Scottish nationality is not linguistic, for there is no Scottish language. There is Gaelic, the language of the Highlands, which today is spoken by only 1·6 per cent of the Scottish population; and there is English, the official language in Scotland since Latin was dropped (a process delayed in the universities until the middle of the eighteenth century and even now preserved in graduation ceremonies). Nearly everyone speaks English in Scotland today, and the vast majority spoke English at the time of the Union. But they spoke English in a peculiar, Scottish, way. In rural districts, this Scottish dialect or dialects was barely intelligible to the outsider, even to a Scot of another district, and it was rich in its own words and phrases. Some of this language has been preserved in literature, through ballads, but its tradition is mostly oral, of which there are many survivals to this day. In the towns and among the educated people, a modified Scots was spoken and written, closer to English, but still distinctively

Scottish. Most Scottish poetry and the early Scottish drama is in this form, but there is little prose literature to compare with it. The absence of a prose literature in Scots does not mean that Scots have confined their literary efforts to poetry. Tobias Smollett, Sir Walter Scott, Thomas Carlyle, Robert Louis Stevenson and James Barrie all wrote prose, and they were Scots. But they wrote *in English*, and when they described Scottish life their feelings were expressed in the mould of the language native to Englishmen.

To some Scots this seems to deny the very existence of Scottish nationality, for they claim that when a nation has to express its thoughts in the language of another nation it ceases to have a life of its own. Thus, the poet and critic Edwin Muir considered that the linguistic division in Scotland means '. . . that Scotsmen feel in one language and think in another; that their emotions turn to the Scottish tongue, with all its associations of local sentiment, and their minds to a standard English which for them is almost bare of associations other than those of the classroom' (Muir, 1936, p. 21). Here is 'a divided Scottish consciousness', which goes beyond literature into all Scottish life: being and thinking Scots and English at the same time. 'To most of us who were born and brought up in Scotland dialect Scots is associated with childhood, and English with maturity' (Muir, 1936, p. 71). This, Muir felt, was fatal for a separate Scottish literature, which had no unity, and also for the Scottish nation, 'for no civilisation can exist without a speech in which it can express both its thought and its passion' (Muir, 1936, p. 70).

Not many political scientists today take such a simple view of nationality or of culture. While a language is a dividing line between some nations, such as the French and the Germans, with others it matters scarcely at all (the Swiss and the Americans). Even when nations which have a pronounced national consciousness but a weak national language, such as the Irish and Welsh, seek to stimulate that language, they need hardly bother, for their nationality does not depend on linguistic differences. And so it is with the Scots. The English language is shared by too many nations to be the touchstone of nationality and it is flexible enough to express the needs of widely varying cultures. Thus the heart-searchings of Scottish literary critics and creative artists have little relevance to the real differences between Scotland and England.

Unfortunately, many insist that Scots must develop and use their own language, whatever that is, and no other. A synthetic 'Scots' or 'Lallans' is the language of Hugh MacDiarmid's poetry, and a curious archaic metre and vocabulary pervades Lewis Grassic Gibbon's trilogy *A Scots Quair*. These forms of expression were the conscious creations of the leaders of Scotland's twentieth-century literary renaissance, and they were attempts to recapture the age (prior to 1603) when Scotland's language and consciousness were 'undivided'. Both MacDiarmid's poetry and Gibbon's prose have been recognised as works of genius, but the relation between the language used by them and the language spoken in Scotland is not resolved. No one in Scotland talks or writes (or thinks?) as MacDiarmid or Gibbon wrote, and indeed many Scots find it difficult to understand some of the words they use. The linguistic nationalists cannot return to a period in Scottish history, if one ever existed, in which Scotsmen spoke a purely Scottish language, and they are absolutely unable to create such a situation today. Most would agree that literary creation in Scotland should use the language which it needs, and which is capable of being understood.

But the cultural dilemma in Scotland is not just about anglicisation. Edwin Muir regretted the influence of English on Scotland's nationality, but he also attacked Calvinism, and a whole generation of modern Scots has grown up to place the blame for all Scotland's apparent shortcomings squarely on the shoulders of the 'Fathers of the Kirk'. The Presbyterian Establishment in Scotland, it is said, imposed the English language on Scotland through the Bible, its catechisms and its sermons; it warned the Scottish people that all art, beauty and pleasure were sinful and must be avoided on pain of hell-fire; it turned a happy, extrovert nation into a morose and unsmiling set of hypocritical Philistines. If this were all true, as Muir seemed to believe that it was, and others today undoubtedly do believe that it was, 'then the Reformation truly signalised the beginning of Scotland's decline as a civilised nation' (Muir, 1936, p. 24).

Yet the Presbyterian scapegoat is really no more convincing than the English *bête noire*. Scotland did not have Presbyterianism imposed on it from outside, although it was in two minds for over a century whether to accept it as its Established religion. The so-called evils of the Calvinist ethos were present in England too, but they were drowned or balanced by other, milder tempers. It would be trite to say that Scotland got the Knox it deserved, but there were certainly many people in Scotland, and beyond (Bonnie Prince Charlie included), who would have gladly replaced Presbyterianism with Episcopalianism or Roman Catholicism, if the Scots had let them.

Similarly, there is a belief that Scotland has always been dominated by ministers of religion. Henry Buckle, who was otherwise percipient, wrote that Scotland seemed to resemble Spain, for:

> Both nations have allowed their clergy to exercise immense sway, and both have submitted their actions, as well as their consciences, to the authority of the Church. As a natural consequence, in both countries, intolerance has been, and still is, a crying evil; and in matters of religion, a bigotry is habitually displayed, discreditable

indeed to Spain, but far more discreditable to Scotland, which has
produced many philosophers of the highest eminence, who would
willingly have taught the people better things, but who have vainly
attempted to remove from the national mind that serious blemish
which mars its beauty, and tends to neutralise its many other
admirable qualities. (Buckle, 1904, pp. 4–5)

There was (and is) intolerance in Scotland, and bigotry, and the
Church has always had great authority – but not in the manner of
the Church in Spain. In the Presbyterian Establishment, the clergy
have only an equal vote with the laity, and the individual minister has
to compete with the authority of his 'elders', the chief laymen of the
congregation. In the past, these elders often tyrannised the Scottish
clergy, watching their every move to see whether they offended against
the Bible's injunctions. They tyrannised the people, too, with their
kirk session inquisitions and public humiliations.

However, they could not contain Scottish individualism (another
paradox). The Scot was religious, intolerant and bigoted, but not
because the Church demanded it of him, rather because he demanded
it of the Church. The late eighteenth-century Church of Scotland
was settling down nicely to a period of broad-minded Moderatism,
in which most views and the arts could be tolerated, when a whirl-
wind of Evangelism swept through the country. People now believed
that there could be only one true road to salvation. The result was
very different in Scotland from that in Spain: while Spain found
unity in Rome, Scotland's Presbyterian path to heaven was as stony
and as ambiguous as those in the Grampian Mountains themselves.
Time after time, the Established Church was forsaken for a 'purer'
alternative, and the record of schisms and reunions among the
Presbyterian Churches must be charted in the manner of the London
Underground map. If the Scot was dominated by his Church, then
there were almost as many Churches as Scots.

Is there no truth, then, in the charge that Calvinism destroyed
Scotland's culture? Of course there is. The Protestant reformers
sought to erase all the symbols of popish idolatry, which included the
entire panoply of art, good and bad, associated with the Roman
Catholic Church. Man should have no images other than God, who
also should not be represented in pictorial form. Dramatic imperson-
ations came under the ban, and the use of musical instruments. The
view was strongly held that the reading of books, other than the
Bible and *Pilgrim's Progress*, might lead towards temptation, and
could certainly not be tolerated on the Sabbath. By the nineteenth
century, Sabbath observance had reached such a pitch in some parts
of Scotland that even walking for recreation or smiling on a Sunday
denoted sin. The Church controlled the educational system, and

impressed upon generation after generation the absolute frivolity of spending time on non-academic or non-utilitarian subjects. Creative activity should proceed along two lines only: the production of abstract theories and the accumulation of wealth. The notion that Man might benefit from paintings, sculpture, music or literature was never considered in a Scot's education, and rarely is today.

Would Scotland have been much different without Calvinism? Certainly, Calvinism took root on fertile soil in Scotland, as it did in other parts of northern and central Europe, but it coexisted with other social forces which in many periods and places were just as strong. Even in its Victorian heyday, Presbyterianism left the industrial masses largely untouched, and in Glasgow and the other cities there existed a proletarian culture which owed little to the Kirk. Rural and Highland Scotland too may have appeared under the domination of religion on Sundays, but during the rest of the week a hard-drinking, hard-toiling and mundane pattern of life was forced on the people by their economic circumstances.

Only a leisured, wealthy society can support organised culture, and Scotland as a whole has never had such a society. Even the Scottish aristocracy was poor by English standards, and those who could afford it lived in London for most of the year. The new-rich industrialists of Central Scotland were the same as their counterparts in the north of England: men who never ceased to work in pursuit of the one thing they understood – material success. Only Edinburgh had the type of society which could sustain the arts. In the eighteenth century, it was known as the 'Athens of the North', and frequented by philosophers, painters and poets. Today, it has the Edinburgh Festival, perhaps grudged on account of its expense by City Fathers and ratepayers, but apparently permanent nevertheless. It was the brainchild of an English opera director, Rudolf Bing, and the artistic directors who followed him have invariably been non-Scottish. So too are the artistic directors of many theatrical enterprises in Scotland.

It is often remarked that the Edinburgh Festival and the other major artistic endeavours in Scotland have failed to produce any great change in the cultural climate. One disillusioned critic (an exiled Scot, who, needless to say, harboured the usual love–hate feeling of exiles for Scotland) wrote of the twenty-first Edinburgh Festival (1967): 'Festival time in Edinburgh seems to have joined tartanry, militarism, Burns and Scott . . . as a constituent of the Great Scottish Dream' (Nairn, 1967).

There is a Scottish Dream, or Scottish Myth,[1] and it is a part of Scottish national consciousness (or unconsciousness?). But as the quotation shows, it is jumbled and inconsistent. Anti-cultural as they may be, the Scots have yet chosen a poet, Robert Burns, as the object of their principal national day of celebration, 'Burns Nicht' (25

January). What feeling for poetry goes into these occasions it would be difficult to say, but the sentiments expressed in Burns's poems are dear indeed to Scotsmen. His simple and lyrical defence of the inherent dignity of man, unbent by privilege; his defiance of the 'unco guid' or affectedly righteous; above all his attitude towards romantic love, which must prevail despite Calvinist morality – all have expressed the Scottish Dream directly to the Scottish people, and to like-minded peoples throughout the world (Russia in particular). In England, no poet has achieved such a popular following, and there is no similar poetic national festival.

Another indication of the way Scots like to see themselves is provided by the Scottish communications media. Scotland has its own newspapers, magazines, television and radio; although the London media circulate in Scotland, they are not nearly as powerful there as is sometimes supposed. The *Daily Express* is published in a separate Scottish edition as the *Scottish Daily Express*, and a comparison of the London and Scottish editions reveals marked differences. A great part of the Scottish version is devoted to Scottish news, editorial comment and sports. Apart from this hybrid (and its sister paper the *Scottish Sunday Express*), there are also purely Scottish newspapers.[2] Three are 'nationals': the *Scotsman*, the *Glasgow Herald* and the *Daily Record*; and there are provincial morning dailies in Aberdeen *(Press and Journal)* and Dundee *(Courier and Advertiser)*. Scottish Sunday newspapers are the *Sunday Post* and *Sunday Mail*.

Table 1.1   *Circulations of the principal Scottish newspapers (1976)*

| | |
|---|---|
| Sunday Post | 1,000,000+ |
| Sunday Mail | 766,484 |
| Daily Record | 676,022 |
| Scottish Daily Express | 345,340 |
| Scottish Sunday Express | 206,560 |
| (Aberdeen) Press and Journal | 112,708 |
| Glasgow Herald | 108,750 |
| (Dundee) Courier and Advertiser | 100,000 |
| Scotsman | 89,576 |

Evening papers in Glasgow, Edinburgh, Dundee and Aberdeen are extremely popular. Eighty-three per cent of morning paper and 74 per cent of Sunday paper circulation in Scotland is produced in Scotland.

*Source:* D. Hutchison (ed.), *Headlines: The Media in Scotland* (Edinburgh: EUSPB, 1978), pp. 78–80.

It is possible to study Scottish society through these newspapers, for the great majority of Scots read only the Scottish (pure or hybrid) press, (see Table 1.1). The two 'serious' dailies *(Scotsman* and *Glasgow Herald)* reflect middle-class society in Edinburgh and Glasgow respectively. The former habitually dwells on the place of Scotland in Britain, and reports at length on Church, educational and legal matters. Its correspondence columns are never silent for long on Home Rule for Scotland, the merits of Scottish education over English, and the threat to Presbyterianism from Episcopacy. The atmosphere is smug, if a little melancholic. The *Glasgow Herald*, on the other hand, spends little time on culture or nationalism. It is firmly committed to the Union, and its readers are the commercial leaders of the Western Lowlands. Densely-packed pages of small advertisements show that its feet are firmly on the ground, and far removed from misty romanticism.

If Scotland is remarkable within Britain in having two 'quality' newspapers of its own, it is also unique in the style of one section of its popular press. Here an examination of the D. C. Thomson publications is profitable. These range from the famous comics such as *Dandy* and *Beano* (which circulate throughout Britain) to the intensely local *People's Journal*, a weekly tabloid with several regional editions. The most important D. C. Thomson publication is the *Sunday Post*, which, with a circulation of over a million, is read by over three-quarters of the adult population of Scotland.

The image of Scotland purveyed by the *Sunday Post* is a curiously archaic one. The comic strip 'The Broons' shows a Glasgow family of the 1920s or earlier, Gran'paw with a Keir Hardie beard and handlebar moustache, and Paw also moustached. As far as can be seen, this is not a historical exercise, but is intended to represent contemporary Scotland. Other parts of the paper reveal similar curiosities. The journalese is chatty or 'couthy' to a degree, and trivial items (never, be it noted, concerning sex) predominate. Here is an example from 17 September 1967:

MRS MCGRAW DISLOCATED HER NECK
TURNING IN THE BED
Last Saturday morning Mrs Zena McGraw, 3 Balhall Crescent, Menmuir, near Brechin, was having a wee long lie.

Oh, it was lovely not to have to jump out of bed and get on with the housework.

She snuggled down into the sheets, and rolled over to make herself more comfortable.

And as she turned – snap! She felt a stab of pain in her neck.

She tried to straighten her head up. But she couldn't.

Heavens! What had happened? Her head was locked at an angle, tilted on one side . . .

So it goes on, and there are more items like it in the same issue.

Editorially, the *Sunday Post* is extremely right wing. It refuses to recognise trade unions and constantly campaigns against socialism, the welfare state ('Never has so much been given to so many for so little. Idleness is encouraged more and more'), and irreligion. Its readers, however, are predominantly Labour in politics, and presumably remain unaffected by this aspect of the paper.

I should say that the *Sunday Post* gives us another aspect of the Scottish Dream. This is the feeling that Scotland is a community in which the individual counts for more than the state, and can do all things by his own effort. But the problems of the individual which can be openly discussed are limited to medical ailments, domestic upsets and tiffs with officialdom. There can be no details of serious crime or sex on a Sunday, for such would destroy the moral fibre of the nation. Instead, trivialities, football and a religious pep-talk (the Frances Gay column). This must be the only popular Sunday paper which has never printed a 'pin-up' photograph during its whole existence.

If this is the self-image of Scotland, how does the reality match up to the dream? Egalitarianism and democracy have been aims in Scottish society from an early date, and their effect can be traced in the social institutions of the country. The educational system, with its ladder of opportunity for the talented, and the Presbyterian Churches with their representative courts, are evidence, not of the total realisation of the aims which were set them, but of a centuries-long national striving in that direction. No such striving is evident in England until much later.

The rest of the Scottish Dream is unfulfilled. The 'unco guid' and the Calvinist morality still oppose the natural man in Scotland, who, when he bursts forth, as he does when drunk or at football matches, is a much more violent creature than the Englishman. Romantic love and lyricism may have been inborn in Burns, but they are conspicuously absent in most Scots. A hard climate and a hard economy do not produce a nation of lovers, nor indeed of a people who show much sensitivity of any kind. One has only to examine the man-made edifices in most of Scotland – which in their ugliness conflict so blatantly with the natural beauty of the scenery – to appreciate this fact. There is no architecture in the world, one feels, so dismal as that of the typical Scottish town, with its monotonous rows of tenements and council houses. Yet even Glasgow is set down at the edge of the Highlands, and snow-topped mountains are visible in winter from near the city centre itself.

The *Sunday Post* picture of Scotland's good-neighbourliness, in which life's problems can be solved by writing to 'the Doc', or 'the Queries Man', is a typically Scottish form of escapism. Scotland has problems of housing, unemployment and religious bitterness which make it a society torn by class and racial tensions. Scots often prefer not to discuss these, and when they think of Scotland they conjure up a picture of the past. The *Sunday Post* does this too, with its back-ward-looking comic strip, and it seems intent on preserving a fictitious Scottish society of days gone by. Here too is the attitude of 'Wha's like us?', and a rigid social conservatism, which together are the most violent contradictions of the democratic and egalitarian myths of Scottish life.

This is about as far as it is advisable to go in assessing national character, a dubious subject. A nation's character changes over the years, and the differences between social classes within the same nation may be as great as the differences which divide nations. An anglicised Scot of the upper class is much closer to his English counterpart than to a worker in the Gorbals, and the social com-position of the regions and cities of Scotland marks each off from the other as effectively as it marks Scotland off from England.

Nevertheless, Scotland is not just an abstraction: it *is* a tangible reality. Just as the foundation of the Scottish state produced the Scottish nation, so today the existence of a wide range of institutions and quasi-institutions which are Scottish perpetuates Scotland and its society. No one who has crossed the border from England into Scotland can fail to be aware that in some sense he has come into another country with a life peculiarly its own. He sees around him the symbols of nationality: a flag, a 'national' newspaper press and other communications media, quite separate from those in England although superficially similar, and the constantly repeated words 'Scotland' and 'Scottish'. There is a Scottish Football League, a Scottish Youth Hostels' Association, a National Trust for Scotland, a Scottish Opera, a Scottish Television, a Scottish Arts Council, and, of course, a Scottish Secretary of State and a Scottish Office.

The visitor who settles in Scotland soon becomes amazed and perhaps perplexed at the more subtle parts of Scottish life. His children have to be educated in a Scottish way, and their teachers must have Scottish qualifications. His dealings with his solicitor bring him face to face with that 'anomaly', Scots law. The more he looks at the law in Scotland the more he is surprised: special licensing laws, special courts, judges and magistrates, and a baffling structure of local and central government to be learnt from scratch. Scotland may be partly anglicised, but you do not find many Englishmen commenting on the fact.

What, then, is the meaning of Scotland? Scotland is a nation, but it is not a nation-state. The state of which Scotland is a part is Britain (the United Kingdom of Great Britain and Northern Ireland). This state is sometimes described as a nation-state, and it is true that British national feeling, or British patriotism, is to be found alongside, and in harmony with, the separate national consciousness of England,

Scotland, Wales and, to some extent, Northern Ireland. Scots can feel Scottish and British at the same time, and it is only occasionally that a real conflict of loyalties develops. This is because Scottish national aspirations and traditions have largely been recognised within the context of the British state, and include many distinctive social and political institutions. Although Britain is not a federal state, it has federal tendencies, both in its constitution and in the spirit in which it is operated. A delicate balance is maintained between the forces of unity and the forces of separation which make up the relationship between the constituent nations.

Scotland has only one-tenth of the population of England, and it is natural that it is subject to a constant process, or threat, of assimilation to the 'predominant partner'. To some in Scotland this poses no problem and is welcomed in the name of progress. To others, however, anglicisation represents the loss of a valued style of life and a superior organisation of society. Many who would never become political Scottish Nationalists, or demand Home Rule for Scotland, nevertheless wish to preserve distinct Scottish institutions and culture. It is unfortunately the case that, irrespective of the merits or otherwise of Scottish life, such attitudes are bound to be viewed in England as parochial and petty-nationalist. Only occasionally in England is much attention paid to the Scottish solutions of social problems, despite the relative similarity of these to the corresponding problems in England. Here an informed debate between Scotland and England is overdue, and could help to remove some of the national prejudices which exist in Britain today.

NOTES

1  Myth, as used in this book, means a self-image, whose truth or falsehood has never been established.
2  Not, however, purely Scottish in ownership. The Thomson organisation owns the *Scotsman* and *Press and Journal* and the *Mirror* group the *Daily Record* and *Sunday Mail*.

# Chapter 2

# The Social Structure

To describe a society is to describe its people and its institutions. But the Scottish people have never confined their activities to Scotland, and their influence on other societies may be as interesting and important as their life at home. To look at Scotland and not the Scots may result in ignoring part of the Scottish 'élite' – the many educated and resourceful Scots who become leaders outside Scotland (see Donaldson, 1966; Gibb, 1937; Clement and Robertson, 1961). In so far as they migrated to other parts of Britain, their position in the wider British society may have an influence on Scotland, and this should be noted. But, important as they have been in the development of the British Commonwealth and the United States, it is within the histories of these countries themselves that their contribution should be assessed.

The population of Scotland, as revealed in the censuses of Scotland since 1801, has shown three marked tendencies over 160 years which help to explain many other features of Scottish social history. In the first place, although it has grown from 1,608,000 in 1801 to 5,229,000 in 1971, the proportion of the inhabitants of Scotland to the inhabitants of England and Wales has fallen in the same period from 18 per cent to under 11 per cent (see Table 2.1). The reason for this is the moving out of large numbers of Scots from Scotland to England and abroad. In recent times this tendency has become especially marked, to the extent that it has aroused political agitation and some despondency within Scotland as to the future vitality of the nation. In 1971, 14 per cent of those born in Scotland were living in England and Wales, which shows that, whatever attractions Scottish society may have, for many they do not outweigh its shortcomings.

The second main feature of the movement of Scottish population is the changed distribution of the people in Scotland itself (see Table 2.2). Thus, while the Highlands and north-east contained 42 per cent

Table 2.1    *Population changes in Scotland, 1801–1971*

| Census | Total (thousands) | Scotland as percentage of England and Wales |
|---|---|---|
| 1801 | 1,608 | 18·1 |
| 1851 | 2,889 | 16·1 |
| 1871 | 3,360 | 14·8 |
| 1891 | 4,026 | 13·9 |
| 1911 | 4,761 | 13·2 |
| 1931 | 4,843 | 12·1 |
| 1951 | 5,096 | 11·6 |
| 1961 | 5,178 | 11·2 |
| 1971 | 5,229 | 10·7 |

*Source: 1971 Census (Scotland).*

Table 2.2    *Growth of population in the regions of Scotland*

| Region | Population (thousands) | | | | | | | |
|---|---|---|---|---|---|---|---|---|
| | 1801 | 1851 | 1871 | 1891 | 1911 | 1931 | 1951 | 1971 |
| Highlands | 303 | 396 | 372 | 360 | 342 | 293 | 286 | 283 |
| North-east | 221 | 350 | 395 | 435 | 467 | 443 | 463 | 452 |
| Tayside | 255 | 381 | 417 | 452 | 454 | 438 | 446 | 453 |
| Edinburgh | 224 | 422 | 509 | 654 | 843 | 876 | 963 | 1,032 |
| Falkirk/ Stirling | 73 | 113 | 125 | 158 | 194 | 200 | 221 | 251 |
| Glasgow | 341 | 938 | 1,259 | 1,678 | 2,191 | 2,329 | 2,451 | 2,506 |
| South-west | 107 | 173 | 159 | 153 | 148 | 147 | 154 | 151 |
| Borders | 84 | 116 | 125 | 136 | 123 | 115 | 113 | 102 |

*Source: 1971 Census (Scotland), Population Tables.*

of the Scottish population in 1801, in 1971 they had only 14 per cent. By way of compensation, the Glasgow region had 48 per cent of the population in 1971 as compared with 21 per cent in 1801. Another way of expressing the change is in terms of urban and rural populations, which in the early nineteenth century were evenly matched, but today are in the ratio of five to one. Two main types of movement can be noted: that from the crofting and rural areas to the towns, and the migration of farmers in the higher farmlands to the more profitable lands lower down the valleys. While the first swelled the populations of the main cities such as Glasgow, Edinburgh, Dundee and Aberdeen, and made city life the typical pattern of existence for most Scots, the latter strengthened the 'high farming' areas of the Lothians, Angus and Aberdeenshire at the expense of the marginal lands of the south-west and the Highlands.

The third principal feature concerns the national origins of the population resident in Scotland. The presence of substantial national minorities in a country often leads to social conflict, especially if such minorities are differentiated from the majority by economic status, religion or education. In Scotland such a minority exists, especially in the west: the Roman Catholic Irish. Irish (both Catholic and Protestant) had settled in Scotland from an early date, but it was during the nineteenth century that their numbers increased until in 1861 the Irish born in Scotland constituted 6·7 per cent of the Scottish population. In Glasgow and Greenock they amounted to around 15 per cent of the population. This Irish group was not cohesive, for it split into antagonistic 'Orange' and 'Green' (or Protestant and Catholic) factions, the former appealing on religious grounds to the native Scots Presbyterians for support. In 1971, the Irish-born in Scotland amounted to only 1·2 per cent of the population, but this should be contrasted with the claim of the Roman Catholic Church to a membership equal to 15 per cent of the adult population. In 1959, of the 530,000 adult Catholics in Scotland, under 20 per cent represented the 'native Scottish' element, and these were to be found largely in the Western Isles. The religious difference, then, can serve to identify and perpetuate 'Irish' sections of the population, even several generations after the movement from Ireland, especially when, as in the case of the Catholics in Scotland, separate denominational schools mark off the minority from the overwhelming, Presbyterian majority.

Since the First World War, another national group has overtaken the Irish as the most substantial minority in Scotland: the English. In 1971, English-born persons in Scotland numbered 279,340, or 5·3 per cent of the population. This is largely the result of the expansion of government offices and projects, and the spreading of English business firms to Scotland. Several differences between the English and Irish minorities are apparent. The English command from the start a higher economic status in Scottish society and are not liable to the charge, which was often levelled at the Irish immigrants, of undercutting the wages of the Scots. Although Episcopalian in religion, this has not proved a matter of social conflict in Scotland, for Episcopal/Presbyterian relations have not in the last 150 years been subject to the same strain among the general population as the Roman Catholic/Protestant division. Moreover, the Scottish Episcopal Church plays down any imputation of domination from England, and nearly all Anglicans in Scotland become members of it and not of any outpost of the Church of England. (There are only two churches of the Church of England in Scotland, one in Edinburgh and the other in Glasgow.) No other minority in Scotland amounts to 1 per cent of the population, although certain groups, such as the Indians and Pakistanis in Glasgow, sometimes attract attention.

Altogether, 9 per cent of the Scottish population were born out-

side Scotland in 1971,[1] but this number (469,490) is small when
compared with the total of Scots-born (775,495) who were enumer-
ated in England and Wales. The latter, however, account for only
1·5 per cent of the population of England and Wales. The old jibe
that 'the noblest sight a Scotsman has is the high road to England'
no longer raises a laugh in Westminster or Whitehall. It has become
economically and politically imperative to stem the flow of population
out of Scotland, not only because this is a vote-catching issue, but
because a balanced economy for the whole of Britain requires the
development of areas in economic difficulties, such as Scotland, and
the decongestion of the prosperous south-east of England. A further
leavening of the Scottish population by outsiders would benefit the
country culturally as well as economically for, although the Scots
who go abroad are frequently tolerant of and friendly to foreigners,
those who stay at home occasionally display nationalism and parochialism which may alarm the visitor. The merits of Scottish institutions such as education, church and folk-culture are enthusiastically
defended by Scots, not on the basis of comparison with other countries
but because they are usually all they know. The critical faculty, long
the intellectual pride of Scotsmen, must benefit from the interaction
of cultures within Scotland, and if the institutions have real merit
they will survive.

THE REGIONS OF SCOTLAND

Although Scotland is in many respects a unity, especially when
Scottish institutions are considered, there are also striking divisions
within the country. Since Scotland, albeit about three-fifths (7,876,584
hectares) the area of England, contains a great diversity of physical
and economic characteristics, this is not surprising. Indeed, it was for
long a major problem for Scottish rulers to keep together the entire
territory which had become known as Scotland, and to prevent the
remote and inaccessible parts from breaking away completely from
central control. In the Highlands, bad communications preserved
much of the chiefs' powers over the clans until their military defeat
in 1746 at Culloden; and today, the Highlands, which contain the
shrinking Scottish Gaelic culture, still display the strongest features
of a separate region within Scotland. Here are separate economic
problems associated with the barren and mountainous nature of the
land, the crofting system, and the distance from the principal markets.
And the human problems are special: memories of the 'clearances'
when Highlanders left their crofts, often unwillingly, to settle elsewhere, and the basic insecurity for the few who try to make their
living there today. On top of this, there is the Highland way of life,
a mixture of religious piety or mysticism and hard drinking, and

mostly incomprehensible and funny to the Lowland Scot. The fight to preserve the Highland way of life from attack from the Lowlands adds another dimension to the more general defence of Scottish values from attack by the English. But the extent to which Gaelic culture is in tune with Scottish culture is open to argument. Certainly the kilt, bagpipes and Highland games are symbols of Scottish tourist-culture today. But these are hardly typical of the average Highlander. And the more essential features of Gaeldom – such as the Gaelic language, the puritanism and strictness of religious doctrine, as well as the elusive Highland temperament – have few counterparts in other areas of Scotland. The Scot of argument, ambition and thrift is another person altogether, at least at first sight. So what is left of the so-called Scottish character? The inhabitants of Orkney and Shetland, it might be added, are prone to deny that they are Scots at all, having been part of the Scandinavian civilisation until well into the seventeenth century.

*The physical divisions*
Geographers have traditionally divided Scotland into three basic divisions: the Northern Highlands, the Central Lowlands and the Southern Uplands. The boundaries between them follow two geological fault-lines, that from Helensburgh to Stonehaven in the north, and from Girvan to Dunbar in the south. While these divisions are satisfactory in a geological interpretation and correspond to the division between an area of hard metamorphic rock, a rift valley with volcanic uplands and a plateau of softer rock, respectively, they have led to some confusion when the same divisions are used outside the geological context. For example, the Northern Highlands should be regarded as seven distinct physical regions: Shetland; Orkney; North-West Highlands; Caithness Lowlands; Western Isles (Inner and Outer Hebrides); Grampian Mountains; North-East Lowlands (with Cromarty and Laigh of Moray); and the Southern Uplands contain three regions: the Uplands proper, the Solway Lowlands and the Tweed basin. With the Central Lowlands remaining as one region physically (although divided in other respects), this gives eleven physical regions in Scotland, instead of three, and the characteristics of these regions are in part social and economic as well as physical. In practice, however, the socio-economic areas have been more broadly defined than the physical, and are subject to a greater variety of interpretation.

*The socio-economic divisions*
Much of the social and economic information about Scotland is derived from the ten-yearly censuses, and in these Scotland is divided into regions which correspond broadly to the three basic physical divisions,

with the central area divided into East Central and West Central. This method of dividing the country for social statistics has limited value, and in recent censuses other regions have been added, which have special relevance to economic and political life. The crofting counties or Highlands and Islands (Orkney, Shetland, Caithness, Sutherland, Ross and Cromarty, Inverness and Argyll) are treated separately as they have special economic problems and have had their own administrative arrangements since the Crofters Act of 1886. The border counties (Berwick, Peebles, Roxburgh and Selkirk) are also considered as a unit. Then there is the Central Clydeside conurbation, of which Glasgow is the focal point.

Scotland can also be divided into regions on the basis of types of occupation, agricultural and industrial. The Department of Agriculture and Fisheries for Scotland distinguishes five regions which are relevant to types of farming (DAFS, 1952). The Highlands for this purpose are not equivalent to the crofting counties, but consist of Argyll, Inverness, Ross and Cromarty, Sutherland and Shetland. They are predominantly crofting, however, with hill-sheep farming. The North-East (Aberdeen, Banff, Caithness, Kincardine, Moray, Nairn, Orkney) is largely concerned with cattle-rearing and semi-arable farming. The East Central area (Angus, Clackmannan, Fife, Kinross, Perth) has mainly cropping farms, while the South-East (Berwick, East Lothian, Midlothian, Peebles, Roxburgh, Selkirk, West Lothian) ranges from the rich arable lands of the Lothians to the sheep farming of Roxburgh and Selkirk. The final division, the South-West (Ayr, Bute, Dumfries, Dunbarton, Kirkcudbright, Lanark, Renfrew, Stirling, Wigtown), is dominated by the large dairying complex around Glasgow.

These divisions are perhaps misleading in some respects. The Lothians, for example, belong with the arable-farming East Central area, while parts of the border counties might well be extracted from the South-East region to form with the upland areas of the South-West region a distinctive farming area largely based on sheep farming. Stock-rearing is important in the border counties, and also in the Western Isles, and dairy farming is prominent in Aberdeenshire and in many of the central counties. Caithness and Orkney must be accounted part of the Highlands as they come under the Crofters Acts, although by farming region they rank as part of the North-East. This is because most of their farms are lowland rather than crofting in character.

Industrial regions are somewhat easier to define, as nearly all Scottish industry is concentrated in the Central Lowlands. The only town of over 50,000 inhabitants outside this region is Aberdeen (212,237), which is the most important fishing port in Scotland, and centre of the North Sea oil industry. It has ancillary shipbuilding and engineering industries, but is largely concerned with marketing and service functions. In the Highlands, industry is small and localised, the principal examples being nuclear energy (Thurso), pulp- and paper-milling (Fort William), tweed-weaving (Outer Hebrides) and whisky-distilling. The last, although a major dollar earner, does not employ many workers, and the Highlands are principally an area of agriculture, fishing and service industries, with tourism growing rapidly in pockets such as the western Cairngorms where ski-ing and other sports have been developed. Oil is now important in Cromarty, Orkney and Shetland.

In the Southern Uplands, the chief industry is textile manufacture, concentrated in the border burghs of Galashiels, Hawick, Innerleithen, Peebles and Selkirk. There is also textile employment in Dumfries, the marketing centre of the South-West area. The border counties resemble the Highlands in that industry is localised, skilled labour is in short supply and there is heavy emigration. This has led to special government plans for the economic development of the area, although there is as yet no agency equivalent to the Highlands and Islands Development Board. There are a large number of retired, professional people in the region, whose opposition to industrial development parallels that of many of the shooting lairds in the Highlands. For example, the Roxburghshire Development Plan, published in 1966, was strongly attacked as a threat to the residential character of the Melrose–Abbotsford area. The advent of Liberal, Labour and SNP MPs in the Highlands and the border constituencies since 1964 is probably an indication that change is favoured by the majority of the occupied population, but it will probably have to be imposed on the social Establishment.

The chief distinction to be made in the central industrial belt is that between east and west. It is still broadly true that heavy industries are to be found in the west, while light industries, along with coal-mining in the Fife–Clackmannan and Lothians coalfields, are predominant in the east. There are other important differences within these subdivisions; and, in the east, Edinburgh stands apart from the other Scottish towns in that its occupied population in manufacturing is only one-fifth of the total number of employees, while service industries account for three-quarters. In Dundee (the other East Central large town), the manufacturing proportion is around half, the same as in service industries; it resembles more closely Glasgow in the west (60 per cent service industries). Apart from the Ayrshire resorts, the West Central area is more consistently industrial.

The east–west division in the whole of Scotland is one of the most important, from the social point of view. In the Highlands the division is partly ethnic, with the Celtic or Gaelic culture in the west, and the Lowland Scots tradition in the east. In the Central Lowlands the industrial division is reinforced by ethnic and religious features. The Irish and Roman Catholic traditions disrupt the unity of the population in the west, while in the east (apart from a strong Roman Catholic minority in Dundee) there is more cohesion, with the English element in Edinburgh and the border counties more readily assimilated than the Roman Catholics. The social division is not so pronounced in the south of Scotland, but even here the South-West has received an Irish population which has helped to distinguish it on religious and political grounds from the eastern border counties.

*Political and administrative divisions*
These divisions have been left to the last as they may in general be considered the most arbitrary and artificial of the recognised territorial units within Scotland. They are, of course, subject to periodic review and have changed considerably in the last hundred years. Most stable are the counties, now used mainly for parliamentary constituencies and Post Office purposes. They number thirty-three, and range in size from Inverness (1,090,690 hectares) to Clackmannan (14,139 hectares).

The county is no longer an administrative unit of local government, having been abolished by the Local Government (Scotland) Act 1973. The old system of local government, which lasted from 1930 to 1975, was a complex mixture of county councils, 'joint county councils' (Moray/Nairn and Perth/Kinross), counties of cities (Glasgow, Edinburgh, Dundee and Aberdeen), large burghs (there were twenty-one at the end), small burghs (176) and district councils (199).

The new system, which became operational in May 1975, consists of Regions and Districts, with three Islands Authorities for the Western Isles, Orkney and Shetland. The nine Regions range in area from Highland (2,509,106 hectares) to Fife (130,538 hectares), and in population from Strathclyde (2,500,000) to Borders (100,000). The fifty-three Districts range in population from Glasgow (860,000) to Nairn (8,900). The Islands Authorities, which cover most Regional functions, range in population from the Western Isles (30,000) to Orkney (18,000).

Two general comments can be made here. First, the number of administrative units has been drastically cut since the late nineteenth century, when the parishes, numbering about 900, were the basis of such local administration as was exercised by the parish councils (1894–1930) and school boards (1872–1918).

Secondly, comparisons with England and Wales regarding the nature of local government units are difficult owing to the completely different traditions which have come down to the present time. Scotland itself is administered by the Scottish Office for certain central government services, and the local government bodies have strong historical roots. There is now a strong contrast with England and Wales, which has retained the counties, some 'metropolitan', and most 'non-metropolitan'. The districts in England and Wales are likewise divided into metropolitan districts and non-metropolitan districts. England has retained a large number of parish councils and parish meetings, while Scotland has established community councils.

The parliamentary divisions in Scotland since 1868 can be summarised as in Table 2.3. The average electorate per constituency

Table 2.3   *Parliamentary divisions in Scotland, 1868–1979*

|         | Burghs | Counties | Universities | Total | Average electorate per division |
|---------|--------|----------|--------------|-------|---------------------------------|
| 1868–85 | 26     | 32       | 2            | 62    | 4,750                           |
| 1885–1918 | 31   | 39       | 2            | 72    | 9,430                           |
| 1918–50 | 33     | 38       | 3            | 74    | 36,330                          |
| 1950–74 | 32     | 39       | —            | 71    | 49,490                          |
| 1974–9  | 30     | 41       | —            | 71    | 52,680                          |

in England and Wales in the general election of May 1979 was 65,577. The difference with Scotland is mainly explained by the number of constituencies in the Highlands and Islands and central city areas which have relatively few electorates (five had under 30,000). The range was Glasgow Central (19,826) to Midlothian (101,482).

Two peculiar forms of parliamentary division have survived in Scotland from nineteenth-century practice: the 'District of Burghs' (as in Kirkcaldy Burghs), and the paired county divisions (as in Caithness and Sutherland). The former extracts from the counties a group of small towns which on their own would not be sufficient to form a constituency, while the latter joins contiguous counties for the same purpose. From 1868 to 1885, there were fifteen Districts of Burghs, but the number dropped to thirteen (1885–1918), then to seven (1918–50), and today stands at three. There were four paired county divisions from 1868 to 1918 (excluding Ross and Cromarty, which is usually taken as one county), and after 1918 an involved system of pairing was introduced which affected the representation of twenty-four counties. In some cases one county was paired with part of another (as in Kincardine and West Aberdeenshire, 1918–50), while the Western Isles constituency is formed out of parts of the counties of Inverness-shire and Ross and Cromarty. Today there are eleven constituencies which involve the pairing of counties or parts of counties, another indication that the Scottish county is often too small in population (if not in area) to be a major political unit. The only English county to be combined with part of another is Rutland (with

Stamford, Lincolnshire). In Wales, Brecknockshire is combined with
Radnorshire (Brecon and Radnor). Both divisions date from 1918.

OCCUPATIONS

In 1971, 45 per cent of the Scottish population were 'economically
active', as compared to 47 per cent in England and Wales; 59 per
cent of the male population and 32 per cent of the female population
in Scotland were thus classified (England and Wales, 61 per cent
males, 33 per cent females).

There is in Scotland a chronic problem of unemployment. Before
the First World War unemployment does not appear to have been
especially severe, partly because of the buoyancy of the heavy
industries which dominated the Scottish economy. Between the wars,
however, the heavy industries and agriculture declined, and in the
early 1930s unemployment rose to 27·7 per cent. Although the percentage unemployed in Scotland since 1945 at its worst (8 per cent
in 1977) represented only about a quarter of the highest total in the
interwar period, the percentage unemployed in Scotland has been
much higher than in Britain as a whole (see Figure 2.1). Further
aspects of unemployment will be dealt with in Chapter 10, in
relation to the long-term economic tendencies.

Fig. 2.1    *Changes in relative unemployment and hourly earnings*

Average hourly earnings: Scotland as a percentage of UK
Unemployment: Scotland relative to UK (UK = 100)

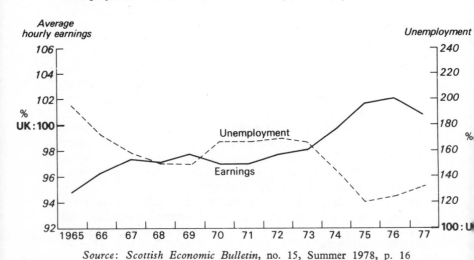

*Source: Scottish Economic Bulletin,* no. 15, Summer 1978, p. 16

Many of Scotland's economic troubles have been traced to the distribution of occupations, which are often held to be insufficiently diversified and too dependent on the heavy industries. In 1851, agriculture was the most important sector of the Scottish economy, with 27 per cent of the occupied population, and the principal manufacturing industry was textiles (18·2 per cent). It was the latter half of the century which saw the emergence of the modern Scottish occupational structure, with the decline of agriculture and the further industrialisation of the Central Lowlands. It is possible to compare 'primary' industry (agriculture, fishing and forestry), 'secondary' industry (manufacturing, including housebuilding), and 'tertiary' services (distribution, transport, domestic, etc.) in terms of the percentage of the occupied population in Scotland and in England and Wales (see Table 2.4). The figures show that the broad tendencies

Table 2.4

A. Percentage of occupied population in primary, secondary and tertiary production, 1881 and 1901 (Scotland). (Figures in brackets are for England and Wales.)

|  | 1881 | 1901 |
|---|---|---|
| Primary | 16·8 (12·4) | 12·0 (8·5) |
| Secondary | 58·1 (57·8) | 60·4 (59·1) |
| Tertiary | 25·1 (29·8) | 27·6 (32·4) |

B. Occupied population in various industries as a percentage of total occupied population, 1881 and 1901 (Scotland). (Figures in brackets are for England and Wales.)

|  | 1881 | 1901 |
|---|---|---|
| Textiles | 12·6 (9·8) | 9·9 (9·1) |
| Heavy industry | 12·1 (11·4) | 15·3 (13·8) |
| Chemicals | 0·9 (1·1) | 1·1 (1·3) |
| Housebuilding | 6·7 (6·9) | 6·2 (7·8) |

Source: T. J. Byres, 'The Scottish economy during the "Great Depression", 1873–96,' unpublished B. Litt thesis, Glasgow University, 1962.

in Scotland and in England and Wales were the same between 1881 and 1901, but that in Scotland primary production, with its lower income per head, was more important. The tertiary sector, on the other hand, with its high income per head, was significantly greater in England and Wales, an indication of the relative poverty of the Scottish economy.

Within the large 'secondary' (manufacturing) category there were significant developments in the same period, and a breakdown of the occupied population into industries. Table 2.4B reveals the decline of textiles and the rise of heavy industry both in Scotland and in England and Wales. However, Scotland was relatively more dependent on the 'heavies', and failed to develop the new light engineering industries (electrical engineering, cycles, motor cars, machine tools, etc.) to the same extent as England. About a third of British shipbuilding tonnage originated in Scotland at this time and there were also large locomotive engineering works. This economic imbalance is discussed again in Chapter 10.

Since 1901, the broad tendencies have continued: the decline of textiles and agriculture, and the rise of metal industries and of tertiary production. Perhaps the differences between Scotland and England and Wales are not now as striking as they have sometimes been made out to be (see Table 2.5).

Table 2.5   *Employment*

A. *Employment by industries, 1975. Percentages of male employees in employment (females in brackets)*

| | UK | Scotland | England | Wales |
|---|---|---|---|---|
| Agriculture, forestry, fishing | 2·2  (1·1) | 3·4  (0·8) | 2·0  (1·1) | 3·1  (1·8) |
| Construction | 9·0  (1·1) | 13·3  (1·3) | 8·4  (1·1) | 10·0  (0·8) |
| Mining, gas, electricity, water | 4·6  (0·9) | 4·5  (0·8) | 4·4  (0·9) | 9·4  (1·3) |
| Distribution | 9·0 (16·8) | 7·5 (17·4) | 9·3 (16·9) | 6·8 (15·0) |
| Professional, scientific services | 8·5 (26·2) | 8·1 (26·9) | 8·5 (25·9) | 7·8 (29·5) |
| Manufacturing | 38·9 (24·3) | 36·0 (23·2) | 39·4 (24·4) | 37·9 (21·9) |
| Other industries and services | 27·8 (29·6) | 27·2 (29·6) | 28·0 (29·7) | 25·1 (29·7) |

B. *Percentage of employees in employment in Scotland, 1975*

| | |
|---|---|
| Agriculture, forestry, fishing | 2·4 |
| Engineering and allied industries | 15·2 |
| Other manufacturing | 15·4 |
| Construction | 8·3 |
| Mining, gas, electricity, water | 3·0 |
| Service industries | 55·6 |

*Source*: CSO, *Regional Statistics*, no. 13 (London: HMSO, 1977).

To some extent Scotland is catching up in the 'new' industries, but this has not yet stemmed the flow of labour out of Scotland. This is despite the rise in earnings in Scotland, relative to that of the rest of the country. Traditionally, Scotland was a 'low-wage' area, but by 1975 manual workers in industry were earning as much as the UK average (Figure 2.1). This was also true for male non-manual workers, but female non-manual workers remained somewhat below the national average.

Gross Domestic Product per head in Scotland has also been rising. In 1968 it was only 90 per cent of the UK GDP, but in 1975 it was 97 per cent. Similarly, personal disposable income per head had risen from 92 per cent in 1971 to 98 per cent in 1975. Consumers' expenditure rose from 93 to 94 per cent in the same period (*Scottish Economic Bulletin*, no. 15, Summer 1978, p. 51). The feeling that wages and salaries are lower in Scotland than in other parts of the country may account for a certain amount of emigration, but unemployment is probably a more serious stimulus.

SOCIAL CLASS

Social class is notoriously difficult to define, and here the analysis will be based on the classes used in the Census. Table 2.6 gives a comparison between Scotland, England and Wales, and some regional and urban areas. Scotland is less 'middle class' than England, but the differences between the nations are less striking than the regional contrasts within the nations. Edinburgh has more than twice the proportion in Class I than Glasgow, and the north of England is in strong contrast to the south-east.

The similarity between Edinburgh and London and the south-east of England is brought out by the figures, and it is possible to detect symptoms of anglicisation of the southern English type in the life of the Scottish capital to a greater extent than elsewhere in Scotland. These are principally to be seen in the schools, the style of life and cultural pursuits, as well as in economic groupings. The Clydeside conurbation, too, is not typical of Scotland as a whole, although it contains much of its population; socially it resembles the Tyneside conurbation. There is little sign of anglicisation, unlike Edinburgh, but of course the strong cultural influence of Ireland is evident in the large Roman Catholic population (around a quarter of the total).

Some light is shed on social class divisions in Scotland by the types of houses people live in. Despite the broad similarity between Scotland and England and Wales in social class, there has never been any similarity in housing conditions. Thus social class and housing are not correlated in the same way in the two areas.

The industrial revolution brought about an overcrowding and a lack of amenities in Scottish housing unparalleled in England and Wales. By 1911, there were as many people in Scotland in proportion to the population living four to a room (8·6 per cent) as there were

Table 2.6    *Social Class – Percentage of economically active males in social classes, 1971*

| Area | Social Class | | | | | | | |
|---|---|---|---|---|---|---|---|---|
| | I | II | III(N) | III(M) | IV | V | NC | I–III(N) |
| Scotland | 4·6 | 14·9 | 9·6 | 39·0 | 18·8 | 19·1 | 3·0 | 29·1 |
| England | 5·2 | 17·5 | 11·8 | 37·5 | 17·1 | 7·7 | 3·3 | 34·5 |
| Wales | 3·9 | 16·8 | 9·1 | 39·5 | 17·7 | 9·9 | 3·0 | 29·9 |
| Central Clydeside conurbation | 4·5 | 12·3 | 11·2 | 40·7 | 16·9 | 12·0 | 2·3 | 28·0 |
| Rest of Scotland | 4·6 | 16·2 | 8·9 | 38·1 | 19·7 | 9·2 | 3·3 | 29·7 |
| Aberdeen | 4·5 | 13·4 | 10·9 | 36·5 | 21·1 | 11·6 | 2·0 | 28·8 |
| Dundee | 4·3 | 12·0 | 9·7 | 38·4 | 21·1 | 11·9 | 2·6 | 26·0 |
| Edinburgh | 8·3 | 16·5 | 13·8 | 34·2 | 15·7 | 8·3 | 3·2 | 38·6 |
| Glasgow | 3·2 | 9·7 | 10·5 | 41·4 | 18·7 | 13·8 | 2·7 | 23·4 |
| North England | 3·8 | 14·4 | 9·7 | 42·1 | 17·0 | 10·0 | 2·9 | 27·9 |
| South-east England | 6·6 | 20·0 | 14·2 | 33·0 | 15·8 | 6·6 | 3·7 | 40·8 |

*Source*: Calculated from the *Census (1971)*, Economic Activity Tables.
The Social Classes are defined as:

    I    Professional, etc., occupations
    II    Intermediate occupations
III(N)    Skilled occupations – non-manual
III(M)    Skilled occupations – manual
   IV    Partly skilled occupations
    V    Unskilled occupations
   NC    Not classified
I–III(N) might be considered the 'middle class'

living two persons to a room in England. In 1931, 35 per cent of the population in Scotland were living more than two to a room, compared with 6·9 per cent in England and Wales. The disparity was emphasised when in 1917 a Royal Commission defined overcrowding as more than three persons to a room in Scotland, while in England and Wales the standard was over two persons per room.

In the interwar period many Scottish local authorities embarked on housebuilding schemes, until in 1976 54 per cent of houses in Scotland were rented from local authorities or new towns (29 per cent in England) (see Table 2.7A). The rents of council houses in Scotland are low by English standards, and are heavily subsidised by the rates. Household expenditure per head on housing in Scotland in 1975 was 22 per cent below the average for Britain, largely as a result of the preponderance of council-house tenants. Private house-owners, on the other hand, pay more for their houses in Scotland, and according to a 1976 survey (CSO, 1977, p. 74), the price-level of houses in Scotland was second only to southern England. Flats in Scotland are relatively cheap and account for almost a quarter of all house sales. Despite the lower level of Scottish incomes, the average income of a Scottish house-buyer is higher than in any other part of Britain so that house ownership in Scotland is more socially exclusive.

Table 2.7   *Housing*

A. *Tenure, 1966 and 1976. Pencentage of households**

| | Owner-occupied | | Rented from local authority, New Town, SSHA | | Rented from private owner, etc. | |
|---|---|---|---|---|---|---|
| | 1966 | 1976 | 1966 | 1976 | 1966 | 1976 |
| United Kingdom | 47 | 53 | 29 | 32 | 24 | 15 |
| Scotland | 29 | 34 | 47 | 54 | 24 | 12 |
| England | 49 | 55 | 27 | 29 | 24 | 16 |
| Wales | 53 | 58 | 26 | 29 | 21 | 13 |
| North England | 38 | 45 | 36 | 40 | 26 | 15 |

B. *Housing conditions, 1971. Percentage of households with exclusive use of basic amenities (hot water, bath, inside WC); overcrowding (more than 1½ persons per room)†*

| | Amenities | Overcrowding |
|---|---|---|
| Scotland | 86·3 | 12·6 |
| England and Wales | 82·1 | 2·9 |
| Aberdeen | 77·5 | 3·8 |
| Dundee | 81·0 | 5·5 |
| Edinburgh | 83·2 | 5·3 |
| Glasgow | 76·6 | 13·6 |
| Highland Region | 88·9 | 5·3 |

*Source*: CSO, *Regional Statistics*, No. 13 (London: HMSO, 1977).
†*Source*: 1971 Census.

Present-day housing amenities in Scotland have greatly improved in recent years. Thus, the 1971 Census shows that 86 per cent of Scottish households have exclusive use of hot and cold water taps, fixed bath and water-closet, compared with 82 per cent in England and Wales. But 13 per cent of the population still live in overcrowded conditions (that is, over 1·5 persons, on average, per room) in Scotland (England and Wales, 3 per cent); in Glasgow, the percentage is 13·6. Further variations within Scotland are set out in Table 2.7B.

Scotland has the worst areas of urban 'multiple deprivation' in Britain. These are areas with poor housing and high male unemployment. Seventy-seven per cent of Great Britain's 'worst five per cent' of these areas in 1971 were in Scotland, and Clydeside had 95 per cent of the 'worst one per cent' of such areas. England, on the other hand, had only 22 per cent of the 'worst five per cent', and 2·5 per cent of the 'worst one per cent' (Department of the Environment, 1975). In the early 1970s Scotland was estimated to have had 14·2 per cent of its population living in poverty, compared with 12·9 per cent in Great Britain (Norris, 1977).

To many observers, the unity of Scottish society is its principal characteristic. They see Scotland as a small country with a close-knit family and social structure, and a set of distinctive Scottish institutions in education, law and religion which reinforce this inter-relationship. At a more popular level, there is the usual stereotype which identifies the Scot as uniformly kilted, dour, individualistic, and so on.

In this chapter, the emphasis has been on the divisions among Scots and within Scotland. Not only is the Scottish-born population increasingly dispersed beyond Scotland, but within Scotland there have always been important national minorities such as the Irish and the English. National consciousness, especially when reinforced by religion, education and a separate style of life, is thus a divisive influence in Scotland. The territorial unity of Scotland is seen to be less striking than its diversity. Scotland is made up of distinct regions: geographic, economic and social. Harmonising these areas within common Scottish institutions is almost as difficult as assimilating Scotland to the rest of the United Kingdom. Finally, the social class divisions of the Scottish population demonstrate the differences between individuals and regions in another light. Clearly, the problem of inequality in social and economic terms is another challenge to the social and political institutions of the country.

NOTES

1   A similar proportion (8·6 per cent) of the population of England and Wales in 1971 were born outside England and Wales; 2·3 per cent were born in the 'New Commonwealth', but in Scotland the figure was only 0·6 per cent. Scotland has always had a high proportion of non-Scots-born: in 1871 the figure was 8·9 per cent of the population, while in England and Wales the 'elsewhere-born' figure was 4·5 per cent.

FURTHER READING

Central Statistical Office, *Regional Statistics* (occasional).
Scottish Office, *Scottish Economic Bulletin* (occasional).

These sources provide the factual information from which an analysis of Scotland's 'social indicators' can be made.

# Chapter 3

# Scottish Social Institutions: Introduction

The continuing strength of Scotland as a nation, despite its *de jure* Union with England since 1707, is largely the result of its having maintained right down to the present day distinctive social, and to a lesser extent political, institutions. Thus the national consciousness of the Scots, unlike that of the Welsh, has always been reinforced by the machinery of government, even although it became fashionable for a time to drop the use of the word Scotland and to talk of 'North Britain': letter headings such as Edinburgh, NB, were common in the late nineteenth and early twentieth centuries.

'North Britain' was a misnomer, because Scotland was not just a region of Britain; indeed, it was impossible to exclude reference to Scotland as long as the Church of Scotland, Scots law and the Scottish educational system (administered by the 'Scotch' Education Department from 1872 to 1918, thereafter the Scottish Education Department) continued to exist. During the eighteenth century and a large part of the nineteenth, government from London was for geographic reasons remote in Scotland; moreover, this was an age of minimum state interference in the social life of the people. Part of the bargain at the Union in 1707 was that Scotland should retain its social institutions, and indeed it is unlikely that England would have had much success in imposing its own on Scotland. Where England tried to alter parts of the Scottish institutions, as in the restoration of patronage in the Church of Scotland (1712), considerable opposition was aroused. Most of Scottish social life was under the control of the Presbyterian Established Church, which in the absence of a strong resident upper class[1] fulfilled the principal functions of social leadership, at least in the rural areas. Its connection with the pre-modern educational system was close, for it appointed the schoolmasters in the state system (who had to be Church members), inspected the schools and organised the teacher-training colleges. Although the last of these bonds was broken in 1906 with the setting up of state teacher-training centres, the Scottish Education Acts allow religious teaching in state schools to include doctrines or catechisms which are distinctive of particular churches. While the Church of Scotland is the main beneficiary of this, the Roman Catholic Church since 1918 has also educated its young within the state system in Scotland.

The practical concern of the Church of Scotland extends beyond education to all aspects of Scottish life and, in the period of the unreformed House of Commons (1707–1832), the General Assembly of the Church acted as a sort of Scottish Parliament, which, if not democratic, was at any rate more representative of the Scottish middle class than the Scottish MPS of the day. The jurisdiction of the Church was held by many in Scotland to be equal to that of the state, and thus the Acts of the General Assemblies were given the force of law. It was only when the Church clashed with the nobility over patronage in the 1830s that the state attempted to overrule its activities. For the most part, the day-to-day life of Scotland, including poor relief and moral and social welfare as well as schooling, was in its charge, and not under the state. Even when the state assumed the functions previously held by the Church (as in the case of most poor relief after 1845), the social leadership of the ministers and elders remained almost intact. For the administration of social services was still carried out at the local level, and at that level the Church provided most of the resident leaders of society. The picture alters somewhat in the 1920s and 1930s, when economic depression demanded a more vigorous role for the central government, and the clergy of the Church of Scotland suffered a set-back financially as a result of the new arrangements for paying their stipends (Church of Scotland [Property and Endowments] Act, 1925: see Chapter 4, p. 45–6). But even today the minister and the elder has a status in Scottish society higher than that of most local church leaders in England, and the General Assembly influences thinking in Scotland and outside on many non-religious issues. For example, it supported African self-government in Nyasaland, thus acting as a strong pressure on the Conservative government: R. A. Butler, the Home Secretary, attended the Assembly debate on Africa in 1959.

The teacher is also accorded higher status in Scotland than in England, as might be expected in a country which has traditionally put a high social importance on education. The country schoolmaster or 'dominie' of the period up to 1914 was next in the social order to the laird and the minister in many areas, but until very recently the economic status of the school house was well below that of the manse. Thus, in the nineteenth century a country schoolmaster earned on average about a third of the minister's stipend and his style of life was markedly inferior. After the 1930s the schoolteacher caught up with, and has now definitely overtaken, the minister in earnings but his status position is not so clear. The country 'dominie' is gone, for primary and secondary education are no longer taught by the same man and the best trained and best paid teachers are in the towns. Moreover, in the country areas many former farm labourers have achieved a higher economic and social position by the break-up since 1918 of the old estates into independent farms. The school-teacher no longer stands out socially from the rest of the people.

In the towns, the schoolteacher was more prosperous, but he had to compete with the merchants, lawyers and other professionals who worked there. As these were more wealthy, on the whole, they could buy better houses, rent better pews in the church and play a more active part in burgh administration. But they all regarded the teacher as an essential part in the social establishment, and in many burgh schools all the resident social classes were taught by the same teachers. This situation did not survive the expansion of the middle class in the late nineteenth century, and after the 1870s the social classes were increasingly educated separately as new fee-paying schools were established for the wealthier. For long, many of these fee-paying schools remained (and some still remain) within the state educational system, and this has enabled more of the middle class in Scotland than in England to find satisfaction within the state system itself. The higher percentage of pupils attending state schools in Scotland (96·4 per cent in 1975, compared with 94·2 per cent in England) means that there is more uniformity in Scottish education and, with the reservations mentioned, a more comprehensive social class cover-age in the state sector. As most of the traditional Scottish national consciousness is transmitted through the classroom in Scottish history lessons and so on, education in Scotland makes everyone aware of nationality. The independent schools in Scotland (1·6 per cent of the pupils) often appear anglicised in contrast, and, indeed, they train their pupils for the English Certificate of Education rather than for the Scottish Certificate and hope to send their best products to Oxford and Cambridge rather than to the Scottish universities. They are staffed largely by English-trained teachers, and are directly copied from the English public schools, even though some of them show a fondness for the kilt as a uniform.[2] However, as they involve such a small proportion of the Scottish pupils (compared with 4·5 per cent in England) their social influence is comparatively weak.

The preservation of Scots law in the Act of Union was the most important indication that Scotland would remain politically distinct from England, even though the parliaments were to be united. For it was necessary to govern Scotland through the medium of its own legal system and, just as important, its own legal profession. While it was allowed that laws concerning 'public right, policy and civil government' might be made the same throughout the United Kingdom, laws affecting the private rights of Scotsmen could be altered only 'for evident utility of the subjects within Scotland' (Article XVIII).

The assimilation process has been nearly complete in commercial and revenue law, and has gone far in social welfare law (outside education), but property laws and other 'private rights' are different from those in England. In criminal law, too, various features of Scots law, such as the majority verdict and the Not Proven verdict of juries, and public prosecutions, have remained to serve as a model for the reform of English criminal law. The practical effect of the existence of Scots law on the cohesion of Scotland is obvious, even though few Scots are aware of the exact differences between their laws and those of England. Not only is Scottish legislation still necessary in Parliament (between five and ten Bills a year relate exclusively to Scotland), requiring the existence of two committees of the House of Commons for Scottish business, but a lawyer in Scotland must be trained in Scotland, where are to be found the only Scots law university faculties. Law in Scotland is thus a closed shop as far as English lawyers are concerned, unless they are prepared to complete their education in Scotland (and very few are).[3] At the same time, Scottish lawyers are unable to pursue their careers in England unless they are engaged on parliamentary business or commerical law, or take an English law qualification. On the whole, lawyers in Scotland seem least affected by the 'brain drain' which draws many of the best educated Scotsmen away from Scotland.

As far as social status is concerned, the lawyer in Scotland is much more consicous of the hierarchy in his profession than his co-professionals in the schools and the Church. The Scottish tradition of egalitarianism, which finds expression in the Presbyterian system of church government and in the educational ladder of opportunity, is strangely absent in the legal profession. At the top of the tree are the 110 members of the Scottish Bar (the Faculty of Advocates) in active service, and from these are chosen the judges of the Court of Session, Scotland's highest civil court. Entry to the Scottish Bar has traditionally been an expensive matter, costing some £450 in entrance fees and other dues in 1966 (they were as high as £350 in 1897), and in Scotland a candidate advocate used not to draw any salary in a law office for a considerable period before his admission to the Bar. It can thus be said that, even as compared with England, the Scottish Bar is socially exclusive and candidates require considerable private means if they are to succeed.

The majority of lawyers in Scotland are solicitors, but within that group there are status distinctions and financial barriers. Those solicitors whose business is with the Court of Session in Edinburgh are segregated from the rest and are members of the Society of Writers to Her Majesty's Signet (WS) or the Society of Solicitors in the Supreme Court (SSC). Solicitors in Scotland as a whole have, since 1949, been members of the Law Society of Scotland. (In Aberdeen, solicitors who are known as advocates are members of the Aberdeen Society of Advocates.) Although the training of solicitors does not impose the same financial strain as does that of advocates, the disincentive exists. The principal law degree in Scotland (LL.B) was until 1961 a second degree following the MA, which meant that the state would not pay law students grants to complete their training. Although there is now a new LL.B first degree, clearly the older generation of solicitors has had to survive a financial disability which is not present in England, where the basic law degrees are first degrees. The first few years as an apprentice in a law office in Scotland are virtually unpaid, making the career of solicitor (as compared to that of teacher or businessman) attractive only to those with some private source of income.

In general, Scots law gives Scotland an objective political identity which is jealously guarded by an important social leadership group, the Scottish legal profession. Scots lawyers defend Scots law and by implication the distinctness of Scotland. Whether the Scots themselves are altogether happy with Scots law is another matter, and the absence of a reforming spirit among lawyers until lately has brought about political protest, especially with regard to the feudal system of land tenure. There is little evidence that the ordinary Scot feels much pride in the Scottish legal system, and its role in socialisation is not great. There would probably be little protest at further assimilation with English law except from lawyers, and certainly nothing like the protest which arises in the educational and religious sphere when anglicisation is suggested. This is because the schools and the Established Church have penetrated the consciousness of the people to a far greater extent than the law, which is only partly Scottish. When the Scot thinks of law, he finds it difficult to disentangle the Scottish from the British elements, but with education and religion the Scottish characteristics are clear. The Scots have been able to control their schools, universities and churches far more tightly than their laws, and they feel more responsible for them today. Scotland has a large degree of self-government with respect to these social institutions, and thus to the Scots themselves must go the credit or blame for the results. What these are will now be examined in greater detail.

NOTES

1 After the Union, most of the Scottish nobility acquired London houses and spent a large part of the year away from their estates.
2 There is also a curious Spartan fetish in some Scottish boarding schools, which ill accords with the climate. Gordonstoun, Keil, Merchiston and Loretto make all the boys wear open-necked shirts and shorts, and Loretto even dispenses with underwear. The wearing of shorts, even by older boys, is common in the independent day-schools of Edinburgh, despite the fierce east wind which prevails in Princes Street.
3 This is true of teaching also, for Scottish qualifications are different from those in England. English teachers who are trained in education can, however, usually get recognition in Scotland.

FURTHER READING

Ferguson, W., *Scotland: 1689 to the Present* (1968).

Probably the best general introduction to modern Scottish history, though tending to the gloomy side.

*Chapter 4*

# The Presbyterian Establishment

In Scotland the Established Church is Presbyterian, while in England it is Episcopalian. Although both are Christian and Protestant, the Church of Scotland nominally adheres to the Westminster Confession of Faith of 1647, and the Church of England to the Thirty-Nine Articles of 1571. In 1960, a far higher proportion of the Scottish adult population were members of the Church of Scotland (37·6 per cent) than the proportion of the English and Welsh adult population who were members of the Church of England and the Church in Wales (10 per cent). Moreover, in England and Wales a mere 23 per cent were members of any Christian church, compared with 60 per cent in Scotland (Highet, 1960).

In 1978, the Church of Scotland had just over a million members, or 26 per cent of the adult population of Scotland. Thus the Church has experienced a sharp fall in membership in under twenty years. Roman Catholic Church membership had also dropped from 827,000 members of all ages in 1966 to 811,000 in 1978.

Membership statistics are controversial, and in the following Table 4.1 a comparison is made with the figures for marriages by denomination in 1977. Religious marriages accounted for 62 per cent of all marriages in Scotland; the Church of Scotland performed 42 per cent and the Roman Catholic Church 15 per cent. Thus all other denominations in Scotland accounted for only 5 per cent of marriage ceremonies. In England and Wales in 1974, 54 per cent of marriages were performed with religious ceremonies; the Church of England and the Church in Wales accounted for 36 per cent, and the Roman Catholic Church for 9 per cent.

The difference between Scotland and England and Wales is thus very marked in religion, and attempts to bring the two Established Churches together in a scheme of union involving the introduction of

Table 4.1   *Religion*

### A. Membership of the Scottish Churches, 1886 and 1966

|  | 1886 | 1966 |
|---|---|---|
| Church of Scotland | 540,061 | 1,240,342 |
| Free Church (including adherents) | 329,541 | c.24,000 |
| United Presbyterian (UP) Church | 177,517 | — |
| United Free Church | — | c.24,000 |
| Total non-Established Presbyterian Churches | 510,307 | c.53,000 |
| Roman Catholic Church (all ages) | 342,500 | 827,410 |
| Scottish Episcopal Church | 29,744 | 53,793 |
| Congregational Union of Scotland | c.12,000 | 30,000 |
| Evangelical Union | 13,210 | — |
| Baptist Union | 9,688 | 18,279 |
| Wesleyan Methodists | 4,653 | 13,212 |

### B. Marriage ceremonies, by religious denomination: Scotland (1977), England and Wales (1974)

|  | Scotland % of marriages | England and Wales % of marriages |
|---|---|---|
| Religious marriages as % of all marriages | 62 | 54 |
| Church of Scotland | 42 | n.a. |
| Church of England and Church in Wales/Scottish Episcopal Church | 2 | 36 |
| Roman Catholic Church | 15 | 9 |
| Methodists | 0·4 | 4 |
| Congregationalists | 1 | 0·3 |
| United Reformed Church (EW) | — | 2 |
| Baptists | 1 | 1 |
| Jews | 0·1 | 0·4 |

*Sources: The Distribution and Statistics of the Scottish Churches* (Edinburgh, 1886); Highet, 1960; Registrar-General for Scotland, *Annual Report 1976*, no. 122, pt 2, p. 138; Office of Population Censuses and Surveys, *Marriage and Divorce Statistics, England and Wales, 1974*, Series FM2, no. 1 (London: HMSO, 1977), p. 32.

bishops in the Church of Scotland arouse intense opposition in Scotland (see p. 49). Scottish Presbyterianism is seen historically in terms of a national struggle against English Episcopacy, and these Myths have a repeated exposition in the Scottish schools. Yet in more recent times (from 1843 to 1929), the conflicts within Presbyterianism were much more serious than the dormant struggle against Episcopacy. They cut down through the middle of Scottish society, instead of being directed at an indifferent foreigner or a small Scottish minority (the Scottish Episcopal Church represents under 2 per cent of the adult population). Largely forgotten today, they were nevertheless an important aspect of the history of modern Scotland, and eventually brought about a reformed and reunited Church of Scotland in 1929.

## THE KIRK DISRUPTED

Prior to 1843, the Church of Scotland contained within its ranks two warring parties, the Evangelicals and the Moderates. The former stood for missionary work at home and abroad, and a zealous puritanism not unlike that of the Nonconformists in other parts of Britain. But they were not Nonconformists in Scotland, and indeed believed passionately that the Scottish Established Church should be maintained by the state and strengthened by the provision of additional churches to cope with the rising population. Most important, they began to assert that the congregation of each church had the right to veto the appointment of a minister they disliked, even when the patron persisted with his nominee. Many held that patronage itself was inconsistent with Presbyterianism; for patronage, abolished by the 1690 Act re-establishing the Church of Scotland, was later foisted on an unwilling Church by the Westminster Parliament in 1712. In the eighteenth century, the Church suffered secessions on account of patronage and dissatisfaction with the connection with the state, and by the 1830s these 'voluntary' churches seemed a real threat to the Establishment. In 1847, most of them joined together in the United Presbyterian (UP) Church, which in 1851 had 465 places of worship and around 200,000 members, drawn mainly from the lower middle class in the Lowlands.

The Moderate party was identified with the maintenance of patronage, and it had a much more easy-going attitude towards dogma and personal behaviour. Many of the Moderate ministers were closely identified with their patrons, and they shared some of the aristocratic tastes in recreation, culture and wine. It was noted with shock by the Evangelicals that they were prepared to arrange the time-table of the General Assembly so as to be able to attend the theatre while in Edinburgh. The Moderates in the Church of Scotland bear some resemblance to the 'Board Churchmen' in the Church of England.

During the period of Whig reforms in the early 1830s, the Evangelicals gained the majority in the General Assembly of the Church, and proceeded to pass two Acts – the Veto Act and the Chapel Act – which were afterwards challenged in the Court of Session and ruled illegal. The former would have allowed congregations to veto the appointment of ministers and the latter sought to give new churches the same rights as the old parish churches. This conflict between

Church and state could have been healed by the intervention of the government but there was little understanding of or sympathy for the Evangelicals on the part of either the Whigs or Tories in England. To the Whigs, the Evangelicals seemed to be demanding more money from the state with no control in return, while the Tories were alarmed at the attack on property in patronage rights.

Thus there was deadlock, and in 1843 most of the Evangelical group within the Church of Scotland withdrew to form the Free Church of Scotland. This soon contained almost as many members as the Established Church itself, and more than a third of the ministers joined it. By 1851 it had 889 places of worship, and sittings were provided for 495,335 worshippers, compared with the Established Church's 1,183 places of worship and 767,000 sittings. A religious census in that year showed that attendance at services was much the same in number for both churches (Howie, 1893, p. 91). The secession was so great that it is called the 'Disruption', and it was certainly the biggest disaster to befall Presbyterianism since the Stuarts. For the number of Presbyterians outside the Establishment was now as high as that of those who remained inside it, and the union of the older secessionists in the United Presbyterian Church in 1847, shortly after the Disruption, gave added strength to the 'voluntary' opponents of the Kirk. The bitterness which grew up between the Established and 'dissenting' Presbyterian Churches pervaded Scottish life for two generations, affecting politics, education, social welfare and family ties. Not only were churches duplicated in every parish, but also schools and, in the cities, teacher-training colleges and divinity halls. An entire alternative Presbyterian system was erected by the Free Church, culminating in a rival General Assembly (whose hall is now used for the Established Church General Assembly).

The membership of the Free Church was of two kinds. In the towns, large numbers of the middle class joined and, with their handsome donations, they built many of the finest churches in their areas. In the country areas, however, other than the Highlands, members were few and poor. The landlords opposed the Free Church from the first, refusing sites for churches and serving interdicts for trespass on congregations worshipping on their lands. With the added threat of eviction, this made Free Church membership hazardous in rural areas for a time. But in the Highlands these difficulties were overcome. There the Free Church swept the board and left the Established Church almost destitute. To a man, the Highlanders joined the seceders and flocked to support the Evangelical ministers. This was partly a result of growing anti-landlord feeling, spurred on by the clearances of crofters to make way for sheep. But it was mainly the new zeal of the Highland religion, akin in spirit to that of the Free Church, which determined the result. Largely untouched by the eighteenth-century Presbyterian secessions, the Highlands adopted an evangelical religion of their own, before the Lowlands. Emotional and dogmatic, it seems to have replaced the superstitious beliefs of the past by Calvin's doctrine of predestination, and to have erected a new set of local spiritual leaders, 'The Men', or chief elders, to direct the lives of the people. Even today in the Highlands something of this religion remains among those Presbyterians who refused to join the union of the Free and United Presbyterian Churches in 1900 and who are chiefly to be found in the crofting counties. It is marked by puritanism and Sabbatarianism, strong anti-Roman Catholic sentiment, and a somewhat hostile attitude to such features of Gaelic culture as singing, bagpipe music, dancing and literature. It holds that organ music in churches is sinful, and to this day only unaccompanied psalms are sung in many churches. (Indeed, in the Church of Scotland itself, it was not until 1863 that organ music was reintroduced, and then only after prolonged controversy: Fleming, 1927, p. 120.)

The Free Church (continuing) today has around 20,000 members and adherents and is nicknamed the 'Wee Frees'. The Free Presbyterian Church (founded 1893) is also predominantly Highland, and has under 7,000 members and adherents. The United Free Church (continuing), which stayed out of the 1929 union, is mainly Lowland and is the heir of the UP Church's voluntary traditions. It has around 13,000 members (all figures for 1976).

The divisions in Presbyterianism destroyed the old basis of the social institutions in Scotland, such as the schools and the poor relief authorities (the kirk sessions), for it could no longer be assumed that the majority of Scots belonged to the Church of Scotland and would trust it to perform important social services on behalf of the people. In one interpretation, the Disruption heightened feelings of social responsibility in Scotland, as was seen in the large number of new schools established by the Free Church (there were 617 Free Church schools, around 40 United Presbyterian Church Schools and 519 Church of Scotland schools outside the parochial system in 1864: Osborne, 1966, p. 7). It brought a more personal involvement in religion for many Scots, especially those of the middle class, not only in their way of life but in their financial obligations to support the new independent churches. But at the same time the sectarian bitterness among Presbyterians, professing the same faith and doctrine and differing only in matters of church government, is difficult to understand today and was often deplored at the time. Churches of the Establishment were called 'synagogues of Satan' by the disruptionists, and the Free Kirkers were 'traducers of the Mother Kirk' to those who remained within the Church of Scotland.

In this situation, certain social services could not be left to the jurisdiction of the Established Church and, two years after the Disruption, the Poor Law Amendment (Scotland) Act, 1845, was passed to transfer poor relief from kirk sessions to partly elected parochial boards. These were controlled centrally by a Board of Supervision, an agency of the government. Poor relief was refused to the able-bodied poor in Scotland under this Act, but the churches continued to support them out of church collections and endowments. Until about 1860, only outdoor relief was given in Scotland, but after that date Scotland copied England in confining poor relief from the state to the inmates of workhouses (Campbell, 1965, p. 211).

The Disruption also shattered the link between the Church of Scotland and the state school system. The Established Church had been closely linked by law with this system, for all schoolmasters were appointed by the parish minister and heritors (chief landowners, who were usually elders of the Church) and had to subscribe to the Confession of Faith and the formula of the Church of Scotland. The presbyteries of the Church had to confirm their appointment by examination and could dismiss them for neglect of duty, immorality or cruelty. The teaching hours and holidays were also fixed by the presbyteries. Inspection of the parish school was undertaken by the minister, and he might also take a hand in the teaching himself (Knox, 1953, p. 24). With the split in the Church, this situation became intolerable, and it became necessary to sever most of the ties between the Church and the schools. The Parochial and Burgh Schoolmasters (Scotland) Act, 1861, removed the obligation on schoolteachers to adhere to the Church of Scotland (an Act of 1853 had already removed a similar obligation on university professors, except in the Faculty of Divinity), and transferred the powers of the presbyteries in the examination of teachers to panels of university professors. Dismissals on the grounds of immortality or cruelty were placed within the province of the sheriff, but the minister and heritors retained the power to dismiss teachers because of negligence or incompetence. This power was given up under the Education (Scotland) Act, 1872, when the school boards took over the remaining powers of the Church in education, except teacher training. The Churches were strongly represented on these boards, and their influence on the teaching in schools was marked. The boards were elected by cumulative vote, and it became the practice in Glasgow that, of the fifteen members on the board, three were nominated by the Established Church, three by the Free Church, three by the Roman Catholic Church, three by labour organisations, with the remaining three independent. The Church members received instructions from their Churches on how to vote (Haddow, 1943, pp. 60–3). In Scotland it was permissible for the catechisms to be taught in board schools. This encouraged the Presbyterian Churches (but not the Episcopalians or Roman Catholics) to transfer their schools to the school boards and so achieve an exceptionally strong public system of education, not at all like that established in England under the 1870 Education Act, where denominational schools remained outside the boards.

The enforced withdrawal of the Presbyterian Churches from a large area of social administration on account of their sectarian disputes may have contributed to a new exclusiveness and obsession with points of dogma and church government which seem today strangely irrelevant to Presbyterianism. Charges of heresy were brought against ministers and professors in the three principal Presbyterian Churches when they sought to modify and reinterpret the ancient teachings of the Old Testament and the doctrine of predestination (Fleming, 1933, ch. II). The most important of these was the trial in 1880–1 of Professor W. Robertson Smith of the Aberdeen Free Church College, when the Free Church General Assembly deposed him from his Chair on account of his opinions on the authenticity of certain Old Testament books. The Church of Scotland and the United Presbyterian Church had their trials too. The principal cases were Robertson Smith (1880–1), Dods and Bruce (1890, acquitted), and George Adam Smith (1902, acquitted) in the Free Church; Ferguson (1878, acquitted) and Macrae (1879) in the UP Church; Robinson (1879) in the Church of Scotland. The UP Church proved the most liberal in theology when it passed its Declaratory Act in 1879 modifying the traditional Calvinism. Unfortunately for the Free Church, a similar Declaratory Act in 1892 led to the secession of two ministers and many elders and the formation of the Free Presbyterian Church the following year.

In the Church of Scotland, the new liberal theology was not finally introduced until 1905, when Parliament passed the Churches (Scotland) Act. The principal Presbyterian Churches were now committed to a much freer interpretation of the Westminster Confession of Faith and the Old Testament, and thus no doctrinal snags of importance arose in the Union negotiations in 1929. Today the Church of Scotland is not narrowly dogmatic and its former belief in Calvinist predestination has disappeared. It is thus misleading to describe the modern Church of Scotland as Calvinist, except as regards church government.

The question of the relationship of the Church to the state was even more disturbing to the peace of Presbyterianism, and for a time also to the stability of the political parties in Scotland. The Evangelical party in the Established Church had always adhered to the doctrine of the sixteenth-century church father Andrew Melville that there were 'two nations' or jurisdictions in Scotland, that of the Church and that of the state. Each was to be supreme within its own sphere, the former controlling spiritual, and the latter temporal, affairs. Unfortunately, there was no way of deciding where the division came, and the Evangelicals claimed that all matters of internal church government, including the rules for appointing ministers and establishing new churches, came within the spiritual sphere. This was unacceptable to the state, which considered that, since public money was directly involved in the support of ministers and churches, it should uphold its supremacy in these matters.

The Free Church left the Establishment on this issue, but it did not at first reject the principle of an Established Church. As the Free Church leader Thomas Chalmers declared, in words often repeated later: 'Though we quit the Establishment we go out on the Establishment principle; we quit a vitiated Establishment but would rejoice in returning to a pure one. We are advocates for a national recognition and national support of religion – and we are not voluntaries' (Burleigh, 1960, p. 354). Thus began the seemingly impossible task of achieving a Church of Scotland, 'Established, yet free'. Whether they liked it or not, the Free Church were in fact voluntaries, for they no longer had any connection with the state or received support from public funds. This led them into intense fund-raising campaigns, and what appeared to outsiders an obsession with money. It certainly seemed to be difficult for a poor man to enter the kingdom of heaven by way of the Free Church (at least in the towns), and inevitably the Free Church grew closer to the United Presbyterian Church, whose voluntary principles they had originally attacked.

As the chances of reforming the Establishment seemed remote, a party grew up within the Free Church, led by Dr Robert Rainy, which sought union with the United Presbyterian Church. Negotiations were begun in 1863 but foundered ten years later on account of the opposition of a strong party of Establishmentarians in the Free Church, led by Dr James Begg of Newington, Edinburgh. Begg relied heavily on support from the Highland wing of the Free Church, which apparently supported the Establishment principle on account of the financial benefits which poor congregations would gain from the state connection. Few Highland Free Church congregations were self-supporting, and they relied on subsidies from the central Free Church Sustentation Fund. It was this Highland 'Constitutional Party' which later contested the legality of the union when it was achieved in 1900, and which was awarded the bulk of the Free Church property by a House of Lords judgement in 1904 (the Free Church case). The reasoning of the Lords was that of Begg in the 1860s: the Free Church was based on the Establishment principle and could not unite with voluntaries without breaking its constitution.

At the same time as the first union negotiations between the Free and United Presbyterian Churches broke down, the Church of Scotland achieved a reform by Act of Parliament which set off a new campaign of ecclesiastical warfare in Scotland. This was the Patronage Act (1874) passed by Disraeli's Conservative government, terminating the right of lay patrons to present ministers to congregations in the Church of Scotland. From now on, ministers would be elected by the congregations which would not have ministers forced on them by landowners and the Crown against their will. This reform was not received with joy by the Free Church, even although patronage was one of the root causes of the Disruption. On the contrary, the Free Church, with Gladstone as their spokesman, attacked the Bill as a cynical attempt to filch Free Church members and lure them back into the Establishment. For it was plain that the election of ministers was the most popular item in the Free Church constitution, and the necessity to contribute heavily to its funds the most unpopular item. So why not get an elected minister, free, in the Establishment?

The only solution to this problem, as far as the Free Church and the United Presbyterian Church were concerned, seemed to be to 'disestablish the Church of Scotland', and Rainy was able to carry the Free Church Assembly on this issue (despite renewed opposition from the Constitutionalists) in 1874. Thus the Free Church and the United Presbyterian Church embarked on a joint campaign to secure disestablishment, a campaign which lasted a generation and prevented the reunion of the Presbyterian Churches (by this time scarcely divided in their doctrines and government) until 1929.

The details of this chapter in Scottish Church history need not be recounted here (see Simpson, 1909, and Kellas, 1964). Most churchmen in Scotland today prefer to forget this episode, though recent, since it brought out the worst in Scottish Presbyterianism – intolerance, arrogance and irrelevance. The more they were alike, the more they hated each other; the more they argued about mundane matters, the more they attributed them to divine intervention; and, while industrial Scotland wallowed in the slums of Glasgow and the crofters starved in the Highlands, the Scottish middle classes argued about church attendances and the size of members' contributions to the church plate in the Establishment and outside.

To the disestablishers the Church of Scotland was responsible for 'a multitude of social and religious ills', and the time had come to 'make a speedy end of this religious scandal and political injustice' ('Memorial to Gladstone from 1,475 Scottish Liberal Clergy', *Scotsman*, 7 November 1885). Such talk from Presbyterian brethren raised the ire of leading men in the Establishment. 'I have sometimes been tempted', cried Dr Story at the 1885 General Assembly of the Church of Scotland, 'to desire that we could go back for a little to the days of the Covenanters, and on the bare hillside meet the traducers of our mother Church, foot to foot and hand to hand.'

The climax was the conversion of Gladstone and the Liberal Party to Scottish disestablishment in 1887, and the promise of legislation by the Liberal government of 1892–5. After Gladstone's retirement in 1894, however, his successor Lord Rosebery did not proceed with the Bill, and it never again received active government support. For years the subject was brought up at Liberal Party meetings, but with Campbell-Bannerman (an Established Church elder) and Asquith as leaders, the party as a whole was lukewarm. Moreover, the Scots were less decided on the subject than the Welsh, who obtained a Welsh Disestablishment Act in 1914. The Church of Scotland was in fact gaining rapidly in membership and prestige at the end of the nineteenth century, and the claims of the disestablishers that it represented a minority of the Presbyterian body were no longer convincing (Table 4.1). The Established Church had recovered much of its lost popularity and, under the influence of leaders such as Dr Norman Macleod and Professor A. H. Charteris, had committed itself to an evangelical and missionary programme not unlike that of the Free Church. It became apparent in the light of the fiasco of the Free Church case (1904) that even a non-established Church was fettered by the state, and that, given a new constitution, an Established Church might have more control over its own affairs than a 'voluntary' church.

The United Presbyterian (UP) Church had united with the Free Church in 1900 to become the United Free (UF) Church, and it might be thought that its non-establishment principles would preclude any talk of joining the state church. But negotiations for union began in 1909, and it became the task of leaders such as Dr John White and Christopher Sands, KC, of the Church of Scotland, to find a formula which could serve as the new legal basis for the Establishment. In April 1912 a memorandum was issued: the Church was to ask Parliament for legislation guaranteeing its freedom from external control in doctrine and government, and, by 1914, Articles of a Draft Constitution giving 'spiritual independence' were passed by the General Assembly. But there were strong minorities in both the Established and United Free Churches who were prepared to challenge such a formula, and the threat of another 'Free Church case' loomed up.

THE KIRK REUNITED

Had it not been for the 1914–18 war, the solution might never have been reached, for it is likely that old attitudes and fears would have prevailed for years to come. But the Scotland that emerged after 1918 was impatient with ecclesiastical squabbles, and the ministers and elders of the churches could see that the grave social problems of the time demanded united action. There was no longer the political barrier of the electoral unpopularity of disestablishment which had dogged the Liberals in the 1890s: very few cast their votes on church questions in the Scotland of the 1920s. A settlement could be reached with the agreement of all political parties: all that was needed was for the Churches to produce an agreed constitution. As before, the initiative was with the Established Church, and it secured parliamentary sanction for its Articles on spiritual independence in 1921 (Church of Scotland Act). These give the Established Church in Scotland far greater powers than its counterpart in England, for it is 'recognised' by the state to be independent in doctrine and government 'as derived from the Divine Head of the Church alone'. In England, the Queen is head of the Church of England, but in Scotland she is merely a member of the Church of Scotland, although she sends her representative, the Lord High Commissioner, to the General Assembly as an observer.

This Act seemed to accept the 'two nations' idea of Melville at last, and to reconcile the warring factions. But even now there was a problem: how to deal with the ancient patrimony of the Church, especially the teinds (tithes) levied on landowners to pay part of the minister's stipend, and other rates. Apart from teinds, the Church's income from public funds included grants from town councils and the Treasury for ministers' stipends, glebe moneys and the general obligation on heritors (landowners) to maintain the churches and manses. The total public income from public funds was under £400,000, less than half the value of members' contributions (Fleming, 1933, p. 108; Gibson, 1961, p. 39).

The United Free Church insisted that all income should be controlled by the Church itself, and many in it found the teinds totally unacceptable. But the Established Church could not be expected to give up its historic rights to 'a national support of religion', and the teinds could not be abolished without compensation. This would mean a compulsory redemption of their value, a proposal which filled the landowners of Scotland with alarm. Instead of paying a small annual sum, they were likely to be forced to compensate the Church 'once and for all' for its loss of income. According to the Duke of Buccleuch, 'it would mean their final ruin' (Muir, 1958, p. 223).

As it turned out, it was the Church which suffered, and not the landowners. The teinds had always been related to the price of grain, so that when the price was high the stipend of the minister was high also. Thus the minister's income kept pace with the cost of living. After much haggling between the Church of Scotland and the landowners, a new proposal was agreed which fixed the annual value of the minister's stipend from the teinds as the average of the years 1873–1922 plus 5 per cent: a figure which in future years was to count for less and less as the value of the pound fell. It was this fact which was to destroy much of the financial security of the Church of Scotland clergy and to affect its status in society. From a position high in the social hierarchy, many ministers, especially in rural areas, soon found their old standard of life difficult to maintain, except in the few burgh churches (often previously United Free Church) which had a tradition of congregational largesse.

The teinds were thus not compulsorily redeemed but standardised at a particular level, and the Church of Scotland immediately lost one-sixth of the revenue from this source (Fleming, 1933, p. 111). The settlement differs from the comparable tithe redemptions of the Church of England in that no large capital sums were paid to the Church of Scotland in compensation for the loss of the ancient revenues. The English Establishment gained £12·5 million at Irish Disestablishment in 1869 and £70 million in government stock at the final redemption of tithes in 1936. The interest and investments from this property have proved more profitable than the fixed annual sum obtained from the teinds. Three-quarters of the Anglican clergy's income is paid from the earnings of this capital, and the income of the Church of England as a whole is derived equally from investments and members' contributions (Ferris, 1962, pp. 165, 174). In the Church of Scotland, on the other hand, with its part-voluntary traditions, members' contributions amount to three times the income from property (*Church of Scotland Year-book, 1967*, p. 28).

At last the great reunion took place, on 2 October 1929. A small minority of die-hards in the United Free Church decided to continue independently, but all the rest combined: 1,457 parish (Establishment) churches and 1,441 United Free Churches, with a combined membership of 1,300,000. When 'adherents' are added, they amounted to about half the Scottish adult population. The Church of Scotland which resulted was a curious amalgam, for features of the constituent churches were allowed to continue, even as far back as the United Presbyterian Church. This Church, merged with the Free Church in 1900, and now with the Church of Scotland, had its own style of Presbyterian government, whose chief expression was the exclusion of the minister from the congregational Committee of Management which controlled each church's finances. This was retained and ministers of these churches have less say in their churches' affairs than the ministers whose churches' ancestry is Established or Free. Those churches which had been part of the United Free Church also retained in their congregations special features: the Deacon's Court manages the temporal affairs of the congregation instead of the kirk session as in parish churches (Cox, 1964, pp. 29–34). For many years congregations retained distinctive attitudes towards their ministers and to financial contributions, depending on their lineage. At first only the churches which were in the Establishment before

1929 derived any income from the teinds, but lately some of this has been re-allocated to other congregations, and the General Trustees of the Church are in sole control over the Church's property as a whole. A model church constitution was drawn up in 1931 so that each congregation would have similar institutions, but the anomalies still continue.

It is usually assumed that the Presbyterian system of church government is democratic, and that there is no hierarchy, either of clergy or laity. 'It is essentially a democratic Church, in the management of whose affairs there is no respect of persons' (Cox, 1964, p. 11). However, this is only partly true. The constitution of the Church certainly adheres to representative government and the equality of ministers (although not equality of stipend), and the Moderator of the General Assembly has no special powers and holds office by election for one year only. But, as in most organisations, it is the committee which rules. These are arranged in a hierarchy of church courts, with each level containing representatives of the level below on the principle of equality between clergy and laity. At the congregational level, the committee is the kirk session, consisting of the elders (chief laymen) and the minister. In many churches the elders are not elected by the congregation (as democratic theory might demand), but are co-opted by the existing kirk session. Until the First World War this usually meant that elders were drawn from the middle class, especially in the Free and United Presbyterian Churches, which sometimes made substantial financial contributions to the church the necessary condition of appointment (MacLaren, 1974). Similarly, the appointment of ministers, in appearance by election of all members of the congregation, is usually the result of the choice of a committee which seeks out the man who will be presented as the sole nominee to the congregation. The committee is elected, and so is the minister, but the congregation rarely has a choice of candidate. Such contests would perhaps be unseemly, but the present-day practice of sending committees to sit at the back of churches in order to hear candidates preach before deciding on 'the call' is almost as suspect a procedure.

Above the kirk session are the superior courts of the Church (presbytery, synod and General Assembly) in which, theoretically, the clergy and laity have equality of representation. But many presbyteries meet during the day, which cuts the attendance of elders, and the General Assembly entrusts a great deal of business to committees which are dominated by the ministers, as are the presbyteries. In 1978 there were almost fifty committees of the Assembly, some of them meeting five times throughout the year, in the morning or afternoon. The members of these committees are nominated by a Nomination Committee, but some large committees (for example, to nominate the Moderator) include representatives of the presbyteries and synods. Most nominations go unchallenged, but there have been frequent attacks on the methods of appointing the committees and indeed on the whole system of committees. In 1972 the Assembly decided to reform its structure of committees, and appointed (of course) a committee, 'the Committee of Forty', for the task. In 1978 the Committee of Forty finally reported that the committees should be replaced by seven boards, with an Assembly Council at the top to take decisions between the annual meetings of the Assembly. Apart from reforming the committee structure, the Committee of Forty recommended changes at congregational level, with part-time unpaid ministers and team ministries. These were all signs that the Kirk in the late 1970s was at last waking up to its declining position in modern Scotland.

The activists who run the Church of Scotland tend to be drawn from a limited group of people. Partly from convenience, but also because most church notables live there, the Central Lowlands of Scotland provide the leaders who run the Church of Scotland and the pronouncements of the Church reflect opinion in that area. On the whole, this opinion is more radical and evangelical (but also more ecumenical) than in Scotland generally, and the General Assembly has occasionally voted against important Committee recommendations, such as those on church unity and morals.

The main qualification to democratic practice in the Church of Scotland is that the members as a whole are not directly consulted about important church matters. These are decided by the General Assembly in conjunction with the presbyteries. These bodies are only vaguely representative of the members, and there are no 'general elections' or party platforms in the Church. The General Assembly consists of the representatives of only a quarter of the congregations in any one year, so that it cannot speak for the Church as a whole, and, although important matters are referred to all the presbyteries, these bodies do not necessarily reflect congregational opinion. Thus there is not even as much direct democracy as under the British parliamentary system, where MPs have a theoretical freedom of conscience to vote as they please, but are in reality responsible to their party and constituency.

The number of Presbyterian church members in proportion to the total population of Scotland hardly changed between 1886 and 1966 (27·3 per cent then, 24·5 per cent in 1966). But only 1 per cent of this proportion was outside the Church of Scotland in 1966 compared with 12·7 per cent in 1886. So the process of Presbyterian reunion has been triumphantly successful and most of the old schisms are healed. Since 1929, the great duplication of churches in Scotland as a result of Presbyterian rivalry has been reversed. By 1979, 1,118 unions of congregations and 384 linkings of congregations had taken place.

The main Presbyterian dissentients today are the Free Church of Scotland and the United Free Church which, bereft of their former glory, still meet in their tiny Assemblies across the road from the Established Church Assembly to attack the latest moves in church unity as 'the menace of Romanism' and to lament the latest breaking of the Sabbath by tourists in the Highlands.

Whether the movement towards church unity in Scotland can widen to include the Episcopal Church in Scotland (76,000 members in 1976) seems now to be much more doubtful. The Scottish Episcopalians have a strong native tradition in some parts of Scotland (for example, the North-East Lowlands), but most Scots equate bishops with England and the old oppression at the time of the Covenanters. The Scottish Episcopal Church accepted the Thirty-Nine Articles of the Church of England in 1804 and its clergy became eligible for benefices in the English Establishment in 1864. To many, the Episcopal membership became associated with the anglicised upper classes in Scotland, whose education was often at English public schools or at the Scottish public school connected with the Episcopal Church, Glenalmond in Perthshire. There are now more people living in Scotland who have been born in England, and many are Episcopalians. Thus, the combined effect of these factors is to make the Episcopal Church appear the 'English Church'.

Despite this, representatives of the Episcopalian and Presbyterian Churches in England and Scotland produced a report in April 1957 which suggested that unity could be achieved if the Presbyterians would accept bishops along with their presbyteries, and if the Episcopalians would accept elders and a General Assembly along with their bishops. This not unnaturally caused consternation in Scotland, with (among the press) the *Scottish Daily Express* somewhat incongruously leading the defence of Scotland's religious heritage. By 1959, most presbyteries had pronounced against the report, which seemed to be asking more of the Church of Scotland in the way of concession than it did of the Church of England. One factor was to cause more bitterness in 1966: the Anglicans, unlike the Presbyterians, reject intercommunion with other churches, and in 1966 the Episcopal Bishop of Edinburgh tried to inhibit an American Episcopal priest from taking sacraments in St Giles Cathedral, Edinburgh (Church of Scotland), as assistant to the minister, the Reverend Dr Harry Whitley. Whitley aroused the Edinburgh presbytery and the General Assembly with the Tirrell case (named after the priest, the Reverend John Tirrell) and brought home to many Presbyterian Scots the fact that, although they were prepared to tolerate Episcopalians in their sacraments, the Episcopalians would not tolerate them in theirs. In this atmosphere, therefore, it was difficult to get the Assembly to vote for a continuation of unity talks with the Church of England.

Other church unions have been discussed, and some may materialise. The Congregationalists in Scotland (separately organised from those in England, who are now mainly in the United Reformed Church) and the Established Church produced a draft formula for union in 1967, but nothing came of it. The Methodists in Scotland for a time negotiated with the Scottish Episcopal Church in parallel with their counterparts in England. In 1978, however, they concluded a plan of union with the Church of Scotland, which would include joint action from the level of the presbytery upwards. This has yet to be accepted by both Churches. Scottish Methodism (membership in 1976 around 20,000) is relatively much weaker than in England and Wales, and although Methodist ministers in Scottish charges are frequently English, the laity feel remote from the English Methodist Church. This has led to plans for union with the Church of Scotland, while English Methodists look to union with the (episcopalian) Church of England.

Finally, there is the Roman Catholic Church. Needless to say, unity with the Catholics is hardly ever discussed, except by Episcopalians. Yet it is the fastest growing Church in Scotland, having increased in size from 342,500 (all ages) in 1886 to 814,000 in 1976. To make this figure comparable with other Churches, only adults are counted, and this gives an estimate of around 540,000 (14 per cent of the adult population and 25 per cent of the total church membership in Scotland). About three-quarters of Scottish Catholics live in the Glasgow region, and their presence has a marked effect on social, educational and political life there. Most of them have Irish origins, and there are many Irish priests in Scotland, although the hierarchy is usually Scottish. In the Outer Hebrides, Argyllshire and Banffshire, an old Scottish Catholic tradition lingers on, untouched by the Reformation; however, these are a tiny minority and seem to have little influence on the Church as a whole in Scotland. Unlike the Church of Scotland, the Roman Catholic Church rarely pronounces on public issues, and does not attempt to be a spokesman for Scottish national opinion. It does, however, exert powerful political pressure in some subjects, most notably education and abortion. The Catholic Church has vested rights in education, since Catholic schools in Scotland are part of the state system. In the late 1960s, the Catholic Hierarchy resisted the abolition of fee-paying, selective Catholic schools in Glasgow, which under Labour Party policy were to become comprehensive, non-fee-paying and non-selective. In the 1970s, pressure to integrate Catholic and non-denominational schools increased, and the Labour Party Scottish conference in 1976 endorsed integration as an eventual aim, although not without the agreement of the Church itself. This agreement has never been granted by the Catholic Hierarchy, although the laity may not fully share their views. A survey in 1967 indicated that 63 per cent of Glasgow Catholics favoured integration of schools (*Glasgow Herald*, 29 April 1967).

Abortion law reform is another policy area which arouses Catholic opposition (and some Protestant opposition as well). Catholics attacked the Abortion Act, 1967, and campaigns against it were mounted. Anti-abortion campaigns were still considered strong influences in Scottish politics as late as 1978, for example during the Garscadden by-election (April 1978).

On moral questions such as these all the Churches are active, and the Church of Scotland may be considered responsible for the exclusion of Scotland from the Sexual Offences Act, 1967, concerning homosexuality. All the major Churches in the United Kingdom accepted the Wolfenden Report on homosexuality (1958), except the Church of Scotland, which opposed a change in the law. It was only in 1968 that the General Assembly voted to support homosexual law reform, after the Act had been passed for England and Wales only. Other moral stands have been taken by the Church of Scotland on free family planning, Sunday Observance and licensing law reform. On these, however, the Church has proved less successful, for changes in the law have occurred in a liberalising direction, and Scotland has either had its own legislation or has been covered by British legislation.

The main social conflict between Protestants and Catholics is to be seen in the Glasgow area, where 'Orange and Green' confrontations are common, even in the paint on city buses. The Orangemen (Scottish Protestant Union and Grand Orange Lodge) organise marches in Glasgow, Airdrie, New Cumnock and Paisley and other towns, to celebrate the Battle of the Boyne and other historic events, and these often lead to violence and arrests. So too do the football matches between Rangers (Protestant) and Celtic (Catholic) in Glasgow and to some extent Hearts (Protestant) and Hibernian (Catholic) in Edinburgh. Rangers do not employ Catholics, but Celtic employ Protestants. The Grand Orange Lodge in Scotland has a membership of around 40,000. Its members are nearly all working class, but it does not intervene in labour or trade union affairs, and in fact is Conservative in politics. Slogans such as 'No Popery' and 'Kick the Pope' are often seen on walls in Scotland but, part from the local violence, Orangeism leaves little mark on Scottish social and political life. Although the links between the Scottish Protestant Union and the Ulster militants, such as the Reverend Ian Paisley, are close, the Church of Scotland remains aloof from the Orangemen, as it did from the Ulstermen who sought to defy the Liberal government over Irish Home Rule in 1914.

Only about twenty ministers of the Church of Scotland in 1966 were associated with Orange Lodges (*Scotsman*, 9 July 1966).

In the past the Churches had a greater impact on party politics in Scotland than they do today. The great electoral strength of the Liberal Party in Scotland between 1832 and 1914, for example, is often attributed to the influence of Presbyterianism on the Scots' political aspirations for 'representative and responsible government'. Thus the ideals of the Victorian Liberal Party in parliamentary reform were already the ideals of Scottish Presbyterians in the running of their own affairs. But the Presbyterian clergy were not all of the same persuasion in politics, and the Disruption of 1843 led to political as well as religious cleavages. In the 1868 election, the ministers of the Free Church and the United Presbyterian Church were Liberal and the ministers of the Church of Scotland Conservative.[1] Many of the church members were influenced by sermons which became increasingly political as disestablishment was threatened. But a large section of the Established Church membership diverged from the clergy to vote Liberal, while, after 1886, the Unionist wing of the Liberal Party (later merged with the Conservatives in all but name) recruited some prominent dissenters. The Roman Catholic Church in Scotland was firmly allied to the Liberal Party from 1886 to the First World War, since the Liberals advocated Home Rule for Ireland. A small proportion of Catholics, however, followed John Wheatley to become 'Catholic Socialists' and to support Keir Hardie's Independent Labour Party. But it was only after Home Rule was granted (1922) that the mass of the Scottish Catholic working class became firm Labour supporters, and the hierarchy relaxed its opposition to the Labour Party. Today, 70–80 per cent of Catholics in Scotland vote Labour, and even middle-class Catholics vote Labour or abstain (Budge and Urwin, 1966, pp. 61–3; Brand, 1978, pp. 150–4). This means that in Glasgow, for example, where the Catholic vote is about 30 per cent of the whole, the Labour Party must not offend Catholic interests. All parties are sensitive to opinions expressed by the Church of Scotland although there is little evidence that it is leading opinion among the electorate. On Africa it is liberal (a result of missionary influence with Assembly committees) but on social and moral issues it is conservative. It has responded to the Scottish nationalist movement by supporting devolution, and in common with the other distinctively Scottish institutions it has a vested interest in the separate identity of Scotland. This does not mean that it believes in separation from England, for the 'threat' to Presbyterianism no longer comes from there but from apathy within Scotland itself.

There is still a 'Presbyterian Establishment' in Scotland, despite the rising membership of the Catholic Church, and religion plays a more important role in Scottish society than in English. For example, it is often noted that the communications media in Scotland are more concerned with ecclesiastical and theological questions: the reports of Assemblies and presbyteries and other church matters in the press, the nightly TV religious epilogues from Scottish transmitters, and so on. But relative to the nineteenth century the Church has lost power. In 1861, the shrewd English observer Henry Buckle considered that the Scots 'submitted their actions, as well as their consciences, to the authority of the Church' (Buckle, 1904, p. 4), and there is evidence that much of Scottish life at that time was in effect subject to a narrow oligarchy of clergymen and elders. One way or another they controlled education, social welfare and limited freedom of expression, and they just failed to make people vote the way they desired. But the Church shed its power voluntarily, in the face of the impossible social demands on its resources of the new industrial Scotland, and today what it retains is influence. Its pronouncements can persuade, but they cannot coerce, and the Assembly debates have improved because of this. The Church of Scotland was the historical inspiration for the 'democratic' Scottish educational system, and this, along with its important foreign mission work, is its greatest social contribution. The intolerance, bigotry and persecution which Buckle found in Scotland are not altogether gone, especially in the Highlands, but they are echoes of the past. Scotland is still distrustful of unorthodox opinion, but the orthodoxy of today is social and not religious.

NOTES

1 The votes of ministers in the Scottish universities' constituencies in 1868 are recorded. This was the last election before the introduction of the secret ballot in 1872.

|  | Conservative | Liberal |
|---|---|---|
| Church of Scotland | 1,221 | 67 |
| Free Church | 33 | 607 |
| United Presbyterian Church | 1 | 474 |
| Episcopalian | 78 | 4 |
| Not classified | 35 | 360 |
|  | 1,368 | 1,512 |

*Source*: G. W. T. Omond, *The Lord Advocates of Scotland, 2nd series: 1834–1880* (London, 1914), p. 245n.

FURTHER READING

Burleigh, J. H. S., *A Church History of Scotland* (1960).
   A good 'official' account of Scottish religion.
Highet, J., *The Scottish Churches* (1960).
   Facts about membership and attendances make this interesting, although it is now out of date.
MacLaren, A. A., *Religion and Social Class: The Disruption Years in Aberdeen* (1974).
   A historical materialist looks at Scottish church life in the 1840s, but the lessons are clear for the modern period.

*Chapter 5*

# Education

One hundred years have passed since the Reports of the Royal Commission on Schools in Scotland (the Argyll Commission) subjected the Scottish educational system to the most rigorous scrutiny it has ever known. Even today there is nothing to compare with it as a factual survey and as an evaluation of the aims of the system in relation to that of England and Wales. Yet the facts and the evaluation are sorely needed because in many respects Scottish education is still living on the legacy of its past greatness, the period when it could claim the admiration of nations such as England which were not so well endowed.

English Education Commissioners in the 1860s waxed eloquent about the virtues of the Scottish system and its benefits to society. One of them reported:

> The wealth of the Scotch people has not yet out-grown their civilisation, as has been the case in England. It seemed to me that in Scotland I seldom met with those barbarians, those very uncultivated rich or substantial people, whom one sees every summer lounging at the Welsh and North country sea-side towns, or hurrying through the Continent. The average middle Scotchman has more humanity and refinement than the average middle Englishman. Education has been more generally diffused; riches have been less rapidly and largely accumulated; and as a consequence these circumstances have again reacted on education; have caused the middle classes to value it more generally than those in England do; and have prevented the creation of that gulf which exists between men of cultivation and the middle classes in England, the existence of which all thoughtful persons, who have had a superior education, must have deplored.

The same social causes, combined with the existence of a better system of primary education than any we have hitherto had in England, have prevented the opening of a gulf between the middle and labouring classes. In England, it is not astonishing, though it is deplorable, that schoolboys should be divided into castes, and that a 'select school' should be the secret wish of parents' hearts. (Fearon, 1868, p. 19)

And of the Scottish universities:

The intensely national and popular character of the Scotch Universities causes their influence to be felt in every part of that wild and rugged country. In every corner of the kingdom; in the Islands as well as the Highlands; among the shepherds of the Grampians and the fishermen of Argyleshire, as well as among the weavers of Paisley, and the colliers of Ayr and Dumfries, the influence of one or other of the universities is keenly felt. (Fearon, 1868, p. 32)

This was in 1867. Today the comparisons are not so favourable. England has largely caught up with Scotland in education (although this took eighty years to achieve), and many would say that it is now ahead in methods of teaching, in the attainments of pupils and students, and in the general relationship of its schools and universities to the needs of society. Certainly, the days when England looked to Scotland as a model seem to have passed. Yet, it is unfortunate that, in the words of the author of a comparative study of Scottish and English schools, 'whatever developments are taking place in England are happening in a mood of sublime indifference to the educational system of Scotland, if not of the rest of the world' (Osborne, 1966, p. 28).

English education has owed a great deal to the example of Scotland in establishing within the British state the principle of 'a career open to talent'. Scotland had made this national orthodoxy since the Reformation in the sixteenth century, but it was far from being accepted in England until well into the twentieth century. The principle is explained, in its Scottish context, by the Argyll Commissioners:

It cannot be too often repeated, that the theory of our School system, as originally conceived, was to supply every member of the community with the means of obtaining for his children not only the elements of education, but such instruction as would fit him to pass to the Burgh school, and thence to the University, or directly to the University from the Parish school. (Argyll, Third Report, 1868, Vol. I, p. x).

To this end education was provided by the state in Scotland.

> The system of education in Scotland essentially differs from that
> in England. In England no public provision is made for supplying
> the people with education. There is no school in each parish which
> is maintained by taxation, and to which every child may demand
> admittance . . . In short, in England there is no attempt, either
> in theory or in practice, at a National System. But in Scotland
> provision is made by Statute for a school in every parish, and the
> schoolmaster holds a public office, from which he cannot be
> displaced at the discretion of any individual . . . In the one country
> there is at least, one public school in every rural parish, created by
> Statute, open to all, and supported by taxation; in the other there
> are no schools which can be considered as national institutions, nor
> is property subject to any tax for the purpose of promoting
> elementary education. (Argyll, Second Report, 1867, p. cvi)

Why Scotland and England differed so greatly in education is a
problem which cannot be ignored by the social historian, but the
answers are not at all clear. In one interpretation, the religious factor
is the key, and the basis of Scotland's schooling is the influence of
Presbyterianism. Certainly, John Knox and some other fathers of
the Church of Scotland put education at the front of their programme
of reform (for example, Knox's *First Book of Discipline*, 1560), and
an educated laity seemed essential to church government. Presbyterian
services, with their long sermons, required some mental response from
congregations, and the Shorter Catechism was an essential part of
schooling until the First World War. There were close links between
the Church of Scotland and the schools throughout the centuries. But
it is possible to see the Scottish concern with education as pre-
Reformation in origin, and as much the legacy of the Catholic Church
or the result of the Scottish kings' desire to attain stability in a
savage society through the training of educated supporters: James
IV's Education Act of 1496 made education compulsory for the sons
of freeholders. As for the egalitarianism of the system, the economic
and social aspects must be considered: Scotland was a poorer
country than England and the upper and middle classes could not
afford to convert the open grammar schools and parish schools into
their own exclusive preserves. Endowments were scarce in Scotland,
and the foundations of Eton and Winchester amounted in 1866 to
more than those of all the Scottish burgh schools and universities
together (Argyll, Third Report, Vol. I, p. xvi). Thus there was
perforce a mixing of social classes in the state schools, with the laird
and crofter sitting on the same classroom bench.

However, this 'democratic' aspect of Scottish education should not be exaggerated. Already in 1867 it was noted that 'very few, if any, children of the highest families, of the oldest large landed proprietors, or of the wealthiest professional men' were to be found in the burgh schools. They had decided to join their social equals in England and were to be found at Eton, Harrow, Rugby, Oxford and Cambridge (Fearon, 1868, p. 20). In Scotland the movement to establish independent middle-class schools was under way: boarding-schools equivalent to English public schools were opened (Loretto, 1829; Merchiston, 1833; Glenalmond, 1847; Fettes, 1870), and also day schools in the cities with fees high enough to keep out the poor boy without a bursary (for example, Edinburgh Academy and the Merchant Company schools in Edinburgh and Glasgow Academy). Wherever wealth increased, the social classes were separated in 'fee-paying' and 'non-fee-paying' schools. Today it may be true that there is more social mixing in Scottish schools than in English, but the class distinctions exist even although they are more subtle.

Until the early 1970s there was within the state system itself a distinct population of pupils attending fee-paying selective schools. Although educating only 2 per cent of all pupils, these schools formed a prestigious group, and to some they represented the best in Scottish education. They included the Royal High School in Edinburgh (proposed seat of the Scottish Assembly), the High School of Glasgow, and Allan Glen's School, Glasgow. The fees charged were very low (£23 per session at Glasgow High School, and £10 at Glasgow Hillhead High School in 1967), and advocates of the selective system claimed that such schools opened an avenue to clever working-class children to obtain a superior education which a local compre-hensive school could not provide. The payment of fees was always part of the Scottish educational tradition, and was justified on the grounds that education necessitated sacrifice and 'self-help': Samuel Smiles, who wrote the celebrated Victorian classic of that name, was a Scot. At the same time, Scotland provided free education before England. Free elementary education was established in 1889 (England and Wales, 1891), and free secondary education in 1918 (England and Wales, 1944).

In 1965 the Labour government embarked on a policy of compre-hensivisation, to cover all of Great Britain. There was some resistance to this in Scotland, even from Labour Party supporters, and especi-ally from the Roman Catholic Hierarchy, which felt that Catholic selective schooling gave opportunities of upward mobility to a largely working-class laity. But this clashed with Labour's educational philosophy, and after a brief campaign to save the local authority selective schools, these disappeared completely with the final closure of Glasgow High School in 1976. The school then reopened as an independent school on another site. By 1976 99 per cent of public sector pupils in Scottish secondary schools were attending comprehensive schools, while in England the figure was only 70 per cent.

Those desiring selective schooling have now to find a place in the grant-aided or independent schools. The former had 2 per cent of all pupils in 1976, and they include such famous schools as George Watson's in Edinburgh, Hutchesons' Grammar School in Glasgow, and Robert Gordon's College in Aberdeen. Their fees are relatively low by English 'direct grant' school standards, but unlike these schools Scottish grant-aided schools did not provide a proportion of free places to pupils nominated by local authorities.

Independent schools (1·6 per cent of pupils in Scotland compared with 4·5 per cent in England) include the equivalent of the English 'public schools'. They are still prominent, if expensive, and serve basically the more anglicised Scottish middle class, as well as some of the English middle class itself. Many of the Scottish upper middle and upper classes send their children to the famous English public schools. It is common to hear strong 'public school' accents in these social groups in Scotland, especially among the landowning class.

The career fully open to talent, then, cannot be accepted as an entirely accurate description of Scottish educational practice, although the very talented could usually rely on winning bursaries and scholarships. In the past, the proportion of the population receiving elementary education in Scotland was high compared to England.[1] In 1871, 78·6 per cent of children between 5 and 13 were receiving education (*1871 Census (Scotland)*, Vol. I, p. xliv), and the Scottish Education Act of 1872 made education compulsory in that age group. In England, the Elementary Education Act of 1870 did not make education compulsory, but by 1880 the compulsory aspect had been fully accepted.

More important, perhaps, was the distinction between Scotland and England in secondary and university education. The Argyll Commission noted that, in the 1860s, 1 in 140 of the Scottish population received secondary education, while only 1 in 1,300 did so in England (Argyll, Third Report, Vol. I, p. viii). The Scottish Education Act was not just an Elementary Education Act as in England; the school boards were empowered to provide secondary education, although this could not be made a burden on the rates. This was a serious financial disability, and secondary education in Scotland suffered a set-back in many schools, for it no longer paid to give advanced teaching in schools which had inadequate incomes from fees and private funds. The government eventually gave grants for secondary education in 1892, but in the meantime, much of the old 'ladder of opportunity' from parish school to university had been destroyed. Unless the country schools had access to private foundations (as many had in the counties of Aberdeen, Banff and Moray) they could not compete with the burgh schools, and the 'dominie' lost touch with teaching up to university entrance standard. From this time a new distinction between primary and secondary schools (ever-present in England) began in Scotland which only the modern all-through 'comprehensive' schooling has eradicated.

Widespread university education was the culminating achievement of the Scottish educational system. In 1865 Scotland had one student for every thousand of the population, a proportion unsurpassed by any other country, and well ahead of England with 1 in 5,800 (Argyll, Third Report, Vol. I, p. ix). With four ancient universities (St Andrews, Glasgow, Aberdeen and Edinburgh) and technical colleges in Glasgow and Edinburgh (now Strathclyde and Heriot-Watt universities), higher education was valued both for itself and as a practical training for the professions and for science and technology. In Scotland university qualifications were demanded or strongly encouraged in order to enter a career in law, the Church, teaching or medicine. Glasgow's technology was important in the industrial development of the Clyde, while farming in the North-East Lowlands (especially stock-breeding) owed much to the study of agriculture and biology at Aberdeen University. Today, Aberdeen also has the Rowett Institute (animal research), for many years associated with Lord Boyd Orr,[2] the Macaulay Institute (soil research) and the North of Scotland College of Agriculture.

The Scottish universities imposed no religious tests on students, and many English Nonconformists, who were barred from Oxford and Cambridge until the latter half of the nineteenth century, came north to study at Edinburgh or Glasgow, where famous philosophy and medical departments existed. Scotland has always heavily subsidised English university education in this way, while only a very small number of those who went to school in Scotland become students in England. Until 1962, Scots were actively discouraged from studying in England by the withholding of local authority grants from students who chose to go elsewhere than to their nearest university, and the English universities for their part have been reluctant to recognise as an entrance qualification the Scottish Certificate of Education, which has the same function as the General Certificate of Education (GCE). Thus 23 per cent of the students at Scottish universities in 1961 were English or Welsh, but only 0·7 per cent of the English and Welsh student population was Scottish (Robbins, 1963, Vol. I, App. I, p. 200).[3]

Despite this, it is the intense localism of most of the Scottish universities which is striking, and not any cosmopolitanism. Almost half the students in Scotland live at home, and at Glasgow the figure in 1977 was as high as 66 per cent. This is quite unlike the way of life of students in the rest of British universities, where less than a fifth live at home. Many of the staff, too, especially in medicine and science, are locally recruited, despite the increasing attraction of work in other countries. This is both a source of strength and of weakness: most Scots, no matter how clever academically, want to study and perhaps even to teach in a Scottish university in preference to any other.[4] This means that the 'creaming-off' process in England (whereby the best students and staff go chiefly to Oxford, Cambridge and London) does not exist in Scotland. Students of all abilities apply to their local university and there is no hierarchy of prestige in the system: all Scottish universities are equal. There is an equivalent quality in the staff: Scottish professorships are sought after for the power they command, a power which extends both inside and outside the university and is greater than in England.

But the drawbacks are obvious. Even if only a small minority of Scottish students would have preferred to enter a university other than their own (compared with about half of students in England and Wales), it is likely that their bliss is the result of ignorance. Far too many Scots, even those with university degrees, complete their formal education and spend their entire careers within the confines of one Scottish city. Quite often, the most culture-bound of all are the Scottish teachers and they transmit their narrowness to the population as a whole. Their awareness of social values and environments other than their own is dangerously small, and they have not experienced any uprooting which could enable them to see their society in a more objective fashion. Of course, large numbers of educated Scots leave Scotland and experience the clash of cultures for themselves, but too few return to make much of an impact on Scottish society. Thus, parochialism must be recognised as the price paid for the strong links between the Scottish university and the community.

The Myth of the crofter's son who became a professor was a popular one, and indeed could be supported by actual examples. Moreover, working-class students amounted to a fifth of the total in 1866, at a time when very few indeed could be found in England (Argyll, Third Report, Vol. I, p. 155). By 1910, 30 per cent of Glasgow students were working-class (McDonald, 1964, p. 83), and in all the Scottish universities the lower middle class has always been well represented. In this way, Scotland provided proportionately twice as many places at university as England until the 1950s, when the great English university expansion got under way. In 1961, the margin had narrowed considerably and Scotland had 5 per cent of the student age group at university compared with 4 per cent in England and Wales (Robbins, 1963, App. I, pp. 15, 26). By 1974, 8 per cent of school-leavers in Scotland went on to university, and 5·6 per cent in England and Wales. When all students in further and higher education are taken into account, Scotland actually comes off poorer today. In 1975, 19 per cent of Scottish school-leavers continued full-time education, compared with 22 per cent in England and Wales. The difference is largely explained by the more flourishing further education sector in England and Wales.

It is now incorrect to say that the Scottish universities have the highest proportion of working-class students: the Kelsall Report in 1957 showed that this was smaller in Scotland than at the English 'red-brick' universities (Kelsall, 1957, p. 9), and the proportion in 1972 was around 30 per cent (Hutchison and McPherson, 1976).

Of course, the absolute number of students has greatly increased. In 1975–6, 40,500 were attending courses at the eight universities, while in 1892–3 the total was 6,488 at the four ancient universities. St Andrews then had only 197 students (3,332 in 1975), but Edinburgh and Glasgow were already large institutions with around 2,000 or 3,000 students each. One of the great innovations of the period was the admission of women to degree courses in 1892, which especially swelled the numbers at St Andrews, and since that time women have enjoyed a much better prospect of a university place in Scotland than in England. In 1976, they constituted 40 per cent of the student population (a third in England and Wales), and in Arts courses often outnumber the men. Where many women in the south attend teacher-training colleges, in Scotland they often prefer to take an Ordinary Arts degree which will bring them a higher salary as teachers. Thus there is a more balanced distribution of the sexes in Scottish universities – a fact which may comfort the many students who are forced to continue living with their parents.

Until well into the twentieth century there was little doubt but that Scotland was a better educated nation than England. At least, there was more education, in the sense of the number of people who were involved in teaching and in being taught. At the present time, there is little to choose between Scotland and England in the amount of education which is being consumed. Scots tend to go to school later and to leave earlier than is customary in England but the same proportion stay on to 18 and gain university entrance qualifications. It is easier to get a university place in Scotland, and Scotland provides 15 per cent of the university places in the United Kingdom, and in this sense is still subsidising the rest of the country.

There remains an important difference between Scotland and England in the part played by the state in education, and in the relationship between the school, education authority and government department. The Argyll Commission showed that before 1872 the number of rate-supported parish schools and pupils was less than a third of the total of schools and pupils in Scotland (Argyll, Second Report, App., p. 24). Thus, although there was a 'national system' of education, the denominational and private sector was larger. After the 1872 Act, however, all the denominational schools except the Catholic and Episcopalian came under the school boards. In 1918, nearly all these schools too were forced to join the state system so that today only 3·6 per cent of pupils in Scotland are not educated in state schools. In England and Wales, denominational schools (especially Church of England and Roman Catholic) are still important, and the 'private sector' accounts for almost 6 per cent of the pupils.

The state, then, has a tighter hold on the people's education in Scotland, and this is accentuated by the somewhat authoritarian role of central and local government in all aspects of schooling. The Scottish Education Department and the education committees of the local authorities have more direct control over schools, the appointment of teachers and the content of education than their counterparts in England and Wales. This is partly a result of the different settlement as to the voluntary schools; in England, even when these have been transferred to the state, the buildings are owned by their trustees and boards of governors are retained for the schools. All state schools in England have separate committees of management, while in Scotland they are directly under the authority of the education committee, on which until 1963 there could not be any teachers (unlike England). Teaching appointments in Scotland are made by the education committees or Directors of Education of the local authorities, not by the headmasters and managers, and the Directors of Education determine much of the organisation of schooling in their areas.

Finally, the Scottish Education Department is relatively stronger than the Department of Education in England and Wales. This is largely a result of historical factors: state education is traditional in Scotland, and the Scotch Education Department and school boards were given powers in 1872 to maintain schools in every parish, while in England the state stepped in to establish a school only if the private sector was deficient. Until 1899, when the Board of Education was established, there was no equivalent of the Scotch Education Department in England, and even then the central government never assumed the same powers of direction that it had in Scotland. Instead power remained localised at the school and local authority level and the Board acted merely as a co-ordinator. Inspection of schools was undertaken principally by the local authority, and there was no dictation of the curriculum from the centre.

The picture is very different in Scotland. Maintenance of schools by the public authorities depended on the reports of Inspectors of the Scotch Education Department, who imposed their standards throughout the country. In 1888 the Scottish Leaving Certificate was instituted, and the examining was in the hands of the Scotch Education Department, which also prescribed the courses of instruction. Any school which presented pupils for this examination (which was a qualification for university entrance) came under the inspection and domination of the Department, and before long every secondary school (except a few independent schools) provided a uniform curriculum. Thus the content, as well as the organisation, of Scottish schooling was controlled by the state, from which stranglehold it was impossible to break loose.

Most of this is still true. There is still a powerful national Inspectorate and a single school-leaving examination authority for Scotland, in contrast to England's diffusion of control. (In England and Wales eight examining boards set and mark their own GCE examinations in co-ordination with a government-appointed Schools Council. There are also fourteen CSE (Certificate of Secondary Education) Regional Examining Boards.) In England, 'the policy-making, or directive power has tended to cluster around the local education authorities: the representation of local interests around the individual school. In the simpler Scottish system the directive agency is the Department: local interest tends to be represented by the education authority rather than the school' (Osborne, 1966, p. 37). There is thus less variation between one school and another in Scotland, and less freedom to experiment in methods of teaching. Everything hinges on state examinations and satisfying the Department. Until about twenty years ago, the Department's policy was to conserve rather than to experiment, and Scottish education stagnated. There were very few Scottish schools in which the teaching had moved on much in fifty years and it was England which was setting the pace. The teachers themselves did not particularly want to change; they continued to look for direction to the central authority. In recent years, the Scottish Education Department has been demanding a new approach, especially in primary teaching, and its influence should prevail, although the national uniformity will no doubt remain. But it will take a generation or more to shake the Scots' faith in their style of teaching, which must next be examined since it is of very ancient lineage and perhaps even part of the Scottish national character itself.

## TEACHING RATHER THAN LEARNING

The aims which teachers and educationists set themselves vary considerably from country to country. In one, the imparting of knowledge and the training of minds to deal with that knowledge is the chief purpose of education. In another, the whole character and behaviour of the pupil is as much the object of schooling as his intellect. The mode which is adopted is rooted in the attitudes of society, but the experiences of the classroom also shape the style of that society, and the relationship between pupil and teacher affects many other formal relationships in adult life.

Most people who come into contact with Scottish education, or perhaps even with Scots, are conscious that the Scottish intellect has characteristics of its own. They see the Scots as 'dour' or 'argument-ative', 'academic' or 'deductive' rather than 'pragmatic' or 'inductive', and a host of analogies can be drawn between styles of thinking in Scots philosophy, religion, law and education to point the differences with England (Buckle, 1904; Davie, 1961). The Scots themselves are aware of national characteristics which manifest themselves at a personal level: while they feel better educated than the English, they are unable to talk well by comparison or to feel assured in company (Budge and Urwin, 1966, p. 123). Thus their apparent intellectual strength is sapped by social insecurity. These generalisations can be heard repeated in many contexts today: by personnel managers in industry or senior civil servants, who notice that Scottish candidates do not show up well at interviews.

This is borne out by the results of entrance examinations to the Administrative Class of the Civil Service (1948–63). While 18·5 per cent of the Scottish graduates who competed by Method I (which places the emphasis on written exams) were successful, only 5 per cent were successful by Method II (which is largely based on 'personality tests'). This should be compared with the figures for all British university candidates (Method I, 18·7 per cent successful; Method II, 9·5 per cent successful). It is interesting that Scots fought shy of these exams (they were only 7·5 per cent of UK and Eire applicants), yet they were very successful by Method I, coming next to Oxford and Cambridge (27 per cent of applicants successful), and well above the next highest, London (9 per cent). Scottish graduates made up 5·3 per cent of the total entrants to the Administrative Class in the period (Oxford and Cambridge, 81 per cent; London, 8 per cent; other UK universities and Eire, 4·4 per cent). (Derived from Minutes of Evidence in *6th Report from the Estimates Committee*, HC 1964–5 (308), p. 29.)

University tutors sometimes find it difficult to make the ordinary Scottish student participate in discussions. And it is undoubtedly true that shyness in company is endemic in Scotland, outside those consanguineous assemblies such as highland gatherings and football matches when all inhibitions are cast aside. In a formal relationship with strangers the Scot is at a loss for words; amongst his own he is loquacious and aggressive.

How far can this be traced to his education? The atmosphere of the Scottish classroom (excluding independent schools) is at first sight daunting to the southerner. Discipline is rigidly maintained by many teachers through corporal punishment with a leather strap or 'tawse' (even in primary schools and girls' classes), and academic success, rewarded by a top seat in class, is the official aim of the pupils. This success can be achieved only by hard work, right from an early age. Even young pupils slog at hours of homework, trying to assimilate the back-log of facts and figures which are imparted by the teachers. Frequent tests and reapportionments of class places keep the pupils on their toes, and prize-givings crown the year's achievements.

There are now progressive primary schools in Scotland, but they are still rather unusual. A Scottish Education Report of the 1960s said:

> Much of the work in the classrooms still follows an orthodox pattern, the time-table conditioning the day's routine . . . The change from traditional arithmetic is very slow, and it is still not sufficiently realised that in mathematics, as in the curriculum generally, the need to meet individual requirements, to provide a stimulating environment, and to give pupils the opportunity of having first-hand experience and direct observation are fundamental principles in any learning situation. (*Education in Scotland in 1966*, Cmnd 3216, p. 20)

In other words, the old didactic and academic approach, unrelated to real life and pupils' needs, lingers on in Scotland, and the pupils have often little opportunity to understand or make use of what they are taught. This danger was realised over a hundred years ago, when the Argyll Commissioners examined the parish schools, and the words of the official reports have changed hardly at all since that time.

> Instead of trying to bring everyday affairs to bear upon the lessons, some schoolmasters seem to think that they must eschew all that is familiar in the schoolroom, and live in a world of pedantry. So it is in the teaching of arithmetic. Children are taught to do their sums by rules and mechanical processes, but they are not taught to understand what they are doing, and why they are putting down figures in a peculiar way. Very few children can explain the meaning of the simplest rules of arithmetic, and teachers do not seem to think that they ought to teach anything but the mechanical art of counting. It never seems to strike them that thought is an element in arithmetic. (Argyll, Second Report, Vol. III, p. 162)

This was the major fault in Scottish education. The widespread schooling of the past produced a high degree of elementary literacy,[5] and a number of examples of cultured, even learned, men in humble positions. But a great deal of Victorian teaching was by rote and failed to penetrate the understanding. 'If teachers would only educate their pupils, and bring out what is in their minds, instead of pouring a quantity of knowledge in upon them, which they forget as soon as they leave school, and which they are too young to find interesting, it would be a great step towards a higher state of education in the country' (Argyll, Second Report, Vol. III, p. 161). When the Argyll Commissioners asked pupils what was meant by their answers to the Shorter Catechism, they got nowhere, yet 'catechising' was the method of teaching in most parish schools. 'When the answers did come, they would normally be in the form of texts or phrases which the children repeated, which were clearly unintelligible to themselves, and when asked to explain them, they would be unable or unwilling to speak' (ibid., pp. 156–7).

This rote learning has not altogether died out in Scotland, despite the recent advances in teaching methods in many primary schools and in the teaching of physics and chemistry in secondary schools (the Scottish curricula in these subjects are probably ahead of England). There is little advanced study at school, since sixth forms of the English type do not exist, the 'Highers' being essentially a fifth-year certificate. What is considered the province of the school in England is transferred to the first year at the university in Scotland, and all students (whether intending Honours or not) sit together in the large Ordinary classes. Over half of all Scottish students in the early 1970s followed Ordinary degree courses, compared with 20 per cent for the UK as a whole. In Arts, these usually cover five separate subjects. A large number of these students carry with them to university the habits of school, where knowledge was dictated by the teacher, and they rely heavily on their notes of the lectures. Since they have neither the time nor the inclination to read widely, their performance in tutorials and exams is generally stereotyped and their grasp of the subject limited. This is probably largely due to the fact that there is more formal teaching by lectures and less tutorial work in Scottish universities than in other British universities. In recent years, however, tutorial work has greatly increased in Scottish universities. Conversely, the Scottish students do know something about several disciplines, and in theory they have had a 'liberal' education.

This liberal education is the second tradition in Scotland (the first being the disciplined inculcation of facts by rote). Some writers have expounded an exalted theory about the universalist comprehension of the pre-1900 Scottish educational process, in which philosophy teaching at the university was the lynchpin (Davie, 1961, p. xvii). This teaching was supposed to relate the disparate studies in the Ordinary Arts degree course of classics, mathematics, science, and so on, and thus give it unity. Even today philosophy or logic is compulsory for Ordinary Arts students at three Scottish universities (Glasgow, Edinburgh and St Andrews), and Honours students take two 'outside' subjects to their specialism, philosophy being a favourite.

Students are prepared for this breadth of study by the non-specialised nature of their secondary school courses. Unlike those in England, where specialisation is carried very far at school, Scottish secondary courses include more subjects throughout, and the Higher passes in the Scottish Certificate of Education, which count for university entrance, are lower in standard than English 'A' levels and are taken a year earlier (at age 17 or 18). But it has traditionally been necessary for university entrance to pass in English, maths or science, and a foreign language at Higher level, and many pupils have five or six Highers to their credit. (In England, the equivalent would be three or four 'A' levels in related subjects.) English pupils, however, do more 'O' levels than is customary in Scotland and for an extra year, so to that extent it is Scotland which is more specialised. Scottish secondary courses begin at the age of 12 (not 11 as in England), which gives one year less for certificate work, and the number of subjects which can be studied to 'O' grade is reduced.

In 1975, 35 per cent of school-leavers in Scotland had no certificate qualifications (including 'O' grade at bands D–E), while in England the figure was only 17 per cent (excluding CSE). But those with 'higher grade' (bands A–C) 'O' passes, or passes at Higher or 'A' level, were 57 per cent of school-leavers in Scotland, and 48 per cent in England. At the 'élite' end of the scale (that is, those possessing university entrance qualifications of at least three Highers or two 'A' levels), Scotland again came out better, with 18 per cent of school-leavers thus qualified, compared with 13 per cent in England (CSO, *Regional Statistics, 1977*, pp. 80, 83).

In the 1960s and 1970s the Scottish universities changed their entrance requirements, partly to allow for specialisation at school, but also to attract more students. There was still a 'general entrance requirement' for the Scottish universities, set by the Scottish Universities Council on Entrance, but the foreign languages and maths/science requirement could be met at 'O' grade instead of Higher, and two universities, Heriot-Watt and Strathclyde, required only English (although even that might not be possessed by all English-based applicants). In practice, each university decides which students it is going to accept, and there are faculty and course requirements. In Scotland, applicants are admitted to faculties, not departments, and are not usually interviewed, as they frequently are in England.

In recent years there has been much talk, and some action, about reforming the examination system and the curriculum. In the 1960s, the process of anglicisation could be clearly seen in the introduction of the 'O' grade examination in 1962 (just Scottish enough to resist being an 'O' *level*), and in the attempt to introduce an 'A' level to replace the Highers. The old Scottish Leaving Certificate (Highers and Lowers, taken as a 'group') was an élite qualification taken by under

10 per cent of pupils, and in 1962 only 61 per cent of those who entered on such courses had completed them to fourth-year standard (91 per cent in England) (Osborne, 1966, p. 221). Yet the initial intake to secondary certificate courses in Scotland was twice as great in proportion to the age group (40 per cent) as in England (Osborne, p. 218). The introduction of the 'O' grade reduced this wastage, and by 1976 three-quarters of the age group were being presented for 'O' grade examinations, and about 60 per cent of the age group achieved one or more passes.

By this time, however, the school-leaving age had been raised to 16 (this happened in 1972), and there was now a much larger group of pupils in the fourth year of the secondary school. In England, a Certificate of Secondary Education (CSE) has been introduced at a standard lower than 'O' level. Now Scotland was once again out-flanked by an English examination, and in 1977 the Dunning Committee recommended 'Assessment for All' through a new system of examinations called the 'Certificate of Education – Scotland'. This would be awarded to all pupils completing Fourth Year Secondary, and would be set at three levels. At the same time, the Munn Report on 'The Structure of the Curriculum in the Third and Fourth Years of the Scottish Secondary School' advocated something of a return to the broad 'core' of subjects in Scottish schools, with compulsory English, maths, science, social subjects and creative subjects. The cost and complexity of these proposals has inhibited their realisation, but they repeat the old pattern of reform in a Scottish context, which is largely inspired by British-wide changes, such as comprehensive schooling and the raising of the school-leaving age and by the example of English examinations.

One English examination which did not find a true counterpart in Scottish schools was the 'A' level. The Scottish Education Department in 1961 proposed that a Scottish 'A' level be introduced, but this was defeated by a typical Scottish combination of theory and expediency. The theorists defended the liberal tradition, and pointed to the 'overspecialisation' in England, where the Two Cultures can never meet. The realists pointed to the shortage of teachers and to the difficulty of running new sixth forms on the English model (at present most students have had schooling only up to fifth year). The crucial factor was the virtual refusal of headmasters to co-operate with the Scottish Education Department, and instead a watered-down 'Certificate of Sixth Year Studies' was introduced in 1968, although it was not intended to replace the Highers as a university or professional entrance qualification, and is taken by only a small minority of pupils. The absence of an English sixth form in most Scottish schools is one of the major differences marking off Scottish students from English, and this has been criticised by some university teachers who feel that Scottish students are less well prepared for university study than English students.

But the content of Scottish secondary school courses has always been regarded as a preparation for university. It has thus been traditional orthodoxy that the same education is given to all, irrespective of whether the pupil desires, or is able, to go to university. This is part of the 'ladder of opportunity' theory, of equal chances for all, but it makes schooling uniform and academic and pays little attention to the needs of all the pupils.

Even those who do get to university may find that they are at sea in large first-year classes, with little contact with staff. There is considerable wastage in Scottish universities: about 18 per cent of the students fail to graduate, a higher figure than in England (12 per cent: *Scotsman,* 24 May 1979), although much lower than in the United States and in other European countries. Once more it has to be remembered that there is a higher intake of the population to university in Scotland than in England, and in general it is part of the 'democratic system' that as many as possible should be permitted to embark on courses, even when it is likely that a large number will fail. In this, Scotland resembles countries such as France which admit large numbers of students to first-year classes and then fail half of them.

Unfortunately, this democratic approach seems to have penalised those who are able to study at an advanced level. Since most attention must be paid to the majority of pupils and students, there is little 'higher learning' either at school or university. We have seen that sixth-form work is rarely undertaken in Scotland (outside certain town schools), and in the universities research students are a smaller percentage of the total than in other British universities. This continues a long-standing difference between Scotland and England, for it was observed by Matthew Arnold in 1866 that:

> The Scotch, as the state of their universities show, have little notion of *la grande culture.* Instead of guarding, like the Germans, the *wissentshaftliche* [sic] *Geist* of their universities, they turn them into mere school-classes . . . and the University [of Edinburgh] recruits its Greek classes from the third or fourth forms of the High School. Accordingly, while the aristocratic class of Scotland is by its bringing up, it faults, its merits, much the same as the aristocratic class in England, the Scotch middle class is in *la grande culture* not ahead of the English middle class. But so far as intellectual culture has an industrial value, makes a man's business-work better, and helps him to get on in the world, the Scotch middle class has thoroughly appreciated it and sedulously employed it, both for itself and for the class whose labour it uses; and here is

their superiority to the English, and the reason of the success of Scotch skilled labourers and Scotch men of business everywhere. (*Arnold's Report*, 1868, p. 622).

As a result, to the Scots, the notion of a liberal education has never in modern times included cultivation of the Arts such as painting and sculpture, music, drama and modern literature. These have always been neglected in Scottish schools in favour of the old academic or practical disciplines such as classics and mathematics, and it is because of this that Scotland has been desperately short of creative artists. The arts flourished in Scotland until the late eighteenth century, but the new-found puritanism of the Church drove them underground and out of the schools. 'Every gateway seemed closed that led into that realm of ideas and feeling which is called the Beautiful' (Simpson, 1947, p. 34). Thus, earlier educational traditions such as the 'song schools' died out, and music was no longer cultivated by the Church. In England, choir schools have always been maintained by many cathedrals and have educated many prominent English musicians, but in Scotland it is only since the 1930s that music has been seriously taught in Scottish schools.

Time spent in school on art, music or drama is usually grudged by headmasters (with some exceptions) as non-profitable in academic terms, and the more able pupils are steered away from certificate courses in these subjects, if indeed any are offered. The attitude of teachers to the arts is transmitted to Scottish life as a whole, and materialism and puritanism combine to strangle many cultural pursuits. Such ventures as the Edinburgh Festival and the repertory theatres, for example, are frequently attacked and are directed mainly by non-Scots. There has been some change in the Scot's attitude to the arts, but it is probably more a result of mass communications from outside Scotland than any inspiration from the schools.

The arts are also inconsistent with Scottish teaching methods, since they imply a degree of self-expression and individuality in the pupils which does not accord with the acceptable pupil–teacher relationship. This, as we have seen, is essentially one in which there is a flow of instruction from the teacher to the pupil, with little informal tuition. The Scottish teacher is nearly always concerned with the intellectual (*sc.* academic) progress of his pupils, and not with the formation of character. He adopts a similar attitude to children of all ages, at one time acting as if they were adults and had no special 'growing pains', and at another treating even the oldest pupils as children.

There is no real development then in the pupil–teacher relationship from childhood to adult responsibility. Scottish pupils are not generally encouraged to take on important duties in the school, such as the supervision of their fellows, and the 'prefect system' is less influential. 'Authority' in school is synonymous with the teachers, and 'obedience' the common lot of the pupils. It is there that educational traditions in Scotland and England have their most subtle distinction. In Scotland, schooling is in essence part-time and has partial aims. The family is of equal importance for the child and is responsible for his moral and 'non-academic' code. The teacher merely imparts information and know-how, and does not try to shape character. The English teacher, on the other hand, is concerned with the life of the pupil as a whole, and for many in England a boarding school education (which removes the child from the family completely) is the most valuable. There the teacher's task is more difficult, and the influence of the school on the lives of the citizens greater. Certainly, in Scotland there is nothing like the nostalgia shown by many Englishmen for their schooldays.

Despite the fact that English teachers are concerned with both academic and non-academic education, and are thus very influential shapers of society, it is the Scots who value a professional training for teachers most highly. Graduation from a college of education is required of all qualified teachers, and until 1970 all men teachers had to be university graduates. This was in contrast to England, where 'qualified' teachers required no specific training in education at all until 1972, and where men teachers need not be graduates.

Now that Scotland and England have come closer together there is perhaps little to choose between them in the quality of teachers or of the education offered. There are still 'black spots' in Scottish education. There is a shortage of teachers in the Strathclyde Region, which includes Glasgow, although the overall Scottish ratio of teachers to pupils was better than that in England by the mid-1970s. In 1975 it was 1:22·4 pupils in primary schools, and 1:15·1 in secondary (England, 1:24 in primary, 1:17 in secondary).

Scottish teachers are supposed to control questions of certification themselves through their General Teaching Council (similar to the General Medical Council for doctors), and thus they have more say in the rules of their profession than English teachers, but the Scottish Education Department and the local authorities decide how many are to be employed in schools. Thus improving standards is as much a political as a professional matter.

Many of the differences between Scotland and England stem from education, as they do from religion. But the similarities between the two countries are greater in education than in religion. The universities in Scotland have copied many aspects of those in England (Honours degrees, tutorials, entrance requirements),[6] and the schools grow daily more like those in the south. This is a matter of economic necessity: Scots must be able to compete for jobs in England on

equal terms with those whose qualifications are English. Their education must be comparable, if not identical. The process of assimilation
has been going on for over a hundred years. As soon as Scots started
failing the new Indian Civil Service examinations in the 1850s because
they had followed different courses of instruction, they demanded a
revision of the university degrees, with more specialisation (Davie,
1961, p. 211). If specialists are required in industry and government,
then the Scots will not retain for long their Ordinary degrees. As it
is, these degrees survive largely because graduate teachers in Scotland
obtain substantial financial benefits compared to other teachers. The
Ordinary degrees serve a practical purpose as much as an academic
one, and would disappear if they had no value economically.

Scottish education is more vulnerable than Presbyterianism. It is
more subject to the assimilation process in British society, and the
grounds for maintaining it as a distinct form seem less clear. Many
outsiders in Scotland are impatient with it, and in general it lacks
the respect given the Kirk. This may be mistaken, for much of
Scotland's importance as a nation has derived from the diffusion and
strength of its educational system. Whether it should consciously
evolve along peculiarly Scottish lines or merely copy England is probably irrelevant. The end product, as a reflection of Scottish society,
is bound to be unique.

NOTES

1   In 1865, 1 in 6·5 of the Scottish population was on the roll of an
    elementary school, and 1 in 7·7 in England and Wales. Some European
    comparisons were: France, 1 in 9; Holland, 1 in 8·1; Prussia, 1 in 6·3
    (Argyll, Second Report, 1867, p. xix).
2   1949 Nobel Peace Prize winner; first director-general of the FAO.
    He did most of his research at the Rowett Institute.
3   There is another interpretation however: in the early 1960s, 5 per cent
    of Scottish university entrants went to universities in England and Wales,
    and 4 per cent of English/Welsh entrants went to Scottish universities
    (Robbins, 1963, Vol. 1, pp. 14, 25). The Scots who went south would
    appear to be mainly the products of the independent schools who sit the
    GCE. Most of the English students go to Edinburgh or St Andrews
    universities. In 1956, the percentage of students who were domiciled in
    Scotland was: 91 per cent at Glasgow, 63 per cent at Edinburgh, 47 per
    cent at St Andrews, 86 per cent at Aberdeen (H. A. Moisley, 'The
    domiciles of Scottish university students', *Scottish Studies*, vol. IV (1960),
    p. 77). In 1976, the corresponding figures of Scottish-domiciled university
    entrants were Glasgow 95 per cent, Edinburgh 77 per cent, St Andrews
    48 per cent, Aberdeen 82 per cent. Dundee had 65 per cent Scottish-
    domiciled, Heriot-Watt 74 per cent, Stirling 66 per cent and Strathclyde
    87 per cent (Scottish Universities' Council on Entrance, *Report for
    1976–7*, p. 12).
4   The Robbins Report gave a picture of university teachers in the early
    1960s. Of those who graduated in Scotland, 65 per cent were teaching

there. They accounted for 51 per cent of the teachers in Scottish universities and 13 per cent of the teachers in all British universities. But in Oxford and Cambridge there was more inbreeding, for 78 per cent of their teachers graduated there (48 per cent inbred in London; 40 per cent at English civic universities.) Scotland came next to Oxford and Cambridge in the percentage of its university teachers with Honours degrees who had first class honours (Oxford and Cambridge 76 per cent; Scottish 65 per cent; London 54 per cent; larger civic 52 per cent). In 1961 there were 8·8 students per teacher in Scotland, and 7·2 in England (excluding Oxford and Cambridge). In 1938 the corresponding figures were 14·0 and 8·9 (Robbins, 1963, Vol. I, App. III, pp. 7, 20, 36, 181–2).

5  In 1855 the percentage who signed the marriage register in writing in Scotland was men 89 per cent, women 77 per cent. In England it was men 70 per cent, women 59 per cent (Argyll, Second Report, p. cvii).

6  Some of the copying, however, has been done by England. Keele (founded by a Scot, A. D. [Lord] Lindsay) adopted the four-year Honours degree and the breadth of subjects, and this is also found in the other new English universities. The Robbins Report encouraged the notion of a wider range of subjects within university degrees, and English education reports in recent years have recommended changes in schools along Scottish lines, especially in curriculum and examinations.


FURTHER READING

Bell, R. and Grant, N., *Patterns of Education in the British Isles* (1977).
    Exposes the great diversity of educational practice in England, Scotland, Wales, Northern Ireland and the Republic of Ireland.
Osborne, G. S., *Scottish and English Schools* (1966).
    Detailed comparison of Scotland and England up to the mid-1960s.
Davie, G. E., *The Democratic Intellect* (1961).
    The now classic work on how Scotland's educational élite became subverted by anglicisation.
Scottish Office, *Scottish Educational Statistics* (occasional).
    Masses of facts, or rather, figures.

# Chapter 6

# Scots Law

## A CONSTITUTION?

Britain is a unitary state; but, unlike most unitary states, it contains two separate and co-ordinate systems of law: the English and the Scots. In this way it seems to resemble a federal system of government in which federal and state laws exist side by side and have equal jurisdiction within their spheres of competence.

The resemblance, however, is only superficial. In a federal state there is a constitution which lays down the respective spheres of federal and state law, and a supreme court or equivalent body to determine whether such legislation is constitutional. Thus the federal government may be forbidden to legislate within the sphere proper to the states, and the states prevented from trespassing into the federal jurisdiction. This is not the case in Britain. There is no constitutional limitation to the powers of Parliament, so the courts of law are not called upon to rule on the constitutionality of Acts of Parliament. The 'sovereignty of Parliament', so dear to English constitutional lawyers, means that 'Parliament is not legally subject to any physical limitation . . . there is nothing whatever to prevent the Government from introducing legislation on any subject-matter whatever. However "independent" an authority may be, it is, in the last resort, subject to the control of the Government. For if the Government has a majority in both Houses it can always secure legislation' (Jennings, 1957, pp. 2, 11–12).

While there is no constitution as such to limit the powers of Parliament, the Act of Union between Scotland and England, passed in 1707, contains restrictions on the freedom of the new British Parliament to do what it wants with respect to Scotland. As this Act of Union was in the nature of a contract between Scotland and England, and came into force as a result of having passed simultaneously through the Scottish and English parliaments, it differs in essence from ordinary parliamentary enactments. Whether it differs in practice is another matter, for apparent breaches of the Act of Union have never been successfully challenged in a court of law, English or Scottish.

In 1953, an interesting case came up in the Court of Session in Edinburgh, in which a Scottish Nationalist, J. M. MacCormick, sought to have the title of the Queen, Elizabeth II, made illegal, since there had never been an 'Elizabeth I' of Great Britain. MacCormick claimed that Article I of the Treaty of Union had been contravened by this title, while the Lord Advocate (the government's chief legal officer in Scotland) declared that the Royal Titles Act (1953), in which the title was apparently authorised, had abrogated Article I of the Treaty of Union. The government's argument was based on the sovereignty of Parliament, while the petitioners expressly denied this principle in relation to the Act of Union. MacCormick lost his case, but the decision of the court gave rise to a peculiar interpretation of the law, exemplified in the Janus-like judgement of Lord Cooper, the Lord President. To Lord Cooper, the principle of parliamentary sovereignty was 'a distinctively English principle which has no counterpart in Scottish constitutional law' (*Scots Law Times*, 24 October 1953, p. 262). In Scotland, before 1707, parliament had not been sovereign, for there had been a belief that the community was sovereign. (An excuse for anarchy?) Thus, the new British parliament after 1707 could not just be the old English parliament writ large: it must contain also the essence of the Scottish parliament.

This opinion involved a very difficult (if not impossible) feat of jurisprudence, and has so far not produced any practical results. Lord Cooper denied stoutly that canons of English law must be accepted in Scotland, and he even got the Lord Advocate (who after all was a Scots lawyer as well as a member of the government) to admit that the British Parliament could not repeal or alter the fundamental conditions of the Act of Union. But this did not help MacCormick, nor has it helped anyone else who has challenged the validity of an Act of Parliament. MacCormick was caught out on a technicality: the Queen's title did not depend on the Act of which he complained. So the challenge to parliamentary sovereignty was avoided, although it seems possible that it might some day take place.

'The question whether judicial scrutiny of legislation is competent in Scotland remains open, and there is as yet no conclusive authority for or against', writes Professor T. B. Smith, a noted campaigner on behalf of Scots law. His theory is that 'there are sound reasons in law for the Scottish courts at least to assume duty as custodiers of the Constitution, and there are ample precedents, in countries which Scotsmen have helped to build, for the appropriate techniques' (Smith, 1962, p. 60). There might then be the growth of some sort of supreme court on the United States model (although that court did not initially have the power of judicial review), but it could hardly be entirely Scottish!

With regard to the domestic affairs of Scotland, it is clearly impossible to shrug off the Act of Union as irrelevant, for, despite certain breaches, it has been observed in essentials. Free trade within the United Kingdom and with its possessions overseas (Article IV), and the preservation of Scots law (including the Scottish courts) and the Presbyterian Establishment (Articles XVIII–XX, with the Act for Securing the Protestant Religion and Presbyterian Government in Scotland) are basic to the Union. But unlike most constitutions, the Act of Union contains no procedure for amendment, and certain Articles, such as the temporary financial and excise provisions, were not expected to last for ever and have long since been repealed. Other Articles were expressly described as valid 'in all time coming as a fundamental and essential condition of any Treaty on Union'. Yet these too have not remained untouched. To take a trivial example, one 'fundamental' clause was the provision that Scottish university professors must subscribe to the Presbyterian Confession of Faith; but we have seen that this was repealed in 1853 (Chapter 4, p. 40). It had become fundamental to most Scots that the clause should go, so it went.

This means that the Act of Union retains validity only so long as its legitimacy, rather than its legality, is established. This applies also to the United States Constitution, which has been so interpreted by the Supreme Court over the years that it no longer expresses the minds of the Founding Fathers but is a reflection of the needs of the present time. In Britain there is no judicial interpretation of the 'constitutionality' of Acts of Parliament, and probably not much case for any, since political pressures represent the demands of society. Scottish MPS and pressure groups speak for Scotland more effectively than the Act of Union or the law courts, just as Congress in the United States determines the reality of the federal system. So those parts of the 1707 bargain which are alive and fruitful today are assured permanence because of public opinion, and those parts which have been scrapped go generally unmourned.

Of course, this assumes 'government by consensus' on the American model, and there have been times when it seemed that the wishes of Scotland were being ignored or trampled on by the 'predominant partner', England. Even so, since 1870 it would be difficult to show that a real grievance existed on this score. Scotland has stood to gain much by the avoidance of such Articles as that which prohibited any special government 'allowances, encouragements and drawbacks' to Scotland (Article VI), nor has any objection been raised to the increases in the number of Scottish MPS from forty-five (1707–1832) to the present seventy-one. While every American knows his Constitution, the Scot is only vaguely aware of the Articles of 1707. This is because many of them have over the years become politically, and legally, dead.

## LEGAL RIGHTS IN SCOTLAND

The rights and duties of citizens under the law in Scotland are similar to those of other British citizens, when considered in broad terms of liberty and obligation. The fundamental freedoms of the individual and the degree of protection afforded by the state are common to Scotland and England. Scotland has no Magna Carta or Habeas Corpus Act in its history, but not many Scots are aware of this, and it is always assumed that these charters of liberty are just as practically relevant in Scotland.

Something of the duality of law in federal countries is reproduced in Scotland. Most fiscal, commercial and social welfare legislation is common to the United Kingdom (with slight adaptation), but a great deal of personal and property law is distinctive to Scotland. Moreover, the system of courts and the organisation of the legal profession is unique, although the differences with England, as with the law itself, are on the whole less material than technical. The short discussion which follows on Scots law must not be taken to be about all law in Scotland, but only about that part of the law which pertains exclusively to Scotland.

## ORIGINS OF SCOTS LAW

Throughout most of the Western world, one or other of two great legal systems has been the inspiration for the domestic laws of the state. The most ancient is that derived from Roman law and is widely adopted in Europe and in Latin America. In its modern guise it is found in the form of national codifications, the most notable being that undertaken during Napoleon I's reign in France. These codifications make the law largely systematic and deductive, for great emphasis is placed on the basic principles of the codes, from which the practical applications to each case can be derived.

The other great school of law is that of English law, which is followed, apart from England, Wales and Ireland, in most of the United States and in the Commonwealth countries. In contrast to the Roman tradition, English law is inductive and empirical, is less based on codes and more on common law precedents ('judge-made' law).

Before the thirteenth century both England and Scotland had similar legal systems, which were predominantly Norman and within the Roman school of thought. But the great fifteenth-century separations of Scotland from England (Wars of Independence) and of

England from France (Hundred Years' War) destroyed the unity of north-west Europe. From 1500 England developed in isolation from Europe, and Scotland in isolation from England. While England threw off the continental influence, Scotland maintained political, religious and legal links with France, Italy and Holland, and so continued to have a more 'continental' system of law. The English universities were closed to the Scots, and they became accustomed to attend those on the Continent, where they learned more of the Roman law tradition and returned to Scotland to teach it in the law schools of the Scottish universities. This amalgam of continental and native influences is found in the institutional writings on Scots law which have given it the strength to survive since the Union: the *Institutions* of Viscount Stair (1681); the *Institutes* of John Erskine (1773); and the *Commentaries and Principles* of George Joseph Bell (1829). The authority of these writers is as great even today as the decisions of the highest courts themselves, and they are still referred to constantly by Scottish judges (Smith, 1962, p. 32). In the words of Lord Cooper, Scots Law consists of 'Roman Law, Feudal Law and native customary law, systematised by resort to the law of nature and the Bible, and illuminated by many flashes of ideal metaphysic' (Cooper, 1949, p. 9). While this may be understandable to some lawyers, Cooper admits that 'it is always a pity to have to credit ordinary people with metaphysical conceptions which it is certain that they never harboured, and which they are probably quite incapable of apprehending' (p. 20). Thus the principles governing Scots law remain something of a mystery to most Scotsmen, and their practical application on occasion irritating.

FEUDALISM

The most disturbing aspect of Scots law is its devotion to feudal property laws. Scotland has 'the most feudal of any system of land laws in the world' (Cooper, p. 17), and all holders of land are either 'superiors' or 'vassals'. For centuries the laws and lawyers of Scotland have maintained the power of the superiors, an oligarchy of large landowners, who acted partly as a counterweight to the power of the Crown and made it relatively weak, but who also restricted the rights of the mass of the people. Over the years the feudal superiors have been propped up by laws of primogeniture and entail (ensuring the permanence of large estates), and, in the eighteenth century and first half of the nineteenth century, the Scottish lawyers used all their ingenuity to manufacture 'fictitious votes' out of the intricacies of the feudal system, so that a handful of landowners could control the political representation of the majority of Scottish seats in Parliament.

In much of Scotland (especially the Highlands), the great majority of the population had no legal tenure in the land at all, so that when economic depression hit the crofters and small farmers they were completely at the mercy of the lairds, who not infrequently turned them out. The Crofters Act (1886) and Small Landholders Act (1911) gave these people legal rights for the first time, and, paradoxically, they are now more secure in their land than any English leaseholder. However, this was done by ignoring the traditions of Scots land law and grafting on a solution which had first been applied to the Irish land problem.

Today the feudal system perpetuates aristocratic control over the development of land in Scotland. Only a small number of 'owner-occupiers' in Scotland are legally full owners of their land, for the feudal superior is the technical owner of the land (except in Orkney and Shetland, where Norse 'allodial udal tenure' prevails). Under the old feudalism the vassal gave services in return for protection given by the superior, but today the superior is concerned only to protect himself. Not only may he have an income from feu-duties but he can also lay down conditions as to the use of the land. These are incorporated in the feu-charter, which the vassal has rarely shared in drawing up and which may be of ancient origin. As it is difficult to escape tenure as a vassal in Scotland, most people who would be freeholders in England are in Scotland not free at all but bound to an involuntary servitude. As an example of how this works, the Marquess of Bute, as feudal superior of the island of Great Cumbrae in the Firth of Clyde, consistently vetoed projects for tourist development, not only from private individuals but from the local authority as well. Under the Scottish feudal system, the tenants-in-chief of mediaeval times become the planning authorities of the twentieth century.

Opinion in Scotland has frequently been roused against the undemocratic nature of the land laws, especially as so much of Scottish society pays lip-service to the democratic Myth. In the 1870s, the farmers agitated against the laws of primogeniture and entail, the game laws (which gave landowners the exclusive right to kill game, including marauding rabbits and deer), and the law of hypothec (by which goods could be seized by the landowner for non-payment of rent). Many of these grievances were redressed by legislation in the 1880s, as was the crofting (but not cottar) insecurity of tenure.

Opposition to aspects of the feudal system grew sharply in the 1960s, and in 1966 the Halliday Committee recommended that all feu-duties and most restrictions on land should be abolished within sixty years, and that a new division of the Scottish Land Court should adjust existing land restrictions to new conditions. Eventually, the Conveyancing and Feudal Reform (Scotland) Act, 1970, and the

Land Tenure Reform (Scotland) Act, 1974, implemented most of these proposals, and now feu-duties are rapidly passing into history. A proprietor may redeem these for a lump sum, and there is compulsory redemption when a property changes hands. This has removed the financial grievance associated with the feudal system, but much of the system remains through the control which the feudal superior still has over the use of 'his' land.

## CIVIL LIBERTIES

By the Act of Union (Article XVIII), 'the laws which concern public right, policy and civil government may be made the same throughout the whole United Kingdom', but no alteration can be made in laws which concern private right, 'except for the evident utility of the subjects within Scotland'. The line between the two is often difficult to draw, and, with the right of appeal in civil (but not criminal) cases from the Court of Session to the House of Lords, the result has been a general assimilation between Scotland and England in the sphere of civil liberties.

But one or two aspects of Scottish constitutional law remain or have been revived. We have already seen that the 'sovereignty of Parliament' is theoretically unacceptable in Scotland. So too is the doctrine that 'the king can do no wrong', which until 1947 meant in England that the citizen was often unable to bring actions for damages against government officials. In Scotland, the king, or the king's servants, could be sued like any other citizen, another instance of the relative weakness of the Scottish Crown. After the Crown Proceedings Act (1947), this right became more readily available in England, but even today the Scottish courts take a tougher line with the administration than those in England. Whereas in England government ministers can decline to produce documents on grounds of public interest, in Scotland the courts have been able to demand the production of evidence if other aspects of the public interest or the interests of justice seem to require it (Smith, 1962, p. 64).

Moreover, the Scottish courts do not proceed in administrative cases on the basis of the English 'prerogative writs (orders)', but on larger principles of natural justice: on condition of course that such cases ever reach the courts at all, for most are decided by administrative tribunals or by ministers themselves. But even here practice may differ, for the distinction between judicial and executive decisions, which in England limits the powers of the courts and enhances that of the government, is less prominent in Scotland. The Scottish courts are 'rather more willing to approach the boundary of what must be left to the administration' (Mitchell, 1964, p. 264).

Magna Carta, Habeas Corpus and Petition of Right are not part of Scots law, but the right to a fair trial, freedom from arbitrary arrest, and free expression of opinion in writing and assembly are protected in Scotland. Many maintain that criminal trials are more fair in Scotland, since there is no public preliminary hearing in a magistrates' or coroner's court during which the evidence for the prosecution is reported in the press. This pre-trial publicity can prejudice the jury against the accused, and in the 1960s was restricted in England by legislation (the Criminal Justice Act, 1967), although the Thorpe case in 1978 showed continuing publicity, and renewed calls for reform along Scottish lines.

Criminal prosecutions in Scotland are undertaken by the state, and not by private individuals, and the Procurator Fiscal (the local state prosecutor), acting under the authority of the Lord Advocate (chief government law officer in Scotland), must decide on the basis of the evidence whether a charge shall be brought. This is a more rigorous procedure than that in England, where a prima facie case is sufficient for a trial to take place, but it may result in some guilty persons escaping trial. In Scotland the odds are in favour of the accused, although 'special defences' such as alibi and self-defence must be declared before the trial and cannot suddenly be produced. No person is forced to incriminate himself in Scottish court proceedings (or in pre-trial interrogations), which means that many accused refuse to speak and are acquitted for lack of evidence; this rule is unpopular among a considerable number of lawyers and policemen in Scotland, who wish to see it changed. The evidence of only one witness is generally unacceptable as proof, although it is typical that an exception has been made in the case of deer-poaching offences in order to serve the interests of landowners. For the rest, the criminal may well escape for lack of corroborative evidence, and the famous Scottish verdict of 'Not Proven' may be given by the jury.

The Scottish criminal jury has fifteen members (civil jury, twelve members), and may return its verdict by a majority vote. This has always been acceptable in Scotland, despite some public uncertainty when murder is involved (as in the famous Not Proven verdict in the Madeleine Smith case in 1857). In the light of the frequency of intimidation of juries in England, it would seem that majority verdicts are more satisfactory, and the Criminal Justice Act (1967) instituted a qualified majority verdict in England and Wales. It has become quite common to hear English jurists and politicians point to the smooth running of these practices in Scotland as an indication of their potential value for England. On 1 July 1967 Roy Jenkins, then Home Secretary, announced that he hoped to abolish committal proceedings in England, and said, 'Perhaps a different system of prosecutions, more akin to that prevailing in Scotland . . . could be applied with profit to England as well . . . I intend to see that a thorough study is made of the possible relevance of the Scottish system

to English law' (*Observer*, 2 July 1967). This was in marked contrast
to the arrogant anglicisers of the past, typified by Lord Cranworth,
who declared in 1858: 'If such be the law of England, on what
ground can it be argued not to be the law of Scotland? The law as
established in England is founded on principles of universal application . . . I think it would be most inexpedient to sanction a different
rule to the north of the Tweed' (quoted in Smith, 1961, p. 85).

There are also examples in private law which show the influence
of Scots law on English law. In 1932, in a Scottish appeal *(Donaghue
v. Stevenson)*, the Lords upheld the Scottish principle that liability for
damages was not restricted by the terms of a contract: the lady who
found a snail in her ginger beer had a right to damages from the
manufacturer, with whom she had no contract. As the Lords' decisions
are highly persuasive on English law even in Scottish appeals, this
introduced into England a wider conception of the law relating to
damages for negligence. Similarly, in 1948, the English law of
'common employment', under which employers had no liability for
injuries caused to employees by other employees, was repealed and
the old Scots law practice adopted (Smith, 1962, p. 705).

With respect to the law of the family and other personal matters
Scotland and England have influenced each other. Scots law is more
liberal in its approach to marriage. The consent of the parents is not
required for those aged 16 and over, and 'irregular marriage',
established through prolonged cohabitation and without any ceremony,
civil or religious, is still legal, though rare. Before 1939 the law provided more grounds for 'irregular marriage', a fact which seems to
contradict the great dominance of the Church in Scottish life.
Scotland resembles certain states in the United States, in that its
lenient marriage laws attract couples from over the border with
England who could not otherwise get married, traditionally to Gretna
Green in Dumfries-shire. This practice declined after the age of
majority was reduced to 18 in England and Wales by the Family
Law Reform Act, 1969. The Marriage (Scotland) Act, 1977, allows
people in England and Wales to obtain marriages in Scotland by post
and thereby abolished the old fifteen-day residential qualification.

Divorce has also been historically more easy to obtain in Scotland
than in England. In fact, judicial divorce was available in Scotland
300 years before it could be granted in English courts, including
divorce for desertion after 1573. The Divorce Reform Act, 1967,
introduced a much more liberal system in England and Wales, and
Scotland was clearly left behind. After much deliberation, and several
futile attempts by backbenchers in Parliament to pass Bills (for divorce
law reform is a Private Member's affair), the Divorce (Scotland) Act,
1976, was passed. This brings Scotland roughly into line with England,
although divorce proceedings in Scotland are relatively more expensive

and cumbersome, since they can only be brought in the Court of Session, Scotland's top civil court. In England and Wales, County Courts can deal with divorces more speedily and more cheaply.

As noted in Chapter 4, Scotland was included in the Abortion Act, 1967, but not in the Sexual Offences Act, 1967, relating to homosexuality. Race Relations and Sex Discrimination laws apply throughout the United Kingdom. English legislation on Sunday entertainments and sport does not apply in Scotland, where local communities can decide these matters. But a big change arrived in 1977 when the Licensing (Scotland) Act, 1976, came into operation. Scotland had always been noted for its restrictive drinking hours, and some areas had voted themselves completely 'dry' through the use of veto polls, conducted on a local basis. Areas in and around Glasgow, and in the Highlands and Islands, were especially fond of banning licensed premises. After a well-publicised inquiry conducted by the Clayson Committee (1973), the Labour government in 1976 put through the reform which allowed pubs to open on Sundays, and on other days at hours between eleven in the morning and eleven at night, with possible extension. Licences are granted by local Licensing Boards to suitable applicants, and the evidence by 1979 is that a liberal interpretation of the Act is being adopted. Meanwhile, veto polls have disappeared, as a result of the local government reform in 1975.

All these reforms could be considered a coming together of Scotland and England in the norms of social life, with Scotland moving away from its more puritanical and religion-dominated past, and England looking to Scotland for ideas to reform its legal practices. It should be emphasised, however, that each country has used its own resources, through committees of inquiry, pressure groups, religious bodies, and MPs, to argue out the case for reform. There has been no imposition of laws on Scotland by the UK government without an indication of consent by the people of Scotland. Of course, had a Scottish Assembly existed, it would have clarified such consent through a vote of its elected representatives sitting in a purely Scottish legislature.

As a last illustration of civil liberties in Scotland, the relationship between Church and state may be briefly recalled. The Church of Scotland, although established by law, is nevertheless practically free of all state control, either through parliamentary legislation or in the appointment of its clergy. This is in contrast to the Church of England, which has often faced obstruction in its wishes in the House of Commons (for example, over the prayerbook), and whose clergy are largely appointed by the Crown or by lay patrons. While many modern states, such as the United States, insist on religious equality, Britain adheres to the principle of state recognition and support for religion. But the Scottish version of this principle has become so watered down that its Established Church gains little apart from prestige from the connection with the state. There are no Scottish 'Crown livings', or seats for Scottish bishops in the House of Lords, and the Lord High Commissioner to the General Assembly of the Church of Scotland, who represents the Queen, is only a spectator and must enter the Assembly by a side door (Muir, 1958, p. 262). The Queen, of course, is not head of the Church of Scotland.

In short, legal rights in Scotland are based on the principles of a weak Crown (that is, Executive), a strong Church, a strong feudal oligarchy, and a predominantly liberal criminal and civil code. There is much waiting to be reformed (and a Law Commission is now sitting) but also much that can serve as an example for England. The fact that Scots law is more similar to the legal systems of continental countries than to English law may bring it into greater prominence in the European Economic Community. The British judge on the European Court is a Scot and Scots lawyer, Lord Mackenzie Stuart. Scots law has already been admired by a prominent French jurist, Levy-Ulmann: 'Scots law, as it stands, gives us a picture of what will be some day (perhaps at the end of the century) the law of civilised nations, namely a combination of the Anglo-Saxon system and the continental system' (quoted in Smith, 1961, p. 4). This is more than most Scots would be prepared to grant, but sympathy from France for a part of the British way of life is especially welcome today. The 'Auld Alliance' between France and Scotland is thus revived to serve modern European integration.

THE COURTS

Scotland has its own system of civil and criminal courts (see Table 6.1), with the exception already mentioned that civil cases can be

Table 6.1   *Principal law courts in Scotland, and in England and Wales*

| Civil Courts | | Criminal Courts | |
|---|---|---|---|
| Scotland | England and Wales | Scotland | England and Wales |
| House of Lords | House of Lords | Court of Criminal Appeal | House of Lords |
| Court of Session | Court of Appeal | High Court of Justiciary | Court of Appeal |
| | High Court of Justice | | High Court of Justice |
| Sheriff Court | County Court | Sheriff Court | Crown Court |
| | | District Court | Magistrates' Court |
| | | Children's Hearing | (Juvenile Court) |

taken on appeal to the House of Lords. At the top is the Court of Session of twenty-one judges,[1] who don different robes to become the High Court of Justiciary in criminal cases. The supreme courts' very rarely sit in the presence of all the judges, but are split into Houses and divisions, so that in the Outer House of the Court of Session and in the High Court it is usual for only one judge to preside. The House and divisions of the Court of Session do not deal with specialised classes of judicial work as in England, for each Scottish judge is assumed to be capable of dealing with every type of case (Cooper, p. 23). This versatility is matched by that of the advocates (barristers) who are also considered to be generalists rather than specialists. This perhaps prevents the Bar in Scotland from producing the great stars of the legal firmament that occasionally shine in the south.

Among the lower courts, the Sheriff Court is by far the most important. The office of Sheriff in Scotland is of greater significance than in England. Until 1747 the feudal barons had a hereditary right to the title in their respective shires, and could dispense 'justice' in these courts over a vast range of criminal and civil cases. This omnipotence had no parallel in England, where the 'over-mighty' subject had long since been subordinated to the 'King's writ'. After the Jacobite rising of 1745, it was time for law and order to prevail in all parts of Scotland and the Sheriff Court assumed its modern form as the main inferior court. While in England the Magistrates' (Justices of the Peace, or JPs') Court, the Crown Court and the County Court are important, in Scotland their functions are largely absorbed by the Sheriff Court. In civil cases, the Sheriff Court can dispose of cases of debt and damages without any pecuniary limit whatever, and in criminal cases 'its jurisdiction is practically universal in that it need not be expressly conferred by the statute creating the offence, but it is limited in that the most serious crimes of all, such as murder and rape, may be tried only in the High Court, and by the fact that its powers of punishment are limited' (Walker, 1963, p. 204). These limitations include up to two years' imprisonment. Appeals lie from the Sheriff Court to the Court of Session or the High Court of Justiciary, and thence to the House of Lords or (Scottish) Court of Criminal Appeal in civil and criminal cases respectively.

There is no counterpart of the Sheriff Court in England, although in civil cases the County Court is perhaps the nearest. However, that court has a more limited jurisdiction, has fewer administrative functions, and does not deal with criminal cases. The English criminal court whose jurisdiction most resembles the Sheriff Court is the Magistrates' Court, but its power of punishment is limited, while the Crown Courts go beyond the limitations of the Sheriff Court.

Until 1975, the office of JP (Justice of the Peace) was widely different in Scotland and in England. English JPs were important lay judges in the Magistrates' Courts, while Scottish JPs sat in the unimportant JP Courts, which dealt only with such things as minor breaches of the peace. More important were the burgh and police courts which were presided over by 'bailies', who were town councillors, and were the nearest counterparts to the English JPs. In 1975, by the District Courts (Scotland) Act, the JP, burgh, and police courts were replaced by District Courts, based on the new local government districts. District Court lay judges are called Justices of the Peace and are drawn from three sources: appointment by the Secretary of State for Scotland, former bailies, and *ex officio* Justices appointed by district or island councils from amongst the councillors, up to a quarter of the council. All Justices require to undergo training. There are also stipendiary magistrates in some District Courts, who are professional lawyers. It is still probably true that most of the local administration of justice in Scotland, unlike that in England, is kept out of the hands of laymen, and is entrusted to professional judges, especially Sheriffs.

The Sheriffs are barristers or solicitors who are appointed and paid by the Crown to administer justice in the six sheriffdoms of Scotland. They reinforce the power of the state as represented by the official prosecutors, the Procurators Fiscal. Their functions are not purely judicial for they are administrative officials as well. The Sheriff may be Commissioner for Wrecks, deal with petitions for adoption of children, and so on. Thus the sixty-three Sheriffs in Scotland are important territorial judges and administrative agents of the Crown, while the English Sheriff is a much more humdrum person with narrow duties, and is unpaid, so that when nominated 'many qualified persons seek to be excused' (Wade and Phillips, 1960, p. 330). The English qualification, by the way, is 'the holding of sufficient land within the county to answer for any damages that may be awarded against him for neglect of duty' (loc. cit.).

Among the other courts in Scotland, the Scottish Land Court is particularly worth mentioning. This court was set up in 1911 and was given powers to decide cases relating to crofts and smallholdings under the Crofters Acts and the Small Landholders (Scotland) Act, 1911. These involve landlord–tenant relations, including fixing fair rents, extending or creating holdings and fixing compensation for improvements. Its establishment showed the dissatisfaction of the Scots with their land laws and with the outcome of cases in the Court of Session, which continually vindicated the vested interests of the feudal oligarchy. Subsequent legislation has greatly added to the jurisdiction of the court, so that it now deals with the majority of agricultural disputes in Scotland, including those concerning government grants and subsidies. A great deal of the bitterness in landlord–tenant relations has now disappeared, and the proceedings of the Scottish Land Court are often friendly, with the parties cheerfully accepting the outcome. The court has five members, of whom the chairman has the status and tenure of a judge of the Court of Session. One of the members must be a Gaelic-speaker. Its proceedings, unlike its powers, seem to resemble the light-heartedness of a picnic party, as this report indicates:

> The land court convenes in the island's (Foula) tiny schoolhouse. Lord Birsay (kilted as always) and Mr Bankier sit at the teacher's table with the black-board behind them, flanked by Mr Cameron and Miss White, who occupy the ends of the table facing inwards . . . No decision was announced by the court that day. Because of difficulties of getting to Foula, the court was one short of a quorum . . . The court adjourned. And now Lord Birsay could discard the judge's mantle. Outside in the sunshine he chatted to the Gears and the Holbourns (parties in the case), and urged them warmly to make up their differences amicably. (*Scotsman*, 23 July 1966)

In the words of the reporter, 'The Scottish Land Court is, quite simply, unique. It is the only court of its kind in the world, and its history and procedure are the objects of the awed interest of legal delegations from abroad.' In some measure, this is also true of the whole of the Scottish legal system.

NOTES

1 One of the twenty-one, Lord Hunter, is at present the full-time chairman of the Scottish Law Commission.

FURTHER READING

Walker, D. M., *The Scottish Legal System* (various editions).
Smith, T. B., *British Justice: The Scottish Contribution* (1961).
    Two contrasting interpretations of the law in Scotland, the former practical and the latter romantic.

# Chapter 7

# The Government of Scotland

## I  Central Government

BEFORE THE SCOTTISH OFFICE (TO 1885)

The Union of 1707 merged the parliaments of Scotland and England in the new Parliament of Great Britain (Great Britain and Ireland, 1800–1922; Great Britain and Northern Ireland after 1922), but there was no fusion of all the agencies of government in a new British form. Thus, while Scotland was to be legislated for by Westminster, it continued to be administered largely by Scottish government ministers and Scottish departments. The office of Secretary of State for Scotland was retained in the British government until the Jacobite sympathies of its holders brought about its abolition in 1746. The Lord Advocate, the chief state law officer in Scotland, was also a government minister and took over some of the political duties of the Scottish Secretary after 1746.

From 1746 to 1827, one of the Secretaries of State had formal responsibility for Scotland, but the real political power was in the hands of the unofficial 'Scottish Manager', who was a Scot with a position in the Cabinet, where he was called upon to advise on Scottish affairs. Henry Dundas (Viscount Melville) filled this role for many years, and was able to dispense much government patronage to Scots in return for their political support in elections and in the House of Commons. In this way he became equally valuable to Scotland and to the government. After 1827, however, there was no one available to take this position and the amount of government patronage had been cut by measures of reform. The Home Secretary was made politically responsible for Scottish administration, and it was this situation which eventually led to a growing volume of complaint that Scotland was being neglected.

During the nineteenth century, the self-sufficiency of the Scottish social institutions, and their almost complete control over everyday life in Scotland, became gradually weakened. The rapid industrialisation of the country, with its consequent social problems, proved too great a strain on the resources of the Church, local government and private philanthropy. The intervention of the central government, with its superior financial resources, was necessary to relieve human suffering in epidemics, famines and unemployment, to mediate or impose settlements in industrial and agrarian disputes, and to regulate and stimulate the economy. It is little wonder that Scots became more and more concerned with government from Whitehall, and less with the traditional local organs of administration.

At the same time, the problem of efficient government in Scotland loomed up for the administration. Having been called upon to perform an ever wider range of functions, it was necessary to administer them in such a way that the special circumstances of Scotland should be taken account of. These circumstances were not just that of a region, but of a national society with its own institutions, including its own legal system and local government structure. Nevertheless, just as there were English lawyers who could see no merit in Scots law, there were English administrators who had no time for any separate administrative arrangements for Scotland. Despite their efforts at a unitary administration, the Scottish institutions remained resilient and time has proved the administrative assimilators even more wrong than the legal ones. Today, a greater proportion of the activities of the central government in Scotland are administered on a Scottish basis than was the case a hundred years ago.

In 1870, the division between the functions of central administration organised on a Scottish basis and those organised on a United Kingdom basis was as follows: all foreign policy, taxation, customs and excise and regulation of trade was the sphere of central departments or agencies. So too was much domestic administration, including education, law and order, local government and inspection of mines and factories. Scots law was still represented in the government by the Lord Advocate, who also had his own department in Edinburgh (the Crown Office). There were also certain distinct Scottish administrative bodies. A number of Scottish boards had been set up in Edinburgh by Acts of Parliament, to administer certain matters within Scotland. These boards were not government departments headed by ministers, but the Home Secretary took a rather vague responsibility for them when questions were asked in the House of Commons. Even after the office of Secretary for Scotland was re-established in 1885 and responsibility was transferred to him, the Scottish boards continued with an independent legal existence, and more were created after that date. Here is a list of these boards: [1]

(1) *Board of Manufactures* (1726–1906). Originally intended to promote industry in Scotland, it was latterly more concerned with industrial design and education in the fine arts.

(2) *Fishery Board* (1808–1939). This body was operative also in England until 1849 and was linked with the Board of Manufactures until 1882. It encouraged Scottish fisheries.

(3) *Board of Supervision for Poor Relief* (1845–94). It also had public health functions after 1863.

(4) *Local Government Board for Scotland* (1894–1919). This body took over the functions of the Board of Supervision.

(5) *Scottish Board of Health* (1919–28). This body took over functions of the Local Government Board and of two short-lived boards, *Scottish Insurance Commissioners* (1911–19) and *Highlands and Islands Medical Service Board* (1913–19).

(6) *General Board of Commissioners in Lunacy* (1857–1913); *General Board of Control* (1913–62). Its function was the supervision of mental health.

(7) *Prisons Commission* (1877–1928).

(8) *Crofters Commission* (1886–1911, 1955–    ).
    *Congested Districts Board* (1897–1911).
    *Highlands and Islands Development Board* (1965–    ).

(9) *Board of Agriculture* (1912–28).

Other Scottish agencies of government in 1870 included the department of the Registrar General for Scotland (1855–    ) and the ancient offices of the Lord Clerk Register (Scottish Record Office), the Lord Lyon King of Arms (heraldry and public ceremonial) and the Queen's and Lord Treasurer's Remembrancer (Treasury representative in Scotland). After 1872, there was a Scotch Education Department, but it was a committee of the Privy Council and operated from London. In 1885, the Scottish Secretary was given responsibility for education in Scotland and the committee became in effect a government department, although it continued to meet as a committee until 1913. In 1918 it became the 'Scottish' Education Department and in 1939 it finally moved from London to Edinburgh.

It can be seen that, despite a certain amount of decentralisation of administration, Scotland in 1870 was not in a strong position in the British government. Although there were Scots in British administrations, there was no Cabinet member specifically charged to speak for Scotland, and the Home Secretaries after 1827 were neither Scottish nor knowledgeable about Scotland. A feeling grew up in Scotland that the country was being neglected, and that urgent measures of social and economic reform were being held up by the indifference of the Cabinet and of the majority of MPs. Scots pointed to the fact that the Lord Advocate, James Moncrieff, had tried six times to secure legislation on a large scheme of educational reform, but had never received the active support of his government and parliamentary colleagues (Omond, 1914, p. 247).

By 1870, it was clear to a majority of the Scottish MPs that a Secretary for Scotland was required, since the Lord Advocate's weight had proved insufficient (he had to be in Edinburgh for much of the parliamentary session). They sent a memorial in 1869 to the Prime Minister, Gladstone, urging the appointment of a Scottish Secretary, criticising the system of boards with its absence of direct parliamentary accountability, and protesting that the legal profession, in the person of the Lord Advocate, ought not to monopolise the government of Scotland (Milne, 1957, p. 13). Gladstone set up a Commission of Inquiry under Lord Camperdown, which turned down the proposal for a Secretary for Scotland but recommended that a parliamentary under-secretary at the Home Office be appointed to advise the Home Secretary on Scottish matters, in addition to the Lord Advocate (Camperdown, 1870). No action was taken on this, and in the 1870s the Scottish MPs became even more restive at the apparent neglect of Scottish interests. This was a period in which nationalism was prominent throughout Europe, and was particularly clamant close at hand in Ireland. Gladstone's mission, on forming his administration in 1868, had been to 'pacify Ireland', and he did so for a time by legislation disestablishing the Irish Church and amending the conditions of land tenure. There were many who wanted similar measures for Scotland, although opinion in Scotland was more divided than in Ireland (at least in southern Ireland).

But while Scots could not agree about the laws which were necessary for Scotland, there was a remarkable unanimity among them that the administration of Scotland needed reforming, and that the country's prestige demanded the re-creation of the ancient office of Secretary for Scotland. In the 1880s, there was a wave of nationalism (the strongest since the Union, and perhaps the strongest even to the present time) which was notable in drawing support not only from the fringe of politics and the less respectable members of Scottish society but from the heart of the Scottish establishment itself.

The various elements in this movement can be noted only briefly here. At the top of the social scale, there was an array of peers and landowners who, anglicised in education and way of life as they undoubtedly were, nevertheless felt that they had a duty to profess loyalty to Scotland as well as to the Queen. They included some of the most famous noblemen of Scotland. There was the Duke of Argyll, the Earl of Fife, the young Earl of Rosebery and others, and they spoke in 1881 in the House of Lords about the 'second-hand' management of Scottish business and the need to re-create the post of Secretary for Scotland (*Hansard*, 13 June 1881). There was also a strong body of Scottish MPs in favour of this measure and some who wanted much more in the way of devolution. Sir George Campbell (Liberal, Kirkcaldy Burghs) had spoken in 1877 in favour of a Scottish Grand Committee of the House of Commons, to consist mainly of Scottish MPs, and had indicated that in time some kind of federal system might be the answer to Scottish and Irish nationalism (*Hansard*, 23 February 1877). Duncan McLaren (Liberal, Edinburgh), one of the most well-known of Scottish MPs and a veteran who had actually proposed a Scottish Secretary in 1853, was also in the campaign. Pressure groups in Scotland were favourable to change. The high cost of promoting private Bills at Westminster had disturbed local authorities and business companies in Scotland, and they welcomed Campbell's proposal to set up a tribunal in Edinburgh to deal with such legislation. The Convention of Royal Burghs, the most ancient pressure group in Scotland (unless the Church be included), lent its weight to the movement, and before long even Free Church disestablishers thought they would have more hope of success with a Scottish Secretary and a Scottish Grand Committee.

The key figure was, curiously, Lord Rosebery. Although only in his early thirties in 1880, he had already become a noted Scottish patriot, and had been elected Rector of Aberdeen University in 1878. His speech to the students there and a later speech in Edinburgh University were on the theme of the need to preserve and study Scottish traditions and history (Crewe, 1931, Vol. I, pp. 109–13). Educated at Eton and Oxford, like many of the Scottish upper classes then and since, he nevertheless tempered his anglicisation with a passionate, if synthetic, Scottishness based on the romantic past. In 1880, he acted as host to Gladstone in his famous first Midlothian campaign, and when Gladstone won the seat and returned to Downing Street in that year, he was soon made aware that he could no longer ignore either Scotland or Lord Rosebery. In 1881, the post of under-secretary at the Home Office with responsibility for Scotland was at last created, and Rosebery was appointed. Now he could see at first hand how Scotland fared at Whitehall. He was naturally appalled (Hanham, 1965). The Home Office had made no special arrangements for dealing with Scottish affairs, and was in no hurry to start. Rosebery found it difficult to obtain even clerical assistance and had to fall back on his private secretary. But he did get an office in Parliament House, Edinburgh, which may be considered the predeccesor of the present-day Scottish Office in St Andrew's House.

Rosebery's discontent was transmitted to Gladstone himself, and there seems little doubt that the personal affection which Gladstone felt for Rosebery, together with his wish not to offend a rising star in the Liberal Party of whom he approved (unlike Joseph Chamberlain), made him listen to Rosebery more readily than to the other voices of Scottish nationalism. Rosebery wanted to see (and no doubt to be) a Scottish Secretary with a place in the Cabinet: a fair return for the great electoral support always given by Scotland to the Liberal Party. 'I serve a country which is the backbone of our party, but which is never recognised', he wrote to Gladstone on 16 December 1882 (Crewe, 1931, Vol. I, p. 159).

But Gladstone could not see what a Scottish Secretary would have to do and, in the interests of economy, he was against creating new government posts. This was too much for Rosebery, who tendered his resignation in 1883. The government now proposed a second-best to a Scottish Office, namely, a Local Government Board for Scotland. Rosebery was asked to be its president; not surprisingly, he refused, and soon opinion in Scotland became strongly agitated about the government's double-dealing. On 16 January 1884, a great rally was called in Edinburgh by the Convention of Royal Burghs to promote the Scottish Secretaryship, and prominent Conservatives – such as the Marquess of Lothian, A. J. Balfour and Lord Balfour of Burleigh (all to become Scottish Secretaries!) – made speeches. With this multi-party pressure, the Liberal government introduced the Secretary for Scotland Bill in 1884, which, although held up for a time, was finally enacted under the Conservatives in August 1885. The first Secretary for Scotland was a Tory nobleman, the Duke of Richmond and Gordon (despite the fact that he had opposed the Bill in private); he was given a seat in the Cabinet although the post was not definitely a Cabinet one until 1892. It was not a Secretaryship of State (that came in 1926) and, with a salary of £2,000 p.a. up to 1937, it ranked much lower than the principal Cabinet posts, which rated £5,000 p.a. or more.[2]

From its creation in 1885 until the present day, the Scottish Office has grown continuously, both in size and in the extent of its functions. It seems likely that it will grow even further in the future until most government activities in Scotland are specially designed for and administered in Scotland. Whether this is because efficiency demands decentralisation (the administrative factor) or because the people of Scotland want a distinct style of government (the political factor) is not so clear today as it was in 1885. Then most administrators, even Scots, opposed the creation of the Scottish Office, and it came about almost entirely through public pressure. At the present time, while there is strong national self-consciousness and support for devolution, there are also many administrators, economists and academics who justify separate Scottish executive agencies on grounds which are not national but technical. This blend of emotion and reason lies behind and sustains the case for the separate administration of Scotland.

THE SCOTTISH OFFICE IN LONDON (1885–1939)

There was now a Scottish Secretary, but the formation of the Scottish Office was not so easily accomplished, nor was it clear just how much power it was going to possess. There were those who wished to see as little as possible transferred to the new department, and before the Office was created there had been a battle over the question of the responsibility for Scottish education. Bureaucrats, such as Sir Lyon Playfair of the Scotch Education Department, and his colleague in England, Sir Francis Sandford, opposed the transfer of education to the Scottish Secretary. So too, strange to say, did the Educational Institute of Scotland and most of the large school boards (Hanham, 1965). But nearly everyone else in Scotland was adamant in pressing for the inclusion of education in the Scottish Secretary's powers, and this was done. Many Scots wanted to call a halt to the anglicisation of the Scottish educational system, but their wishes were not realised with the creation of the Scottish Office, as many Scottish Secretaries were anglicised and one, Sir George Trevelyan (1892–5), was actually English. Moreover, Sandford was appointed the first Permanent Under-Secretary at the Scottish Office, and the Secretary of the Scotch Education Department from 1885 to 1904 was (Sir) Henry Craik; both of these men were favourable to educational assimilation with England. But the potentialities of a distinctly Scottish educational administration were there and twentieth-century Scottish Secretaries and educational administrators have been more rooted in the Scottish system, for good or ill.

Apart from education, it seemed that nothing of great importance was to come under the Scottish Office. However, a wide range of functions was included in its powers, so that from the start the Scottish Secretary had to concern himself with a great assortment of subjects, probably more so than any other minister. The 1885 Act transferred from the Home Office to the Scottish Office the bulk of the responsibility for local government services and for the Scottish boards, and certain powers were also transferred from the Privy Council, the Treasury and the Local Government Board for England.[3]

But the Home Office was most reluctant to lose its hold over Scotland; in particular, the final say in matters of law and order was apparently retained by the Home Secretary. Thus the Lord Advocate, who had day-to-day responsibility, was not subject to the authority of the Scottish Secretary. This brought confusion, for most people (including other Whitehall departments) believed that the Scottish Office was the only department which dealt with Scottish matters. They were soon disillusioned when the Home Office undertook to suppress by military force the disorders then prevailing in the Western

Isles. The Home Office believed that all powers of keeping the peace were its own, while the Scottish Office would merely co-ordinate local authorities in providing the police force. But this involved a division of power and responsibility which neither the public nor the government was prepared to accept. When he became Secretary for Scotland in 1886, A. J. Balfour soon secured the transfer of legal and judicial authority to the Scottish Office (in September 1886), and these and most of the remaining Home Office functions in Scotland, except inspection of factories and mines, were legally put under the Scottish Secretary by the Secretary for Scotland Act (1885) Amendment Act, 1887. (The Lord Advocate, by the way, was no enthusiast for the extension of the powers of the Scottish Office, no doubt because he feared a diminution of his own influence if he were subordinated to a Scottish minister. This had also been the attitude of previous Lord Advocates, including James Moncrieff in 1870, despite his frustrating experiences in the office: Hanham, 1965, p. 239; Omond, p. 260.)

The Home Office also had guarded jealously its rights over administrative appointments and had forced the Scottish Secretary to submit his proposals to it and not to the Queen direct. Here, too, Balfour secured a victory, and from 1887 onwards a vast array of Scottish patronage (including Regius Chairs in the universities, the members of many public authorities and most judicial appointments) came under the control of the Secretary for Scotland. Since Lord Salisbury's second administration (1886–92), however, the Prime Minister has decided, after consulting the Scottish Secretary, who is to fill the principal legal offices in the government (Lord Advocate and Solicitor-General for Scotland) and in the courts (Lord President of the Court of Session and Lord Justice-Clerk). Until 1955 JPs in Scotland were appointed by the Lord Chancellor, but their appointment is now in the hands of the Scottish Secretary. Minor legal appointments are made by the Lord Advocate, and chairmen of many administrative tribunals since 1958 are appointed by the Lord President.

Another department which has always been suspicious of the Scottish Office, as indeed of all government departments, is the Treasury, and from the start it opposed the administrative appointments and salaries proposed by the Scottish Secretary. Threats of resignation from Scotland were in the air, and the Cabinet had to intervene to overrule the Treasury officials, so as to grant the required staff. The Treasury was always of the opinion that the new Scottish Office would have very little to do, and this was echoed by MPs in the House of Commons; but, in fact, the officials were if anything overworked.

After this brief period of controversy, which lasted until 1887, the Scottish Office settled down to become the unchallenged agency of the central government for 'purely Scottish affairs', and the Scottish

Secretary was regarded as 'Scotland's Minister'. After 1892, Cabinet membership was assured, and most Scottish Secretaries have been members of the House of Commons (especially since 1914). The final accolade was promotion of the office to one of 'His Majesty's Principal Secretaries of State' in 1926, which gave equality of status with the chief Cabinet ministers.

The functions coming under the responsibility of the Scottish Secretary grew rapidly as the activities of government expanded generally in the United Kingdom. In 1911, legislation relating to agriculture and national insurance and the creation of new Scottish boards brought new responsibilities, and there was much expansion in the field of public health after the appointment of the first Scottish Board of Health in 1919. This last development coincided with the appointment of a Parliamentary Under-Secretary for Health in the Scottish Office. However, the Scottish Office before 1939 was not the Scottish Office as we know it today. In the first place, it operated from Dover House in London. Here were the private office of the Secretary, the General Department which took on the Home Office's Scottish duties, and, legally distinct from the Scottish Office, part of the Scottish Education Department, and the Lord Advocate's Office. In Edinburgh, the Scottish Office had only a small pied-à-terre before 1914, nothing from 1914 to 1935, and from 1935 to 1939 a small division amounting to about thirty civil servants. At the same time, Edinburgh contained all the other Scottish boards and departments (including much of the Education Department[4]), so that the bulk of Scottish administration was carried on in Scotland while the political control and liaison between departments was in London.

There was thus a marked twofold division in the old system of central administration under the Secretary of State for Scotland: the geographic division already mentioned and also a more subtle legal division of functions. The Scottish Office proper was concerned merely to assist the Secretary for Scotland in carrying out his duties, which were essentially 'control and liaison' of government bodies in Scotland. These bodies – the boards, the Scottish Education Department and other departments created in 1928 to supersede certain boards (Department of Health for Scotland, Department of Agriculture for Scotland, Prisons Department) – were concerned with their particular functions only, which had been vested in them by Act of Parliament. They were also technically independent of the Scottish Secretary, since the powers they performed were vested by law in them and not in him (Gilmour, 1937, p. 21). Yet he was the minister held politically responsible for their actions.

The nearest parallel to this confusing situation might be the position of the Prime Minister, whose Office is not vested with administrative functions like other departments but who has a vital role in co-ordinating the work of all government departments. Unlike the Prime Minister, the Scottish Secretary does have powers conferred on him by statute, but it is interesting that these have not limited his political responsibilities. In 1937, the Gilmour Committee on Scottish Administration reported:

> It is a peculiarity of the functions of the Secretary of State that, quite apart from his statutory duties, he has a large nebulous sphere of duties in which he is supposed to represent the Scottish point of view, and to safeguard Scottish interests . . . (Gilmour, p. 25)

> The Secretary of State is regarded as the mouthpiece of Scottish opinion on the Cabinet, and is expected to express Scottish views on many questions which do not directly concern the Departments for which he is responsible. Moreover, there is an increasing tendency among Scottish people to appeal to the Secretary of State on all questions affecting the social and political life of Scotland. (p. 65)

This is a problem still unresolved today, for it is common to hold the Scottish Secretary responsible for the results of government policies in Scotland which may not have come within the field of the Scottish Office.

Before the organisation of the Scottish administration was reformed in 1939, there had been considerable criticism of its constitution, several official inquiries and some minor reforms. In 1914, the Royal Commission on the Civil Service condemned the system of boards on administrative grounds, and recommended their substitution by ordinary departments composed of civil servants. These would include the top civil servants of the administrative class, who had been absent in the boards since the higher business of administration had been the province of the board members, appointed from outside the civil service. The board members sometimes brought little specialised knowledge to their work, and had to learn their duties in the early years of service. The Haldane Committee on the *Machinery of Government*, 1918 [Cd. 9230], attacked boards on political grounds also, echoing the complaints of Scottish MPs since the 1860s that there was no clear ministerial responsibility for their actions. As an example of this, the Fishery Board in the 1930s made a by-law which the Scottish Secretary refused to confirm, and an expensive inquiry followed (Gilmour, p. 11).

In 1928 the first line of complaint – administrative shortcomings – was dealt with by the conversion of all but two of the boards to departments with the usual civil service recruitment and career structure (although not until 1935 were administrative class civil servants employed in the Departments of Health and Agriculture for

Scotland). However, the second difficulty – unclear political responsibility – remained, and the Scottish Secretary was seemingly still not master in his own house.

With a strong Secretary such as Walter Elliot (1936–8), change was inevitable, and the departmental Committee on Scottish Administration already referred to was set up under the chairmanship of Sir John Gilmour (MP, Glasgow, Pollok), an experienced politician who had been Scottish Secretary himself from 1924 to 1929 and Home Secretary from 1932 to 1935. Its Report, published in 1937, is a turning-point in the history of the Scottish Office, and perhaps also of Scotland, since it accelerated the movement towards political separatism and re-established Edinburgh as an administrative, as well as legal and religious, capital in Scotland.

As in the 1880s, Scottish administrative reform took place against the background of popular nationalism, although it seems to have been more independent of it in the 1930s. There was acute economic depression in Scotland and attention was focused on the apparent shortcomings of the government's efforts. Both Walter Elliot and Sir John Gilmour were Glasgow MPs and it was Glasgow which had the worst economic conditions and the most militant nationalism of the period. In 1928 a Glasgow lawyer, J. M. MacCormick, founded a nationalist party; in 1931 Compton Mackenzie was elected Rector of Glasgow University by the students as a Scottish Nationalist.

The Gilmour Committee's Report is not marked by any nationalism, however; its theme is sober practicality. It was impracticable, it said, to separate the Scottish Office from the other Scottish departments by a distance of 400 miles. In future they should all be in Edinburgh, except for a small parliamentary and liaison office. Moreover, all the administrative functions exercised by Scottish agencies should be directly vested by law in the Scottish Secretary, eliminating the quasi-independence of the Scottish departments. It suggested the absorption of most of the Scottish agencies into four main departments: the Department of Agriculture for Scotland, the Scottish Education Department, the Department of Health for Scotland and the Scottish Home Department. This would introduce a standard constitution for each and would enable the Scottish Secretary to distribute the work among them as he thought fit; and it would finally abolish the Education Department's link with the Privy Council. The staff of these departments would be borne on separate establishments and each would have an administrative (not political) head. These heads of departments would have direct access to the Secretary of State, and would not be subject to the Permanent Under-Secretary of State, as are the Divisions in other government departments. But they would meet regularly under the chairmanship of the Permanent Under-Secretary, and he would occupy a key role in co-ordinating the affairs of the whole 'Scottish Office', a term which could now be used to cover the entire administrative organisation of the Scottish departments. Nevertheless, the distinction between the 'functional' departments and the Secretary of State's private Office (still sometimes wrongly referred to as the Scottish Office) was to remain.

Even before the Gilmour Committee reported, the move to Edinburgh was in progress. The Scottish Education Department, for example, had moved forty-four officers up from London in 1935, and Division 4 of the Scottish Office (mostly local government and economic development) had also moved to Edinburgh in that year. In anticipation of the concentration of forces in Edinburgh, a new government building, St Andrew's House, was already under construction on the site of the old Calton Jail, and a provisional allocation of space therein had been made for seven government agencies. Undeterred, the Gilmour Committee made its own allocations for its new departments and these were adopted when the building opened in 1939. Today St Andrew's House (Old and New) is the main evidence that Scotland is treated separately within British administration.

To summarise the position by the end of the period 1885 to 1939: the Scottish Secretary had been upgraded to a secretary of state and given a ministerial assistant, and the Scottish Office had expanded greatly from its modest beginnings in 1885 – in 1885, it numbered seven; in 1937, 117. The staff of all the Scottish departments and boards in 1937 was well in excess of 2,000, the principal establishments being: Department of Health, 796; Department of Agriculture, 555; Fishery Board, 229; Scottish Education Department, 214 (Gilmour, pp. 66–86). Yet the organisation of the Scottish government agencies was obscure, impracticable and unpopular. Public opinion and administrators alike demanded a logical and well-defined Scottish Office and more administration from Edinburgh. This would make Scottish government more efficient, and at the same time allay some of the national discontent.

All the time, of course, the powerful central government departments, such as those concerned with finance, trade, industry and transport, were operative in Scotland and were quite distinct from the Scottish agencies, although informal or formal consultations with these were becoming more common. While these may have possessed the powers of decision in the really vital matters, along with the Prime Minister and the Cabinet, the Secretary of State for Scotland was now identified with all government policy in Scotland and his reputation suffered when there was economic distress (as there often was after 1920). In this respect, the Scottish Secretary's position was not essentially altered by the reforms of 1939, or by later changes. The government of Scotland remained subject to British departments over a wide field, and was of course subject to the will of the Cabinet even in matters coming within its own administrative sphere. Obviously, there was plenty of scope for a further nationalist demand that the Scottish Office be strengthened, or alternatively that it be abolished in favour of complete Home Rule for Scotland.

## SCOTTISH ADMINISTRATION SINCE 1939

The Reorganisation of Offices (Scotland) Act, 1939, implemented the Gilmour Committee's recommendations, and the new Scottish Office was established with four administrative departments whose functions were directly vested in the Secretary of State for Scotland. These departments (Home, Health, Education and Agriculture) had their headquarters in St Andrew's House, Edinburgh, and the small number of staff retained in London at Dover House were there to assist the ministers in the parliamentary, legal and liaison work of the Scottish Office. Most of this staff and the ministerial staff in St Andrew's House were not operating within any of the four administrative departments, but they, too, had their liaison officers in London.

The new department, the Scottish Home Department, took over the old statutory functions of the Scottish Office as well as those of the Prisons Department and the Fishery Board. The Registrar General, the General Board of Control, the National Galleries and the Keeper of the Records were among the minor Scottish agencies which remained outside the direct responsibility of the Secretary of State (Milne, p. 19), but all the important Scottish functions were now vested in him.

From 1939 until the present day the main development has been the general increase in the functions performed by the Scottish Office, partly because of greater government activity, but also through the transfer of functions from other departments. There was a major reorganisation of departments in 1962 and 1973, so that the departments are now the Scottish Development Department, the Scottish Economic Planning Department, the Scottish Home and Health Department, the Scottish Education Department and the Department of Agriculture and Fisheries for Scotland. A summary of the functions of these and of the United Kingdom departments in Scotland is given in Table 7.1.

The period commences with the exceptional wartime administration under Thomas Johnston as Secretary. Johnston, a socialist and ex-editor of *Forward*, the Glasgow Independent Labour Party (ILP) newspaper, recounted in his *Memories*:

Before I was completely hypnotised into accepting the post of Secretary of State for Scotland I had mustered up sufficient sense to table prior conditions.

'What are they?' I was asked [by Churchill].

(Me): 'First, I should want to try out a Council of State for Scotland – a council composed of all the living ex-Secretaries for Scotland, of all parties; and whenever we were all agreed upon a Scottish issue, I could look to you for backing.'

(The PM): 'That seems a sort of national government of all parties idea, just like our Government here. All right, I'll look sympathetically upon anything about which Scotland is unanimous.' (Johnston, 1952, p. 148)

The Council, comprising Johnston and the five living ex-Secretaries, came into being at the end of 1941.

Churchill was much too busy fighting the war to be concerned about Scotland, and in these circumstances the Scottish Office and 'Council of State' (its official title was 'Scottish Advisory Council of ex-Secretaries') were virtual rulers of Scotland. Any stimulus to Scottish industry and agriculture was acceptable, and Johnston got sanction for the setting-up in 1943 of the North of Scotland Hydro-Electricity Board which has since revitalised the Highlands. To counteract the absence of a Scottish Board of Trade, Johnston established the Scottish Council on Industry, an independent body composed of representatives of Scottish economic interest groups, whose funds supported it. This greatly improved the Scottish Office's industrial contacts, for three Scottish departments, as well as nine United Kingdom departments, sent representatives to the Council meetings. The result was a rapid improvement in Scottish production and, between 1942 and 1945, 700 new industrial enterprises were created, involving 90,000 jobs. The Council merged in 1946 with the Scottish Development Council (established in 1930), a private body, to become the Scottish Council (Development and Industry). It is now one of the most important pressure groups in Scotland and, although it is not a government agency, it advises the Scottish Secretary on industrial policy.

During the war the Scottish Office increased its share of government functions with the addition of electricity (North of Scotland only – the South of Scotland did not come under the Scottish Office until 1954), Crown Lands and an equal say in the Forestry Commission, with a separate Scottish Committee sitting in Edinburgh, and the power to subsidise and develop agriculture was greatly extended. A second Parliamentary Under-Secretary of State was appointed in 1941. Johnston summed up the wartime record in Scotland: 'We had got Scotland's wishes and opinions respected and listened to, as they had not been respected or listened to since the Union' (Johnston, p. 169). This he felt had been the result of his 'experiment in political co-operation for Scottish national ends'.

It was no use hoping, as Johnston seems to have done, that after the war such co-operation between the parties could continue, and with the resumption of normal politics the Scottish Office lost much of its influence and independence in the administration. Clement Attlee, the Labour Prime Minister from 1945 to 1951, was less inclined to leave the Scottish Office alone to run Scotland, and the great programme of nationalisation and social legislation naturally increased the relative power of the central authorities and ministries which operated them (except for the National Health Service which in Scotland came under the Scottish Secretary). The immediate post-war period thus saw an increase in 'remote control' from London, and it seemed that the task of postwar reconstruction was also in the hands of London ministries and not the Scottish Office. Someone at the Treasury, however, issued a memorandum in June 1946 which stressed that the staffing of the Scottish regional offices of United Kingdom departments ought to be done 'with the greatest possible care, and with particular regard to the effect on Scottish opinion and the adequate representation in Whitehall of the Scottish point of view'; that these should 'devolve upon their Scottish representatives sufficient authority to enable Scottish business to be settled on the spot, with the minimum of reference to London, and should ensure that in the settlement of large matters of principle, Scottish aspects are fully considered'. The position of the Scottish Secretary as 'Scotland's Minister', with an interest in trade and economic development, is pointed out, and departments concerned with these are urged to invite Scottish Office representatives to their regional committees (quoted in Balfour Report, 1954, p. 121). But a succession of weak Scottish Secretaries (Johnston having become chairman of the Hydro Board, the Scottish Committee of the Forestry Commission and the Scottish Tourist Board) were unable to make Scotland's needs strongly felt in the Cabinet, or to take independent action themselves. The familiar sequence of economic distress leading to nationalism showed itself again, and the Scottish Labour Party itself passed resolutions in 1945 and 1947 urging an inquiry into the treatment of Scotland in Parliament and in the administration. This was the nearest approach to the party's pre-1929 advocacy of a Scottish parliament, and in subsequent years it moved away from such nationalism. Others in Scotland, however, became more nationalist, and 2 million are reputed to have signed the Scottish National Convenant in 1949, demanding a parliament for Scottish affairs within the framework of the United Kingdom.

The Labour government was prepared to make certain changes in the arrangements for Scotland. It introduced various co-ordinating committees: the Distribution of Industry Panel for Scotland, entirely departmental and under the chairmanship of the Board of Trade, which deals with the location of factories, the scheduling of development areas and the distribution of government grants to industry; the Scottish Board for Industry, which included non-departmental representatives and was appointed by the Chancellor of the Exchequer but chaired by the Board of Trade, and which, until its disappearance in 1966, advised on industrial conditions in Scotland; and also such official bodies as the Highlands and Islands Advisory Panel, which comprised Highland MPs, representatives of local authorities and other persons chosen by the Scottish Secretary, until it was superseded by the Highlands and Islands Consultative Council in 1966. In a White Paper on Scottish Affairs in 1948 (Cmd 7308) the government promised a Scottish Economic Conference composed of representatives of interests and government departments (the Council met only seven times between 23 April 1948 and May 1950) and also announced important increases in the powers of the Scottish Grand Committee in the House of Commons (see below, p. 125). A more searching inquiry into Scottish affairs was rejected as inopportune in view of the need 'to make immediate progress by concentrating on the practical measures proposed' (Cmd 7308, p. 4).

This had to wait until the Conservatives took office, and once more it was Winston Churchill who gave a new stimulus to the Scottish Office. As Prime Minister for the second time (1951–55), he appointed his old Chief Whip, James Stuart, as Scottish Secretary, and added a Minister of State and a third Parliamentary Under-Secretary to the ministerial team at the Scottish Office, making five ministers in all. As in the case of Johnston, Stuart was able to rely on the support of Churchill in cabinet disputes (Stuart, 1967, p. 162), and he also set up two inquiries of importance for Scottish government.

The first was a Committee under Lord Catto to inquire into the practicality of making separate statistical returns relating to: (i) government revenue and expenditure in Scotland and the rest of the United Kingdom, and the balances available for general expenditure from Scotland and the rest of the United Kingdom respectively; (ii) Scotland's share in Britain's imports and exports; and (iii) Scotland's imports from, exports to and balance of payments with other countries, including the rest of the United Kingdom. The Report was somewhat inconclusive for, although Scotland received a greater share of domestic expenditure, the proportion of general expenditure (for the benefit of the whole United Kingdom, such as that on defence and government contracts) actually incurred in Scotland was probably smaller: the Catto Committee did not know. Such expenditure, of course, has relevance to unemployment, income per head and the general prosperity of the area in which it is incurred. The second and third questions of its remit could not be answered since it claimed that Scotland was part of one unified economic system with complete freedom of trade (this has not prevented others attempting to answer them in later years).

No sooner had the Catto Committee reported (July 1952) than a Royal Commission was set up 'to review with reference to the financial, economic, administrative and other considerations involved, the arrangements for exercising the functions of Our Government in Scotland and to report'. Thus the Scottish Office once more came under scrutiny, along with the other departments (but not the nationalised industries) in Scotland. The thorny question of parliamentary devolution was excluded, but the Balfour Commission (its Chairman was the Earl of Balfour, nephew of A. J. Balfour) was much more nationalist in tone than had been the previous inquiries.

The introductory chapter of its Report referred back to the Treaty of Union as 'the voluntary union of two proud peoples each with their [*sic*] own distinctive national and cultural characteristics and traditions' and admitted that it was now widely held that a deterioration had occurred in the relationship between Scotland and England. Its main conclusion was that 'Scotland's needs and points of view should be known and brought into account at all stages in the formation and execution of policy' (Cmd 9212, p. 121). The possibility that such needs and points of view might be different from those of England was not considered, for it sanguinely declared that 'the vital community of interest between Scotland and the rest of the United Kingdom must be recognised'. While no evidence was sought on parliamentary devolution, the nationalist organisations and the Communist Party voiced strong views in favour of a Scottish parliament. But the other principal pressure groups in Scotland, such as the Convention of Royal Burghs, the Association of County Councils and the industrial and trade union organisations, did not concur. Thus the Commission could go on confidently to provide a solution within the context of the existing constitutional framework, which indeed struck it as already devolutionary. The office of Scottish Secretary, it considered, was an 'invaluable asset to Scotland', and the Commission trusted that it would continue to exercise responsibility for its existing functions. The only material suggestions were that the Scottish Office should take over: (i) highways, from the Ministry of Transport; (ii) appointment of JPs, from the Lord Chancellor; and (iii) animal diseases, from the Ministry of Agriculture. These were not major changes; JPs and animals were transferred in 1955, and trunk roads in April 1956. On the subject of the United Kingdom departments, the Commission trod warily, and no suggestion was made for a Scottish Board of Trade, one of the principal absentees in

Scottish administration. Greater co-operation with the Scottish Office was urged, and also the dropping of the obnoxious title 'Regional Controller' of these departments in favour of 'Scottish Controller' (athough non-Scots could be appointed).

Such a Report was not designed to appease nationalism in Scotland but, with the economic recovery of the mid-1950s, this became less necessary. There was little interest in Scottish government for several years after 1954, and the next episode in this history of administrative reform in Scotland commenced as usual with another downturn in the Scottish economy. In 1958, unemployment in Scotland rose to 3·8 per cent (Great Britain 2·1 per cent) and increased to 4·4 per cent in 1959 (Great Britain 2·2 per cent). The relative depression in Scotland produced a swing against the Conservatives in the 1959 election (contrary to the English result), and considerable unease was felt by Scottish industrial pressure groups. One of these, the Scottish Council (Development and Industry), itself composed of the principal Scottish economic organisations and strongly connected with the Scottish Office, commissioned an inquiry into the Scottish economy under J. N. Toothill of Ferranti's (Edinburgh), and this received the blessing and co-operation of the government departments in Scotland.

Its Report (published in Edinburgh in 1961) included a chapter on the machinery of central government in Scotland (chapter 22), with special reference to its efficiency in promoting regional economic development – an approach to economic planning which has derived some of its present-day acceptance by British governments from the impetus provided by the Toothill Report. There was nothing nationalist about the Report: in fact it was less romantic than the Balfour Commission. But in its advocacy of Scottish ('regional') planning and development it went beyond the milk-and-water proposals of the Balfour Report. It called for a new department in the Scottish Office to co-ordinate regional development measures and to take over the existing industrial and planning functions of the Scottish departments. This department should include an economic unit to advise on economic and industrial policy in Scotland and on the availability of economic statistics. More radical reforms were not suggested. There was no need for a Scottish parliament, a Scottish Treasury, a Scottish Board of Trade or a Scottish Minister for Economic Affairs. 'We think it is unrealistic to advocate the separate policies which separate departments imply. The Scottish economy is inextricably interwoven with that of England' (Toothill, 1961, p. 174). This was broadly in line with official thinking on the subject, as might be expected, even though it was barely consistent with the notion of Scottish economic planning which was seen as the function of a new Scottish department.

This department was in fact established on 2 June 1962, and was named the Scottish Development Department. It took over the statutory duties of the Scottish Home Department with regard to industry and development, electricity, roads and local government, those of the Department of Health for Scotland relating to housing, town and country planning and environmental services, and the Secretary of State's non-statutory responsibility for the general oversight of the Scottish economy. Another new department was created, the Scottish Home and Health Department, which became responsible for law and order, the National Health Service and associated welfare services (but Child Care remained under the Scottish Education Department, where it had been since 1960). The other two departments continued as before, although it should be noted that in 1960 the Department of Agriculture had become the Department of Agriculture and Fisheries for Scotland when Fisheries were transferred from the Home Department.

The establishment of a whole department devoted to 'development' was described by one expert in administration as 'a new phenomenon in British government' (Willson, 1966, p. 79), and it pre-dated the United Kingdom Department of Economic Affairs set up under the Labour government in October 1964. The Scottish Development Department and Scottish Development Group (an interdepartmental committee) produced the first regional economic plan of the 1960s (*Central Scotland: A Programme for Development and Growth*, Cmnd 2188, 1963), the forerunner of many such plans for other parts of Britain. After that, interest in the Scottish economy and the powers of the Scottish Office in economic planning grew greater. This was partly the result of the resurgence of Scottish nationalism in the mid-1960s, and partly the result of a stronger initiative from the Scottish Office in economic matters. These two strands were not necessarily connected, but they did reinforce each other. A Scottish Economic Plan was issued in 1966, and the Scottish Economic Planning Board and Council set up. The Highlands and Islands Development Board began in 1965, and the Scottish Development Agency in 1975. A new department, the Scottish Economic Planning Department, was established in 1973, and took on key functions such as electricity, transport and oil support services, as well as the economic planning powers.

At the same time, inquiries into the economic relationship between Scotland and the rest of the UK continued. The Treasury and the *Scotsman* issued 'Scottish Budgets' in 1969, and these were followed by studies for the Commission on the Constitution (1969–73), academic works and party literature. Most of these echoed the Catto Committee's findings, until in 1973 and 1974 the implications of North Sea oil revenues changed the balance-sheets dramatically in Scotland's

Table 7.1  *Central administration in Scotland, 1978 – principal functions of government agencies*

| UK or GB | Secretary of State for Scotland |
|---|---|
| Treasury | Responsible for the Scottish Office, |
| Inland Revenue | consisting of the following |
| Customs and Excise | departments: |
|   Taxes, duties, interest rates | |
|   Public expenditure | Scottish Home and Health |
| Department of Trade |   Department |
| Department of Industry |   Law and Order |
| Department of Employment |   National Health Service |
| Department of the Environment | Scottish Education Department |
| Ministry of Transport |   Education (except universities |
|   Railways, ships |     and research councils) |
| Ministry of Defence |   Social work |
| Department of Energy |   Libraries |
|   Oil, coal, gas |   The Arts |
| Department of Health and Social | Department of Agriculture and |
|   Security |   Fisheries for Scotland |
|   Social Security only |   Land settlement, crofting |
| Department of Prices and |   Forestry |
|   Consumer Protection |   Agricultural price supports |
| Department of Education and |     (UK/EEC) |
|   Science |   Agricultural education |
|   Universities and research |   Fisheries |
|   councils only | Scottish Development Department |
| Ministry of Agriculture, Fisheries, |   Local government |
|   and Food |   Housing |
|   Animal health, food only |   Roads |
| Home Office |   Transport |
|   Immigration, cruelty to | Scottish Economic Planning |
|   animals |   Department |
| Foreign and Commonwealth Office |   Economic planning |
|   Passports |   Industrial incentives |
| Civil Service Department |   Manpower services |
|   Recruitment and conditions |   North Sea oil support services |
|   of civil service |   New Towns |
| |   Electricity |
| |   Highland development |
| |   Tourism |
| | Central Services |
| |   Finance and personnel |
| | |
| | *Lord Advocate* |
| | Lord Advocate's Department |
| |   Legal advice to government |
| | Crown Office |
| |   Public prosecutions |

favour. At that point, economists and politicians had to decide whether to count oil revenues as a Scottish or a British resource. This dilemma is still unresolved.

## SCOTLAND AND THE CENTRAL GOVERNMENT TO 1979

Since 1885 the central government functions in Scotland have been the responsibility either of Scottish departments (after 1939, collectively called the Scottish Office), or of United Kingdom or Great Britain departments and public corporations.[5] The functional division has been based on the assumption that some services are essentially Scottish, while others must be organised on a British basis. Thus education, law and order, agriculture, fisheries and local government are agreed to be Scottish, while social security, taxation and customs and excise are by consent United Kingdom functions.

Where there is less agreement is the division between the Scottish and United Kingdom departments in the economic planning and industrial field, and the arrangements to 1979 illustrate this dilemma (see Table 7.1). Thus, while the Scottish Office deals with economic development in Scotland, so too do the Treasury, the Department of Trade, the Department of Industry, the Department of Transport and the Department of Employment. Similarly, fuel and power is divided between the Scottish Economic Planning Department (electricity) and the Department of Energy (gas and coal). A co-ordinated transport policy is also difficult to achieve in Scotland, given the division between the Department of Transport (railways) and the Scottish Development Department (roads). Much of the political discontent in the Highlands and certain other rural areas was about rail closures, and some constituencies may have changed hands because of these. Yet the Scottish Office has little control over the railways, and pressure must be directed at an often unsympathetic Whitehall department.

Thus to the public, the respective spheres of operation of the Scottish Office and the other departments are cloaked in mystery when policies relating to unemployment, factory building and general economic affairs are involved. It becomes very difficult in Scotland to say which minister is responsible for these policies, and clearly 'Scotland's Minister' is only one of the many involved. Unfortunately for him, as we have seen, he is often blamed when things go wrong, and it might appear that the office he holds is unrewarding. He is expected to cover the fields of at least six English ministers (admittedly for a tenth of the population), to travel incessantly between London and Scotland, and to endure the difficulties of the geographical separation between Parliament and his department. Yet where public opinion is most sensitive and votes get lost (over social services, unemployment and general economic welfare) he is weakest, although he has of course a voice in the Cabinet and can emphasise there the political implications of neglecting Scotland.

Many of the problems of the Scottish ministers are shared by the civil servants of the Scottish Office. They too have to be generalists rather than specialists: most are in one of the five specialised departments, but as they are fewer in number than the corresponding administrators in Whitehall departments they range over a wider area in their work. Moreover, they have to commute between St Andrew's House and Whitehall (at least the top ones do). They soon develop a loyalty to Scotland, which is somewhat different in quality from the loyalty which civil servants in other departments have for their departments. Scotland is a nation, not just an administrative unit, and in a sense the Scottish Office men are nationalists. They argue the case for Scotland within the administration, and the wide range of their functions make them aware of Scottish needs as a whole. Most of the top civil servants in the Scottish Office (about four-fifths) are Scots and have probably been more democratically educated than their English counterparts. They share some of the Scots' suspicion of Whitehall and wish to see more administrative decentralisation. So too do the Scottish sections of the United Kingdom departments, and their close contacts with the Scottish Office in interdepartmental committees make them share some of the loyalty to Scotland. These United Kingdom department men may not be so Scottish in origin, but they often become Scots by adoption.

In 1977 there were about 65,000 civil servants in Scotland, representing about a tenth of the British total. Only 11,000 civil servants were in the establishment of the Secretary of State for Scotland, although these included most of the senior officials. Altogether, nearly 180,000 people were employed in public administration (central and local) in Scotland.

In the 1960s and 1970s, the system of Scottish administration came increasingly under attack, and led to renewed demands for devolution. The Secretary of State for Scotland was considered to be over-stretched in his responsibilities, while still lacking crucial economic powers. His accountability to Parliament at Question-Time was limited to an appearance once in every four weeks or less, and his civil servants in Edinburgh seemed remote from parliamentary control. Criticism has also been levelled at the methods of work and policy outputs of the Scottish Office (Mackintosh, 1964). In general, many felt that the whole system of Scottish government should be made responsible to a directly-elected Scottish legislative body.

It is generally admitted that the strain on the Scottish Secretary is very great as he struggles to master the diffuse activities of his department and to cope with the constant travel. An addition to the ministerial team of five or six has been suggested, and even another

Cabinet minister. This is resisted by former Scottish Secretaries on the grounds that Scotland's voice must be heard undivided in the Cabinet, and in any case the proposal would hardly be consistent with retaining a small Cabinet. There is a danger, nevertheless, that when ministers are overtaxed or absent from their departments, the civil servants may play a disproportionate role in policy formulation and that ministers may not know what is going on. On the face of it, such factors are present in the Scottish Office, and it may well be that the bureaucracy is stronger in Scotland than England. We have seen that in education in Scotland, for example, the central government officials wield relatively greater power, and in economic planning too the voice of St Andrew's House is decisive, even when pseudo-independent bodies such as the Highlands and Islands Development Board and the Scottish Development Agency are set up.

The office of Secretary of State for Scotland is potentially a glamorous one. Former Secretaries like to speak of it as 'almost a Prime Minister in Scotland', and as national representative in the Cabinet it ought to carry great prestige. But even in Scotland it has hardly caught the imagination of the people. Few understand its powers, and most suspect, probably rightly, that the Scottish Secretary is greatly circumscribed by Cabinet control. Until 1966, there was no official residence in Scotland for Scotland's minister, but he now has Bute House in Edinburgh, albeit owned by the private National Trust for Scotland and financed privately.

The holders of the post of Scottish Secretary have rarely gained striking political successes or been impressive statesmen. In the early period noblemen predominated, whose imagination was severely limited. Only John Sinclair (Lord Pentland), between 1905 and 1912, was outstanding. Then, between the wars, pedestrian figures came and went, with the brief exception of Walter Elliot (1936–8). In the second war, Thomas Johnston made unprecedented progress but he has not been matched since, except perhaps by William Ross (1964–70, 1974–6).

The Scottish Office has the reputation of being something of a dead end for aspiring politicians but this is only partly true. Apart from A. J. Balfour (1886–7), who became Prime Minister (1902–5), and Sir John Gilmour (1925–9), who became Home Secretary (1932–5), few Scottish Secretaries have been transferred to other Cabinet positions (perhaps they do not want to be), but the junior ministers in the Scottish Office often rise to prominence elsewhere – for instance, in recent years, Thomas Fraser, Margaret Herbison, Lord Home and Judith Hart, all of whom became heads of other departments. Of course, Scots do not see the Scottish Office as the sole object of their ambition, and Scottish prime ministers are something of a tradition in British history – they include Aberdeen, Gladstone, Rosebery,

Campbell-Bannerman, Ramsay MacDonald and Home (and Balfour had a Scottish father). On the other hand, there have been English ministers in the Scottish Office, including one Scottish Secretary, Sir G. O. Trevelyan (1886, 1892–5). An English Secretary of State for Scotland would probably not be acceptable today, any more than an English Secretary of State for Wales, and in this sense there is more national consciousness now than in 1886. But it is a fact that despite the proliferation of Scottish government agencies since that date government is more centralised today. The increase in government activity has strengthened the real policy-makers (the principal United Kingdom ministers) who have the substance of power. The shadow is left to the Scottish departments, who may however gain a trick or two if the political climate is favourable: that is, if there is a danger of losing seats through inaction.

Thus the lack of a Scottish Office in 1870 did not mean that Scotland was more governed from London than it is today. On the contrary, such government as then existed was in the hands of local leaders in church, school, shop and castle. Assimilation throughout Britain has proceeded ever since, by popular demand, and in essentials will continue. However, at a certain level, there must be local self-rule and, in Scotland, the retention of national identity. What this level should be is uncertain and continues to be the subject of constant examination.

DEVOLUTION

A major inquiry into devolution was undertaken by the Royal Commission on the Constitution ('Kilbrandon Commission'), and it reported in 1973 (Cmnd 5460). It recommended the setting up of a Scottish Assembly, to be elected by proportional representation for a fixed term of four years. There would also be a Scottish Cabinet and 'Premier' responsible to the Assembly. Finance would come in the shape of a grant determined by an exchequer board, independent of the UK and Scottish governments.

At first it seemed as if the Kilbrandon Commission's recommendations would not be acted upon, because of the lack of political pressure, but the successes of the Scottish National Party in the February 1974 elections inspired the Labour government to lay alternative proposals before Parliament. By September 1974, these had hardened into a definite scheme (Cmnd 5732), and eventually, in November 1976, legislation was introduced in the form of the Scotland and Wales Bill. This failed at the guillotine motion vote in February 1977, but a second attempt, the Scotland Bill, 1977, reached the statute book in July 1978. It failed, however, to pass the referendum test set by Parliament against the wishes of the government (see pp. 147–8).

The Scotland Act, 1978, followed broadly the recommendations of the Kilbrandon Report, although there was to be no proportional representation, and the office of Secretary of State for Scotland in the UK government was to remain, with several important functions reserved to the continuing Scottish Office. A complex set of 'checks and balances' was to operate between the UK and devolved governments.

It was a scheme of government which lay somewhere between a federal system and a local government system (for detailed analysis, see MacKay, 1979; Bogdanor, 1979). Opinions vary as to whether it could have worked well or not. Certainly it did not fully satisfy the demand in Scotland for devolution, since for some it went too far, while for more it did not go far enough. For nearly everyone it was exceedingly complicated, and had no clear benefit to be set against the cost of additional civil servants, politicians, and so on. Nevertheless, devolution remains on the agenda of Scottish and British politics, and the pattern of the history of Scotland points to its revival and subsequent implementation in the near future.

NOTES

1   Boards of the nationalised industries and other public corporations have been omitted, and also advisory boards (for example, the Scottish Board for Industry, 1945–64).
2   The Lord Advocate was paid £5,000 per annum at this time, just as the Lord Chancellor was (and is) paid more than the Prime Minister.
3   Powers transferred to the Secretary of State for Scotland under the 1885 Act were: from the Home Secretary: Poor Law, Lunacy (except criminal lunatics), Public Health, Wild Birds Protection, Public Works Loans, Fishery Board, General Register House in Edinburgh, Registration of Births, Deaths and Marriages, Vaccination, Marriage Notices, Police, Division of Burghs into Wards, Markets and Fairs, Prisons, Public Parks, County General Assessment, Roads and Bridges, Locomotive Regulation, Sheriff Court Houses, Rivers Pollution, Burial Grounds, Food and Drugs, Local Taxation Returns, Alkali, Salmon Fisheries, School Sites, Parliamentary Divisions, Assessor of Railways and Canals; from the Privy Council: Board of Manufactures, Public Health; from the Treasury: Assessor of Railways and Canals, Board of Manufactures, General Register House (except salaries); from Local Government Board for England: Loans by Public Works Loans Commissioners, Alkali.
    The Privy Council retained Scottish education, through its committee the Scotch Education Department, but the Scottish Secretary became its Vice-President. (*Scottish Administration: Report of Committee* ('Gilmour Report'), Cmd 5563 (Edinburgh: HMSO, 1937), pp. 61–3.)
4   Until 1922 the Head of the Scottish Education Department was stationed in London, as well as half of the staff. By 1937 only 23 of the 125 officers were in London, and there were also 66 inspectors in Scotland (Gilmour Report, p. 71).

5 UK departments cover Northern Ireland (for example, Defence, Inland Revenue, Customs and Excise), GB departments do not. But it is sometimes difficult to say which are UK and which GB (for example, the Department of Trade).

FURTHER READING

Kellas, J. G., *The Scottish Political System* (1973, 1975).
    A textbook for students of Scottish politics.
*Scottish Government Yearbook* (annual).
    Articles on current issues, and facts on elections and publications.
Pottinger, G., *The Secretaries of State for Scotland, 1926–76* (1979).
    Entertaining sketches of ex-Scottish Secretaries, by well-known ex-Scottish Office civil servant.

# Chapter 8

# The Government of Scotland

## II *Local Government*

There is a continuous history of local authorities in Scotland from mediaeval times to the present day. In particular, some ex-burgh councils can trace their development back to the twelfth century, when royal charters established their privileges in trading and their right to self-government through provost, bailies, Dean of Guild (architectural inspector) and council. Other burghs, many of which gained similar local privileges, were established by nobles and bishops (burghs of barony and burghs of regality), and at the time of the Union in 1707 there were 66 royal burghs and about 150 burghs of barony or regality. In the landward areas of the counties, on the other hand, there was little escape from the direct rule of the feudal superior and his sheriff court, and until 1889 the only approach to a county council was an amorphous body known as the Commissioners of Supply. These Commissioners were the substantial men of property in the county, who collectively saw to it that law and order was maintained (eventually by police forces), that the rates were collected, and that the parliamentary electors were registered. Much of local government until the latter half of the nineteenth century was in the hands of the kirk sessions, and we have seen already that their jurisdiction extended to schools, poor relief and to the enforcement of 'temperance and morals'. Justices of the peace also helped to keep order and supervise the upkeep of roads.

In all the successive reforms of the system of local government in Scotland, evidence of the past was allowed to remain so that the great continuity might not perish. Until 1975, there were still burghs in Scotland whose only meaningful title to a council and local government powers was a charter granted by David I or William I, and there were still two counties (Nairn and Kinross) which retained county councils but had no 'county powers' because they were too small. This situation produced the Royal Commission on Local Government in Scotland (1966–9), whose report led to a revolution in the structure of local authorities and the distribution of their powers. It did not make a clean break with the past, for the Scottish tradition in local government is stronger than its tradition in central government. But the disappearance of the burghs and counties may well have caused as much regret as the absorption of the Scottish government and parliament in that of Great Britain.

## LOCAL AUTHORITIES, 1870–1929

The years between 1870 and 1929 were the age of civic improvement. Vast city populations such as Glasgow demanded water, sanitation and the maintenance of public health. Glasgow's problems were enormous, with terrible overcrowding and slums, yet its record is a notable one. Through private Acts of Parliament it gained one of Britain's best water supplies in 1859 by piping 30 miles from Loch Katrine; it inaugurated slum clearance with its City Improvement Trust (1866); and it municipalised the supply of gas (1869) and electricity (1891). The other large burghs had similar projects, and all developed an intense pride in their achievements. The middle-class population had since 1833 been qualified to elect the burgh councils in seventy-nine burghs and in these there was a strong belief in independent self-rule, expressed in parliamentary elections by a solid Liberalism. Many of the other burghs, which had not been given elected town councils in 1833, were soon given the right to call themselves police burghs, with power to provide many local services and to elect commissioners to serve alongside their self-appointed councils. By the Town Councils (Scotland) Act, 1900, the constitutions and powers of these police burghs were brought in line with the other burgh authorities.

The counties needed less collectivism perhaps, and they looked, often in vain, to the paternalism of the lairds for their improving measures. By the Local Government (Scotland) Act of 1889, elective county councils were established. Many of the clauses of the Act were strongly opposed by the (Liberal) majority of Scottish MPs at the time, as the powers given to the county councils seemed weak in comparison with those of the burghs, and the Commissioners of Supply were retained to share with the councils the control of the police. One important amendment was forced on the government by the Scottish MPs: the money made available under the Act from probate duties was applied to the freeing of education in Scottish state schools and not to the relief of the rates as originally proposed. In all, twelve amendments which received the support of a majority of the Scottish MPs were rejected by the government, a factor which strengthened the feeling in the Liberal Party in favour of Scottish Home Rule.

Apart from the burgh and county councils, there were other local authorities in this period. The relief of the poor as well as water supplies and public health in rural areas was in the hands of parochial boards (1845–94) composed of elected members, representatives of kirk sessions, heritors (landowners) and burgh magistrates. These were superseded by parish councils (1894–1930), which were elected by the ratepayers and performed a similar variety of minor local functions. Education was under the school boards (1872–1918), later education authorities for the counties and the five largest burghs (1918–30), which were elected separately from the other local authorities. Finally, district committees composed of councillors looked after roads and public health in their areas, and in time a variety of other bodies appeared: burgh police commissions, county road boards and county joint committees. By 1900 there were 200 burgh councils, 33 county councils, 869 parish councils and almost 1,000 school boards.

Such a profusion of local agencies was bound to be unsatisfactory, and the wonder is that it was not curtailed sooner. In England, the 1902 Education Act had replaced the school boards as education authorities by the county and county borough councils, but in Scotland similar action was inexplicably delayed (Knox, 1953, p. 175). Even in 1918 the Scots were reluctant to adopt the English solution, and they did not do so until the radical reform of the Local Government (Scotland) Act of 1929 inaugurated a new system of local authorities in Scotland.

## THE SYSTEM FROM 1930 TO 1975

The 1929 Act abolished all the existing local authorities other than burgh and county councils, and set up a simpler system in which there were initially:

(1) 4 all-purpose authorities – Glasgow, Edinburgh, Aberdeen and Dundee – known as counties of cities;
(2) 35 county councils and joint county councils:
    (a) 29 county councils exercising complete 'county powers' (that is, they were all-purpose authorities in the landward or non-burgh areas, performed most major functions in small burghs, and education and valuation in large burghs),
    (b) 2 joint county councils (Perth-Kinross and Moray-Nairn), performing all county functions in these counties except for the 'small burgh services' (see (4) below) in the landward areas, which were reserved for

    (c) the 4 county councils of Perth, Kinross, Moray and Nairn;
(3) 20 large burghs, with populations over 20,000 exercising all
    local functions except education and valuation;
(4) 171 small burghs (under 20,000), whose functions were reduced
    to housing, sanitation, streets, licensing of public houses,
    amenities and other minor matters; and
(5) 199 district councils, which superseded the parish councils
    and district committees, but retained only very minor functions,
    principally recreational facilities.

In 1974 there were 21 large burghs, 176 small burghs, and the same
number of city, county and district councils as before. There were
also a number of joint committees composed of representatives of
several local authorities, which combined to provide certain services:
13 water boards, 20 police authorities, 11 fire areas, and others relating
to burial grounds, the probation service and valuation. Since 1947,
five New Towns have been established in Scotland, with special
powers in town and country planning and housing, but these belong
strictly to central, not local administration, since their Development
Corporations are appointed by the Scottish Secretary and are financed
out of taxes rather than rates. Curiously, however, the New Town
of East Kilbride is now also a District Council, and the New Town
of Cumbernauld part of a District Council, with the powers of these
local authorities.

The details of the electoral system and of the procedure of the
old local authorities in Scotland need not detain us here. In general
these were the same as in England and Wales, with a few exceptions
mentioned below. Triennial elections of all the councillors took place
in the counties, and annual ones in the burghs, where a third of the
councillors retired every year. There was also a similar committee
system, through which councillors of all parties shared in the administrative as well as the policy-making deliberations of the council. The
individual councillor might also be concerned in Scotland with
assessing the priorities on the housing waiting-list for his ward, a
notable piece of patronage.

But some differences in Scottish local government procedure were
striking. There were no aldermen in Scottish councils. All the
members of the councils were directly elected by the people, so that
none of the undemocratic consequences of having a quarter of the
council co-opted as aldermen (in English county and borough councils)
arose in Scotland. However, aldermen were abolished in the new
English local government system which began in 1974.

But while Scotland had no aldermen, it had its bailies. These were
burgh magistrates, elected by the councillors from among themselves
to act as judges in the burgh or police courts. As we have seen in

Chapter 6, these courts have been replaced by district courts, and the bailies by justices of the peace. Some of the justices are chosen by the district councils from their members, and a few are still informally called 'bailies'. The chief magistrate of the burgh in the old system was the Provost (or Lord Provost in the 'counties of cities' and in Perth), and there are still Provosts in the new city District Councils. In England, the equivalent is the Mayor, but he was the only magistrate on the council in the old system, and today all magistrates (JPs) are appointed by the Lord Chancellor. From this it can be seen that Scotland takes a different view from England of the judicial capacity of its elected representatives.

## THE SYSTEM SINCE 1975

The present system of local government was established by the Local Government (Scotland) Act, 1973, and came into operation in May 1975 (Table 8.1). It was the result of years of discussion and inquiry, including a Royal Commission on Local Government in Scotland (the 'Wheatley Commission'), which reported in 1969 (Cmnd 4150).

The alleged faults of the old system were many, and they were summarised by Wheatley as 'complications, illogicalities, expense and ineffectiveness'. In other words, there were too many small authorities, and they could not perform their functions adequately. They were particularly unsuited to the planning of industrial regeneration in Scotland, and the Clyde valley region had numerous authorities so that there was no planning authority for the whole region.

The Wheatley Commission recommended that the old authorities be reduced in number, and that they be divided into two tiers, a regional tier and a district tier. The most important powers, such as transport, roads, water, education and economic planning, would go to the regions, while the districts would keep housing, physical (town and country) planning, and environmental services.

The reformed system, as passed by Parliament in 1973, was not exactly as the Wheatley Report had suggested. After the Report came out in 1969, there were strong campaigns in many parts of Scotland against some of the recommendations. For example, the Borders, Fife, the Western Isles, Orkney and Shetland all sought to be separate authorities. Suburbs round Glasgow resisted incorporation in the city district. All these were successful in persuading the government and Parliament. However, those who opposed the establishment of a giant Strathclyde Region (with half the population of Scotland) failed to get their way, and Strathclyde has remained the major problem of the new system.

This was not the only aspect of local government to come under attack, for the whole operation of the system seemed ambiguous. It

Table 8.1   *The Scottish local government system, 1978*

I   *Regions*
Functions: strategic planning, transport, roads, water, sewerage,
education, social work, police, registration.

|  | *Population* | *Hectares* |
|---|---|---|
| Strathclyde | 2,466,300 | 1,372,724 |
| Lothian | 756,246 | 175,516 |
| Grampian | 460,000 | 870,398 |
| Tayside | 402,000 | 766,524 |
| Fife | 339,185 | 130,538 |
| Central | 271,500 | 263,060 |
| Highland | 186,460 | 2,514,933 |
| Dumfries and Galloway | 143,434 | 637,151 |
| Borders | 100,370 | 467,159 |

II   *Island Authorities*
Functions: as for Regions, but joint administration with Highland
Region for police, fire, aspects of education and social
work.

| Western Isles | 29,701 | 290,085 |
|---|---|---|
| Shetland | 20,352 | 142,589 |
| Orkney | 18,014 | 88,062 |

III   *Districts*
Functions: local planning, including urban development and
countryside, housing, environmental services, museums,
art galleries and libraries (the last three jointly with
regions in some districts).
Fifty-three districts, the largest of which are:

| Glasgow City | 830,000 |
|---|---|
| Edinburgh City | 463,923 |
| Aberdeen City | 212,237 |
| Renfrew (incl. Paisley) | 211,116 |
| Dundee City | 192,765 |

was supposed to represent local democracy, yet some of the authorities were much too large to be based on any local community.
Strathclyde, as noted before, had half the population of Scotland,
and ranged from island communities to Glasgow. The Highland
Region occupied about a third of the map of Scotland (see frontis-
piece). Even the districts combined disparate urban and rural areas.

On top of that, the amount of independence which the local
authorities had from central government seemed to make a mockery

of local autonomy. Scottish local government is even more dependent on government grants than English local government, with the Rate Support Grant covering a higher percentage of current expenditure (in 1978–9, 68·5 per cent in Scotland, 61 per cent in England). The Scottish Office exerts numerous controls over local authorities, approving loans, capital expenditures, school-building, and so on. In the 1970s, national pay policies and 'cash limits' on local expenditures removed almost all their freedom of manœuvre in finance. Yet such freedom could be said to be essential to local government decision-making.

In Scotland there are special social and economic issues which are focused on local government. The most important of these is housing. As we saw in Chapter 2 (pp. 25–7), Scotland has a much higher proportion of council housing than England. This has placed a heavy burden on the rates, and ratepayers pay more in Scotland than in England as a result. The situation is made worse by the low level of council rents in Scotland. As the Allen Committee on rates remarked in 1965, 'The high level of rates in Scotland matches the low level of rents; indeed one subsidises the other' (Allen, 1965, Cmnd 2582, p. 140). The Labour Party has retained control of many local authorities by supporting a low rents policy, while the Conservatives have defended the non-council tenant ratepayer. In the 1970s, council rents rose more sharply, largely through the central government exerting coercion on defiant authorities. Rent and rate rebates were introduced to compensate individual householders whose income was low. This ironed out some of the worst features, but the contrast between Scotland and England remains. Rents and rates are the very stuff of Scottish local politics, to which has been added in recent years the sale of council houses. The Labour Party nationally favours this, but once again local Labour-controlled councils are reluctant to disturb their 'client' vote.

Housing is not a priority in the budget of the working-class Scot, who perhaps feels he needs to spend more than the Englishman on fuel, clothing, food and tobacco (see Family Expenditure Surveys, HMSO). It is even said that the poor quality of many council houses makes these items more necessary, especially as the climate in Scotland is rigorous.

Industrial mobility is hampered in Scotland because so many are tied to council houses and will not move to another town for fear of losing their privileged form of tenancy. Length of residence and not employment in the area is the main factor in the allocation of council houses, so that when a council tenant moves to another authority he goes to the bottom of the waiting-list. In general, the 'class warfare' between council tenants on the one hand, and private owners and tenants on the other, is a disturbing aspect of Scottish society. Where the council tenants comprise the majority of the local electorate, as they often do in the large towns, they can virtually subsidise themselves out of the rates. This leads to strong political opposition between the council and non-council groups, with the latter constantly frustrated.

COMMUNITY POLITICS

One of the features of the 1970s has been the development of community politics, and this gives hope for a new vigour in Scottish local democracy. Scotland has been relatively backward in this respect compared with England, where voluntary organisations have sprung up in great profusion. Nevertheless, the 1970s have seen much activity at the grass roots in Scotland, notably in the large cities, where many groups, including tenants' action groups and ratepayers associations, have been established. The Local Government Act of 1973 brought in community councils and schools councils, and these have represented people in a more direct way than the local authorities themselves. So far, their record has been patchy. In some areas there is apathy, in others great activity. Often the local authorities are jealous of the community councils, and seek to ignore them. But along with the voluntary bodies they do represent a new mood in Scottish society, and one which stands in stark contrast to the old authoritarian 'élitism' of kirk, school and council. It is obvious that they are sorely needed to counterbalance the giant, bureaucratic structures which have replaced the old local authorities.

FURTHER READING

Scottish Information Office, *Scottish Office Brief on Local Government in Scotland.*
*Scottish Government Yearbook* (annual).
  Unfortunately, no analytical work exists on Scottish local government.

# Chapter 9

# Parties and Pressure Groups

There are three channels of information and political pressure between Scotland and the government of the United Kingdom. The first has already been discussed: the Scottish departments of government. But these departments would have little influence, or even point, were it not that strong public opinion and pressure groups exist in Scotland to demand a separate and more favourable treatment for Scotland and Scottish interests in government policies. Thus Scottish politicians and administrators can point to the outside pressures which are brought to bear on their activities, and use these pressures as a political argument in support of their proposals.

All government departments do this, of course, but none has the combined strength of Scottish public opinion and organised interests to fall back on, as has the Scottish Office. Conversely, in England the comparable interest groups must diffuse their pressure among many departments. The English regions are as yet not all easily identified, and few have distinctly regional interest groups.[1] Moreover, English interest groups seem to conflict more with one another than the Scottish ones, whose common aim is 'a better deal for Scotland'. In Scotland a sort of log-rolling takes place, in which each group backs the other in anticipation of similar support in the future. The clearest example of this is the Scottish Council (Development and Industry), in which business, trade union and local government interests combine to promote each other's welfare in the name of Scottish development. There is little division in Scotland about the need for new projects such as steel mills, roads and bridges, while English areas often fight among themselves for these.

The third flow of pressure is exerted through Parliament by the Scottish MPs and the political parties. Were Scotland totally united as a nation in its political and economic aims (as to some extent the pressure groups' log-rolling might indicate), there would be little need for separate political parties: all Scots would be Nationalists. But in fact Scotland is split politically between the major parties, and until the late 1960s resembled England and Wales (but not Northern Ireland) in its support for the two-party system. For most of the period under review in this book, Scottish politics have operated *through* rather than *against* the British party system, and it is with this in mind that recent Scottish history must be approached. It can then be appreciated how great a contrast the late 1960s and the 1970s present to this picture. For the main distinctively Scottish party, the Scottish National Party, which originated in 1928, could only achieve 5 per cent of the votes by the general election of 1966, yet was to rise to 30 per cent in the election of October 1974, falling to 17 per cent in 1979. Thus the party system in Scotland moved from a two-party to a three-party system in less than a decade.

## SCOTLAND IN PARLIAMENT

Despite their party differences, the Scottish MPs[2] have always been identifiable as a group. After the Union of 1707 they often acted together to secure some concession to Scotland, notably at the time of the Porteous Riots in Edinburgh (1736), when the English majority in the House of Commons seemed to be particularly vindictive towards the Scots. More generally, the Scots MPs bartered their votes in Parliament for government patronage, which generally benefited their political supporters back home.

In the nineteenth century, less venal co-operation among Scottish MPs was usual. Informal meetings would take place in the House of Commons, at which Scottish MPs discussed issues relating to Scotland and thrashed out their policy differences. This seems to have coincided with a willingness on the part of the English MPs and British ministers to let the Scots have their way on matters which concerned only Scotland. As an ex-Lord Advocate, J. B. Balfour, stated in the House of Commons on 3 August 1886: 'It has been the custom for the Scotch Members, in conference with the Government, to come to an understanding on Scotch questions; and effect has invariably been given, not only by the Government, but by the House, to any understanding thus arrived at by the Scotch Members' (*Hansard*, 3rd Series, Vol. 308, col. 972). Thus many clauses of the Crofters Bill (1886) had been changed as a result of a meeting held between the Scottish MPs and the government. This corresponds with the traditional aloofness of English MPs when Scottish business is discussed. Compare Sir George Trevelyan on 2 April 1894: 'Nothing is more striking – it is one of the best-known phenomena of Parliamentary life – the indifference which English Members show to the details of Scotch Debates' (*Hansard*, 4th Series, Vol. 22, col. 1121).

The Scottish MPs were not all united in their political allegiance or their political opinions. They split into Liberals and Conservatives (and Liberal-Unionists after 1886) as in England, but there could be no guarantee that the party which controlled the majority in the whole House would also be in command in Scotland. This was to be the stumbling-block to the procedure outlined by J. B. Balfour, for how could a government accept policies for Scotland which had been determined by the opposition? Yet not to do so would deny the Scottish autonomy which Balfour claimed existed.

From 1886 to 1892 the Conservatives controlled the House of Commons, while 60 per cent of the Scottish MPs were Liberal. Thus, on most Scottish divisions, the English MPs overruled the Scots. This was particularly resented in Scotland during the passage of the Local Government (Scotland) Bill, 1889, when twelve amendments backed by a majority of Scottish MPs were voted down, and Scottish Home Rule sentiment was strengthened as a result. Many in the Liberal Party not unnaturally started to support some form of Scottish devolution, since Scotland was so Liberal, but the party leaders were reluctant to see the Liberal votes in the House of Commons diminished by the banishment of the Scottish MPs to Scotland. Once in power again (1892–5), they devised an alternative scheme to satisfy the Scots: one which would provide a sort of autonomy for the Scottish MPs but keep them at Westminster. The Scottish Grand Committee was introduced on 27 April 1894 as a substitute for a Scottish parliament, and as a practical way round the congestion of Bills in Parliament at the time. The Committee consisted of all the Scottish MPs, with fifteen other MPs added to ensure that the balance of parties in the House as a whole was accurately reflected in the Committee (this of course meant that the outsiders would be mostly Tories). Violently attacked as revolutionary by Conservatives such as A. J. Balfour, this device nevertheless maintained parliamentary sovereignty intact, since only the committee stage of non-controversial Bills was to be entrusted to the Committee. Controversial Bills, and the other stages of non-controversial Bills – including that of the second reading, in which the principles of the Bill are debated – were to be decided in the House as a whole. Thus the Scots could always be overruled by the English if necessary.

This Scottish Grand Committee was in existence for only two years (1894–5), during which time it did useful work on the Parish Councils Bill and other minor Bills. Then it disappeared under the Conservatives, to reappear in 1907 as a standing committee during the Liberal administration of Campbell-Bannerman. It was to be the only specialised legislative committee in the House of Commons, and remained so until the Welsh Grand Committee was established in 1960. All the other legislative committees are non-specialised and may deal with any type of Bill. In 1922 the Scottish Committee had to be temporarily abandoned since its constitution proved incompatible with the party situation then prevailing in the House. The 1922 election had brought the Conservatives to power, but the Labour majority in Scotland was so large that not even fifteen additional Tories from England could redress the balance on the Scottish Committee. Thus all Scottish Bills had to be kept on the floor of the House (Jennings, 1957, p. 272). Apart from this episode, the Scottish Committee continued to take non-controversial Bills relating exclusively to Scotland at the committee stage until 1948, when its scope was considerably widened.

The White Paper on *Scottish Affairs* (Cmd 7308, 1948) noted that many MPs had desired an improvement in the handling of Scottish business in the House and had asked for an extension of the Scottish Committee's work to include second reading debates and consideration of the Scottish Estimates. This was accepted by the government, and the Committee assumed these functions in 1948. It was *not* intended that all Bills relating exclusively to Scotland[3] should go to the Grand Committee:

The types of Bill to which, in the Government's view, it would be suitable and convenient to apply the new procedure would be Bills of a technical nature applying only to Scotland, which though debatable, are not controversial in a Party sense; certain Bills which make for Scotland provision similar to that already made or proposed for England and Wales; and certain Bills of purely Scottish interest for which time cannot immediately be found under existing arrangements (Cmd. 7308, p. 4)

And so it proved in practice: between 1948 and 1959, less than a third of Scottish Bills were referred to the Committee for second reading, and a little over two-thirds for the committee stage. The others were dealt with by the House as a whole or by another committee (Burns, 1960). As any ten MPs can require a second reading debate on a Scottish Bill to be held in the whole House, and any six MPs can obtain a debate in the House after the Grand Committee debate, the independence of the Scottish MPs is non-existent in theory. In practice, however, few English (or Scots) MPs have so acted, and since it is on the responsibility of a minister that Bills are referred to the Committee, discipline is assured. What constitutes a 'controversial' Scottish Bill is left vague: such Bills as the Deer Bill, 1958, and the Licensing Bill, 1961,[4] have gone to the House at second reading stage, and minor Bills often go through the Committee of the Whole House without debate.

In 1957, the duties of the Scottish Grand Committee relating to the committee stage of bills were transferred to a new Committee, the Scottish Standing Committee, now consisting of sixteen Scottish MPs with up to thirty-four additional MPs. The Scottish Grand Committee continues, as before, to consist of all the Scottish MPs, with not less than ten and not more than fifteen MPs added to bring the balance of parties on the Committee nearer that of the whole House. The duties of the Grand Committee are now (a) second reading debates, (b) Scottish Estimates (up to six days per session), and (c) debates on Scottish affairs (up to two days per session).

Since the introduction of the Scottish Standing Committee, increasing use has been made of the Scottish Committees, and a second Standing Committee was created, starting in the session 1962–3. The proportion of Scottish Bills referred to the Grand Committee for second reading in recent years (1958–70) has been much higher, and over five-sixths of Scottish Bills have been committed to the Grand and Standing Committees (Edwards, 1972). The division of labour between the Scottish Committees has allowed Scottish members to participate more easily in other committees, which often sit simultaneously. They are thus now able to play a larger part in British legislation. As for the English MPs in the Scottish Committees, it is an established convention that unless they have special knowledge of Scotland they play no part in the debates. Indeed, assignment to a Scottish Committee is considered equivalent to penal servitude by most English MPs, and they are retained there only for party reasons (Hughes, 1966). Proposals to remove the Committees to Edinburgh, where they could 'get at' St Andrew's House, have until recently been unacceptable to governments and the majority of Scottish MPs alike. The party balance would be difficult to maintain outside Westminster and, in any case, Scottish MPs are usually anxious to be statesmen of Britain as well as of Scotland.

On the whole, the Scottish Committees have improved the position of Scotland in Parliament, but it would be a mistake to infer (as many do) that some sort of Home Rule has been granted there. The British government, and the House as a whole, retains control of all Bills, and a small minority of MPs could wreck the Scottish Committee machinery. That they do not do so is evidence of party loyalty and apathy, not a belief in devolution. The same applies to the procedure for Scottish private legislation, which since 1899 has been different from that for English or Welsh private Bills. It gives the Scottish Secretary special powers to make Provisional Orders where in England Bills would have to be passed, and inquiries where necessary are held in Scotland and not in London. But ample safeguards remain to ensure that opposition can be made effective to such proceedings, from England as well as Scotland. Once more, the position of Scotland in Parliament is a favoured, but not independent, one.

POLITICAL PARTIES

The party political history of Scotland since 1870 is complex, and only a brief outline can be attempted here. Scotland has its own problems which require political solution, but it is equally concerned with British and foreign issues – scarcely surprising, in view of the exceptionally strong links between Scotland and the outside world, as a result of emigration and Scottish overseas trade and investments. Most Scots feel a personal interest in the British connections overseas and in the armed forces, and the 'Imperial Mission' was as strong in Scotland as in England. It was reinforced by a parallel missionary zeal, that of the Presbyterian Churches, whose activities throughout the world were out of all proportion to their size. Thus British policies abroad have always been important to Scotland, and are eagerly discussed in the press, Church courts and political meetings.

Moreover, there are few internal British political issues which do not affect Scotland. With the principal exceptions of church, educational and legal matters, Scotland is included in the major British social and political legislation, either directly or in corresponding 'Scottish' Acts. Scots are as involved in the results of British policy-making as the English or Welsh and cannot afford to resort to 'parish-pump' politics. However, they have distinctly Scottish problems to settle as well. Some of these – like the high levels of unemployment and emigration, and the poor housing – require special treatment within the context of British general legislation. Others are so peculiarly Scottish – for example, the difficult ecclesiastical relations before 1929, and the perpetual problems of the Highlands – that a completely separate policy must be devised, with perhaps special administrative and legal machinery to carry it out.

The political parties in Scotland reflect this duality of interest. On the one hand, they are British parties (with the chief exception of the Scottish National Party) and represent the Scottish electorate with regard to policies for the whole country. But they are also Scottish parties, since they are given varying degrees of autonomy within the British parties to form their own Scottish organisations, hold Scottish conferences and formulate the Scottish policy for their parties. They press this Scottish policy on their parties as a whole through the British party organisations and through their MPs in Parliament. It is the duty of the Scottish Whip in each party[5] to convey the feelings of the Scottish MPs to the Chief Whip and to party leaders, as well as to keep discipline on the party's behalf. The Scottish MPs in each party also meet as a group to discuss their strategy, especially regarding work in the Scottish Committees, where they in effect take the place of the parliamentary party as a whole.

Table 9.1  Seats won by the parties, 1868–1979

| Election | Scotland | | | | | | England | | | | | | United Kingdom | | | | | |
|---|---|---|---|---|---|---|---|---|---|---|---|---|---|---|---|---|---|---|
| | C | LU/NL | L | Lab | Com | Others | C | LU/NL | L | Lab | Com | Others | C | LU/NL | L | Lab | Com | Others |
| 1868 | 8 | | 52 | | | | 223 | | 240 | | | | 279 | | 379 | | | |
| 1874 | 20 | | 40 | | | | 288 | | 171 | | | | 352 | | 242 | | | 58 |
| 1880 | 7 | | 53 | | | | 203 | | 256 | | | | 238 | | 349 | | | 65 |
| 1885 | 10 | | 57 | | | 5* | 218 | | 242 | | | 5 | 249 | | 325 | | | 96 |
| 1886 | 12 | 16 | 39 | | | 5* | 283 | 56 | 125 | | | 1 | 316 | 77 | 187 | | | 90 |
| 1892 | 10 | 12 | 45 | | | 5* | 236 | 32 | 196 | | | 1 | 267 | 48 | 269 | | | 86 |
| 1895 | 19 | 14 | 39 | | | | 298 | 51 | 115 | | | 1 | 341 | 70 | 177 | | | 82 |
| 1900 | 21 | 17 | 34 | | | | 292 | 47 | 124 | 1 | | 1 | 334 | 68 | 184 | 2 | | 82 |
| 1906 | 8 | 4 | 58 | 2 | | | 109 | 18 | 289 | 48† | | 1 | 134 | 23 | 376 | 54† | | 83 |
| 1910 (Jan.) | 8 | 3 | 59 | 2 | | | 213 | 26 | 191 | 34 | | 1 | 242 | 31 | 275 | 40 | | 82 |
| 1910 (Dec.) | 7 | 4 | 58 | 3 | | | 210 | 29 | 190 | 35 | | 1 | 237 | 35 | 272 | 42 | | 84 |
| 1918 | 32 | | 34 | 7 | | 1 | 322 | | 107 | 45 | | 18 | 384 | | 160 | 62 | | 101 |
| 1922 | 15 | 12 | 16 | 29 | 1 | 1 | 312 | 38 | 39 | 95 | | 8 | 344 | 59 | 57 | 142 | 1 | 12 |
| 1923 | 16 | | 23 | 34 | | 1 | 227 | | 123 | 138 | | 4 | 257 | | 158 | 191 | | 9 |
| 1924 | 38 | | 9 | 26 | | 1 | 355 | | 22 | 109 | 1 | 5 | 415 | | 42 | 151 | 1 | 6 |
| 1929 | 22 | | 14 | 36 | | 2 | 226 | | 35 | 226 | | 5 | 260 | | 59 | 288 | | 8 |
| 1931 | 50 | 8 | 8 | 7 | | 1 | 406 | 23 | 20 | 29 | | 14 | 473 | 35 | 37 | 52 | | 18 |

| Year | C | NL | L | Lab | Com | Oth | C | NL | L | Lab | Com | Oth | C | NL | L | Lab | Com | Oth |
|------|----|----|----|-----|-----|-----|-----|----|----|-----|-----|-----|-----|----|----|-----|-----|-----|
| 1935 | 37 | 8 | 3 | 24 | 1 | 1 | 335 | 23 | 10 | 116 |  | 8 | 390 | 4 | 20 | 158 | 1 | 12 |
| 1945 | 25 | 5 | 2 | 40 | 1 | 3 | 162 | 7 | 5 | 330 | 1 | 12 | 200 | 13 | 12 | 396 | 2 | 17 |
| 1950 | 26 | 5 | 1 | 37 |  | 1 | 245 | 7 | 2 | 251 |  | 1 | 285 | 13 | 9 | 315 |  | 3 |
| 1951 | 29 | 6 | 1 | 35 |  |  | 263 | 8 | 2 | 233 |  |  | 307 | 14 | 6 | 295 |  | 3 |
| 1955 | 30 | 6 | 1 | 34 |  |  | 287 | 5 | 2 | 216 |  | 1 | 332 | 12 | 6 | 277 |  | 3 |
| 1959 | 25 | 6 |  | 38 |  | 1 | 310 | 5 | 3 | 193 |  |  | 354 | 11 | 9 | 258 |  | 1 |
| 1964 | 24 |  | 4 | 43 |  |  | 259 | 2 | 3 | 246 |  | 1 | 301 | 2 | 12 | 317 |  | 1 |
| 1966 | 20 |  | 5 | 46 |  |  | 218 | 1 | 6 | 285 |  | 1 | 252 | 1 | 6 | 363 |  | 2 |
| 1970 | 23 |  | 5 | 44 |  | 1** | 292 |  | 2 | 217 |  |  | 330 |  | 6 | 288 |  | 6 |
| 1974 (Feb.) | 21 |  | 3 | 40 |  | 7** | 268 |  | 9 | 237 |  | 2 | 297 |  | 14 | 301 |  | 23 |
| 1974 (Oct.) | 16 |  | 3 | 41 |  | 11** | 252 |  | 8 | 255 |  | 1 | 276 |  | 13 | 319 |  | 27 |
| 1979 | 22 |  | 3 | 44 |  | 2** | 306 |  | 7 | 203 |  |  | 339 |  | 11 | 268 |  | 17 |

*Crofters (allied to Liberals after 1892).
**Scottish National Party (SNP).
†Includes 'Lib.-Labs'.

- C Conservative
- LU Liberal-Unionist (to 1912; allied to Conservatives)
- NL National Liberal or Liberal National (from 1922; allied to Conservatives)
- L Liberal
- Lab Labour
- Com Communist

THE LIBERAL PARTY

A historical survey of the parties in Scotland since 1870 must begin with the Liberal Party, since every general election from 1832 until 1918 (with the sole exception of 1900) gave that party a majority of the Scottish seats (see Table 9.1). After 1918, the Liberals remained relatively strong in Scotland, and fourteen years before the Liberal revival in 1974 Scottish Liberal MPs amounted to almost half the party's total in the House of Commons. Clearly, the great Liberal strength before the First World War had a different basis from the present-day Scottish Liberalism, which is strongest in the Highlands and Southern Uplands. Alternatively, it could be that only these areas today preserve the features of Scottish society which in the nineteenth century and after were conducive of pronounced Liberalism.

What these features were, and the collective identity of the Liberal supporters before 1918, must remain largely a matter of speculation. The size and distribution of the votes by constituencies is known, as are many social statistics about these constituencies, but the motivations and characteristics of the voters for the various parties can be deduced only imperfectly. There were no survey questionnaires until recent times, and the political sociologist of the past was usually the journalist or the party agent. The Scottish election results show that, in a Liberal country, the burghs were the most Liberal, and some had unbroken Liberal records from the Reform Act of 1832 to the First World War.[6] Here, presumably, the proud independence of the local councils and townsfolk, with their tradition of self-government and freedom from aristocratic or landed control, drew the voters to the Liberal Party, which at that time represented the urban middle class. This independence is shown in the absence of bribery in Scottish burgh elections. A parliamentary report in 1870 says:

In England and Ireland the Borough Elections are often extremely corrupt. In Scotland, it is stated, without contradiction, that bribery is almost unknown. This is attributed in a great measure to the superior education of the Scotch people; and partly to the fact that the constituencies being comparatively new, there exists no corrupt class, long familiar with the traditions of bribery, similar to that which in many English and Irish boroughs has not only retained in itself, but spread through the constituency the desire for corrupt expenditure. (Camperdown, 1870, p. 135)

Municipal self-government was paralleled by self-government in the Presbyterian churches, and the burgh Presbyterians were particularly insistent that congregations should be freed from the outside interference of patronage. They asserted the right to appoint their ministers, and left the Established Church in large numbers in order to practise it. After 1843, there was a majority of Presbyterian 'dissenters' in most burghs, and even the remaining Church of Scotland members were restless under patronage. We have already seen (Chapter 4, p. 43) that they secured its abolition in 1874, evidence that some form of 'democracy' was deemed essential by the Kirk.

A similar passion for democracy (or representative government) was the hallmark of Gladstonian Liberalism, and Gladstone in his Midlothian campaigns consolidated his party's hold on Scotland. His sermonising and moral fervour was manna to the Scots, and they idolised him. Unfortunately, he threatened their bread and butter in 1886 by proposing Irish Home Rule, and many deserted him to form the Liberal-Unionist Party (see below, p. 136). Some compensation for the Liberals was gained by the support of the Roman Catholics, who were naturally Home Rulers, but this had the adverse effect of driving more Presbyterians out of the party. The combination of materialist and religious pressure was acute for the Liberal Party in the Central Lowlands, and they lost many burgh seats there. Although much was recovered in 1906, a new 'Unionism' (or Conservatism) had become firmly established in the towns as a companion to the more traditional Conservatism of the counties. This county Conservatism was very marked in the period 1835–59, when the Liberals generally held a minority of the county seats. After then, with the exception of the elections of 1874 and 1900, the Liberals controlled most counties, and indeed attained unparalleled supremacy there from 1906 to 1918. Only the extreme south-west corner was safe for the Tories, the remnant of an earlier political stronghold.[7]

The influence of the lairds was always a factor in the rural districts, especially before the extension of the franchise in 1884. The electors in each constituency were often only a few hundred and might easily be subject to intimidation by the landowners. Yet there is evidence that a sturdy independence characterised many of these people too. The 1870 Report already quoted drew these distinctions between county elections in different parts of Britain:

> In each of the three countries [England, Scotland and Ireland] it is alleged that intimidation by landlords prevails in County Elections. In England tenants generally vote in accordance with the wishes or known opinions of their landlords. In Scotland they have in some recent instances voted almost in a body against their landlords. This has been attributed partly to the nature of the relations between landlord and tenant in Scotland, which are usually of a more strictly commercial character than in England, partly to

the fact that the Scotch tenant farmers take a very warm interest in certain public questions in which they consider that their own and their landlord's interests are not identical.

Nevertheless, there is evidence that in certain counties – for example, Wigtownshire – tenants were accustomed to vote with their landlords, and in that county politics became a struggle between the Earl of Stair (Liberal until 1886) and the Earl of Galloway (Conservative) (Maxwell, 1932, p. 150). In other counties – namely, Argyll, Sutherland and Bute – one landowner was able, up to the extension of the franchise in 1884, to control sufficient votes so as to ensure that his influence would prevail: these were the co-called 'pocket counties' (Hanham, 1959, p. 24). Evictions of tenants for their political activities took place, and were perhaps more common in Scotland than in England. One prominent farmer, George Hope of East Lothian, who stood as a Liberal candidate in 1865, was put out at the end of his lease, and there were alleged political evictions as late as the 1880s (see Gladstone Papers in the British Library).

It is notable that once the crofters gained the vote in 1884, and security of tenure in 1886, they returned independent Crofter radical candidates to Parliament, in opposition to the lairds. They were also opposed to the official Liberals, but after 1892 the Crofters were allied to the Liberal Party, and today there are still many staunch Liberals (and many new ones too) in the Highlands. Other strong Liberal areas were the North-East Lowlands and the Borders, and they too have a tradition of Liberal representation. Both had lairds who were politically important, but the Earl of Aberdeen was a friend of Gladstone, and the Border lairds were engaged in constant political feuding. Thus the many small farmers could continue to think for themselves (which usually meant voting Liberal).

Most of the industrial county seats in the Central Lowlands were Liberal, but they became very marginal after 1886. Tory employers captured some, and in others Labour candidates (such as Keir Hardie in Mid-Lanark, 1888) began to make inroads. As a factory boss or mine-owner, the Liberal was more exposed to class hostility than the burgh shopkeeper, and there was also Orangeism to alienate the Protestant working class from the 'Home Rule = Rome Rule' party. Much of this anti-Catholic sentiment sprang from material considerations. The Irish Catholic undercut the Scot's wages and rendered his trade unionism futile.

In general, the pre-1914 Liberal tended to equate his picture of Scottish values with the ideals espoused by the Liberal Party ('I am a Liberal because I am a Scotchman' (Reid, 1885, p. 64). These values included the belief in democratic institutions (however qualified in practice), in the career open to talents, and in the duty of every man to make his own way in the world unaided and unhampered by privilege. In large measure, this was also the Liberal creed, and as long as such myths were powerful in Scotland the Liberal Party was secure there.

Scottish Liberal Party organisations date from the 1870s, when some local associations (especially in the burghs) and two regional associations (East and North of Scotland; West and South of Scotland) were founded. In 1881, the regional associations merged to become the Scottish Liberal Association, which held conferences open to all local associations (in 1918 the name was changed to the Scottish Liberal Federation). A rival National Liberal Federation of Scotland was set up in 1885 to promote disestablishment, but in 1886 it joined the official body (Kellas, 1965a). The Scottish Liberal Association supported British Liberal policy faithfully, and took a more radical stand on such issues as the Miners' Eight-Hours Day than the party down south. But it had little belief in the 'New Liberalism' of Asquith Haldane and Lloyd George, which brought collectivism (in the shape of the welfare state) within the party's programme. The Scottish Liberals were individualists and believers in 'freedom': freedom of trade, of religion (at least within Protestantism), and of political, if not cultural, expression. Thus the peculiarly Scottish issues which they promoted were Church disestablishment, crofters' and small tenants' rights, and Home Rule for Scotland. National insurance, pensions, and a minimum wage were much too socialist, and they viewed with alarm these parts of the new Liberal policy.

They were also reluctant to come to an electoral understanding with the Labour Party, such as had been reached by the party in England and Wales at the election of 1906. There, many Labour candidates had been elected because the Liberal Party agreed that no opposition would be provided, in return for Labour support in certain other constituencies. In Scotland no such pact had been forthcoming (except in one case, Dundee), and Liberal and Labour candidates stood as political enemies. The absence in Scotland of 'Lib-Lab' MPs or Liberal-supported Labour MPs was the result of the strength of the Liberal Party in Scotland compared to Labour, and of the doctrinaire socialism of the Scottish Labour Party leaders. Neither side would compromise over its principles, although to the ordinary voter of the time there was little to choose between them. Indeed, the Liberals were as radical as the Labour Party on most libertarian issues, while the socialist ideas of the Labour leaders were not electorally popular.

All this was changed by the First World War and its aftermath. The old nineteenth-century myths could no longer support the Liberal Party, for many had been shown to be insufficient. Those that remained, albeit weaker than before (such as individualism and self-help), seemed now more the hallmark of the Unionist Party, as the main opponent to socialism. Yet even now the former strength of the Liberal Party in Scotland gave it a special momentum, and until 1924 it put forward the highest number of candidates. As late as 1929–31 there were fourteen Liberal MPs in Scotland, out of a total of fifty-nine Liberal MPs for the whole country. Thereafter, the 'Independent' Liberal total (that is, those who did not support the Coalition government) dropped to eight in 1931 and to three in 1935, disappeared altogether in 1945, but stabilised at one from 1951 to 1964 (see Table 9.1, pp. 128–9).

All this time there were a larger number of 'National Liberal' MPs allied to the Unionists, and Liberalism in Scotland, as elsewhere, was torn apart in contending factions. The problem of the party was which of these factions it should regard as 'official'. Right up to the late 1950s all sorts of political animals were calling themselves 'True Liberals', from near-socialists to true-blue Tories, and the internal affairs of the party consisted largely of squabbles over 'credentials'. The Scottish Liberal Association (which became the Scottish Liberal Federation in 1918) backed the Asquith wing rather than the Lloyd George Coalitionists in 1918, but it supported the National Liberals of the 1931 Coalition and not the 'Independent Liberals'. Then it apparently followed Sir Herbert Samuel into opposition to the Coalition, but found itself hopelessly split at the election of 1935. While the chairman of the General Council of the Scottish Liberal Federation and many office-bearers wanted to support the National government and fix an electoral agreement with the Tories on National candidates, the majority of activists did not.

A vote of censure at a special meeting on 17 October 1935 forced the resignation of the National Liberals and led to a reorganised Scottish Liberal Federation in 1937. Its principle was total independence of the Liberal Party elsewhere, and the Scottish Liberal Party now reserves the right to run its own affairs and formulate its own policy. It has its own chairman, and its conferences often pass resolutions, such as those demanding a Scottish parliament, which differ from those passed by the English and Welsh Liberals. Attempts to absorb the Scottish Liberal Party in a British organisation have always been rejected, but observers from Scotland attend the English Liberal conferences, and the Scottish Liberal MPs are an integral part of the Parliamentary Liberal Party, sharing the Liberal Whip.

It was in 1937 that Jo Grimond was first adopted as a Scottish Liberal candidate. He entered Parliament in 1950 as member for Orkney and Shetland. On succeeding to the Liberal leadership at Clement Davies's retirement in 1956, his influence prevailed, both in Scotland and in Britain as a whole, to give the party its present 'radical' image. His emergence on the British political scene had been preceded by many struggles within the Scottish Liberal Party. The old-guard of the interwar period in Scotland had been aristocratic and socially conservative; the new Liberals were young and forward-looking. Eventually, in the election of 1964, they broke through to win four seats from the Tories and to press their reforms on the House of Commons. Although the MPs returned were from Highland or rural seats, considerable support was given the party in the non-industrial towns. Wherever the class hostility and urban economic distress was least, the Liberals found votes. They spoke for regional interests, including the Scottish national interest in a separate parliament, and assumed that these interests could override the other divisions in society.

But in this last respect they were soon to be eclipsed by the Scottish National Party. The Nationalists effectively captured the 'third-party vote' from the Liberals after 1966, and while the Liberals in England shot ahead in 1974 to win over a fifth of the vote, in Scotland they stuck at 8 per cent. A new leader from Scotland, David Steel, took over from Jeremy Thorpe in 1976, but the Scottish fortunes of the party remained a shadow of the successes of the 1960s. In 1979 they retained their three seats and their share of the total Scottish vote. Liberals are still strong in some rural areas and middle class suburbs (especially in Edinburgh), but the rise of the SNP put an end to the Victorian Liberal claim that to be Scottish was to be Liberal. No one now doubted that the most 'Scottish' party was the SNP.

## THE CONSERVATIVE OR UNIONIST PARTY AND ALLIES

In 1870 the Conservative Party in Scotland was in very poor shape. It had only eight seats in Parliament out of a total of sixty Scottish seats, and these were entirely in rural constituencies. Although the Tories had never come near to a majority in Scotland since the débâcle of 1832, they had always been strongly represented in the counties, where the lairds' influence could often be brought to bear on the voters. Not that Scottish Conservatism was entirely rural, for most lawyers, especially in Edinburgh, were Conservative. So was Dr Thomas Chalmers, the Evangelical city minister and founder of the Free Church. His Tory ideas were based largely on Church and state relations, for many clerics distrusted the Whig or Liberal materialism which threatened to withdraw or reduce the financial support which the state gave to its religious Establishments. Thus many Church of Scotland ministers voted Conservative, and frequently preached Conservatism as well. That their congregations rarely followed them in politics is shown by the voting figures, and the Scottish Conservative Party of the 1870s had a very narrow base indeed. It was run by landowners, lawyers and churchmen, all of whom believed that they had a divine right to rule. The Scots would not accept this, for did their religion not prescribe equality and self-government, and their economic situation self-help? The English Conservative leaders were well aware of the plight of their party in Scotland, and tried valiantly to introduce a more bourgeois image. They set up a committee in 1876 to investigate the Scottish situation, and it recommended that professional agents should do what the lairds patently could not do: convince the people that there was more to Toryism than deference (Crapster, 1957; Urwin, 1965, 1966).

But the unpopularity of the landlords in Scotland was so great that no amount of organisation (and here the Tories as usual were more efficient than their opponents)[8] could greatly improve their prospects. In 1885 they still had only ten seats, and if Gladstone had not dropped the bombshell of the Irish Home Rule Bill in 1886, they might have continued to languish. Perhaps Home Rule brought to a head a simmering discontent with the 'radicalism' of the Liberal Party in the 1880s, for many businessmen already were shaken by Gladstone's anti-imperialism, and several Whigs – for instance, the Dukes of Argyll and Fife – had deserted the party over the land reform programme in Ireland and at home. Certainly, Irish Home Rule was the turning-point for the Conservatives in Scotland, for they gained the alliance of a new political group, the 'dissentient' Liberals, or Liberal-Unionists. These were the Liberals who opposed Gladstone's Irish policy, and, with sixteen Scottish seats in 1886, they completely transformed Scottish politics. Because of the close links between Scotland and Ireland through trade, immigration and Presbyterianism in Ulster, the Scots were especially sensitive about Home Rule, and the Liberal-Unionists made greater inroads into the Liberal Party in Scotland than elsewhere.

What the Liberals lost, the Tories gained, for although few Liberal-Unionists were prepared to call themselves Conservative for many years, an electoral pact was quickly established which ensured that there would be no opposition between anti-Home Rule candidates. The Conservatives began to adopt the label 'Unionist', and this eventually (1912) became the official name of the party in Scotland when the Conservative and Liberal-Unionist organisations merged, and was not finally abandoned until 1965 (it is now the Conservative and Unionist Party). Thus the old, bad odour of Scottish Conservatism was expurgated, and the fresh air of Unionism introduced.

The Liberal-Unionists were to begin with not at all like the old Conservatives. They were strong in the burghs and industrial county seats, and were radical on certain matters – for instance, land, education and local government reform. Some were disestablishers, and some were even Scottish Home Rulers (well, they wanted Home

Rule *all round*). But alliance to the Conservatives was traumatic for these radicals, and by 1895, if they had not returned to the Liberal Party, they were almost indistinguishable from other Conservatives. Perhaps the Scottish Unionist Party was more to the left than the Conservative Party in England, but this would be difficult to prove. Robert Boothby and Walter Elliot may be cited as examples here, and the post-1918 infusion of former Liberal individualists and anti-socialists made a difference. However, the interwar period brought back some of the pre-1886 pattern of politics to Scotland, with urban and industrial areas anti-Conservative (now Labour, not Liberal), and the rural or residential areas Conservative. The lairds never again had a monopoly of the party, but they tended to be more influential than the urban Unionists, partly because they were more sure of their political supporters in their safe seats.

In the 'consensus' period from 1931 to 1945, Scottish Conservatives and their allies, the National Liberals, were secure. The urban Scot, though unemployed, seemed afraid of socialism, and the farm worker felt that the Labour Party represented the towns, trade unionism and an alien spoon-fed culture. These men were often 'radicals', who had promoted land reform and anti-landlordism in the past, but there now seemed no alternative but to vote for the lairds. It was felt that the economic depression in the towns and on the farms was not so much the fault of the bosses or the lairds as the impersonal judgement of God or of economics. The escape lay in emigration, not the vote, and in any case, what remedy did the 'left' offer? By 1945, the remedy, and the apparent need for it, was made clearer, and many Labour MPs were returned. However, Scotland did not swing away from the Tories as violently as the electorate in the south, and it has generally been less inclined to sudden changes of opinion. This may be the result of the relatively static nature of Scottish society, in which outside influences and arguments have less power. Quite often, the personality of the candidates is important, especially in the Highlands, where party politics are based mainly on local issues and the best means to achieve the agreed end: more government aid to stop emigration.

Outside the rural areas the Unionists were not at all secure, and by the late 1950s even these could not be depended upon. From 1955 to 1974 the party's strength in the House of Commons fell from thirty-six to sixteen, and bitter self-appraisals, reminiscent of the 1870s, were heard at party conferences. Young Tories of the cities blamed the domination of the party by lairds for the losses, and one Highland Unionist MP, Sir David Robertson (Caithness and Sutherland), made his protest against his party leaders' indifference to Highland problems by resigning the Whip and becoming an Independent MP (1959–64). His seat was captured by the Liberals in 1964 and by Labour in

1966. As in the 1870s, the electoral weakness of the party led to a shake-up in its organisation, and a tighter control from Edinburgh and London has replaced the virtual independence of the constituencies. Even the name of the party was changed to 'Conservative and Unionist' in 1965, a sign that the dividend from the name 'Unionist' was at last of no electoral significance. No one in Scotland believed that they were anything but Conservatives, especially with Jo Grimond and David Steel so close at hand to denounce their 'false Liberalism'.

Scottish Conservatism is more complex today than it was before 1886. In that period, it was largely associated with the anglicised, Anglican (Episcopalian) and absentee gentry, and was a small, rural party. After 1886 it recruited the powerful Unionist wing of the Liberal Party, whose votes and ideas gave it the strength to be a major party in Scotland, and filled it with enough of the old Liberalism to carry it through to the 1920s, when most 'libertarian' Liberals became Unionists.

There has never been much that is distinctive about Scottish Conservative policy. The partial autonomy of the party organisation has produced no challenge to the programme or party leadership in Britain as a whole: certainly nothing comparable to the activities of the Ulster Unionists. The Irish Unionists are separatists in respect of Ulster's political affairs. The Scottish Unionists are British Conservatives, consider the British Conservative Party leaders as their leaders, and accept British Conservative Party policy, even on Scotland, as their own. Here is a source of their weakness, for a policy for Scotland must be initiated in Scotland, and the party which appears to have none loses votes. Edward Heath seemed to impose a policy of Scottish devolution on the party in 1968, while Margaret Thatcher gave no support to an elected Assembly after 1976. Meanwhile, Scottish Conservative conferences vacillated from year to year, trying to stay in harmony with the views of the party leader.

The Conservatives today most strongly represent the view that 'Scotland is British'. They ally with business in Scotland (the CBI, the Chambers of Commerce and the National Farmers' Union), but also with the radical middle class. They have been unable to match the appeal of the party in England, and the condition of Scottish Conservatism illustrates how nationalism, and some special features of Scottish society, such as the preponderance of council housing, and religion, have worked to their disadvantage. For the SNP took more seats from Conservative than from Labour; council tenants have strongly voted Labour, as have Roman Catholics. In these ways, Scotland presents a special problem for the Conservative Party.

## THE LABOUR PARTY

The first political party in Britain to attempt the independent representation of working-class men in Parliament, with a distinct
programme of its own, was the Scottish Parliamentary Labour Party,
founded by Keir Hardie and Cunninghame Graham in 1888. It was
this party which provided the example, and many of the leaders, for
the Independent Labour Party (founded in 1893), which extended
these aims to the rest of Britain (Kellas, 1965b; McLean, 1975). The
Labour movement in Scotland at this time was nevertheless not a
strong one in political or industrial terms. Since the collapse of
Chartism, its political side had virtually disappeared within the all-
embracing Liberal Party, and the industrial wing of the movement
was less effective than in England. Trade unionism in Scotland had
to contend with Irish blacklegs, a shifting labour force and the
fragmented pattern of industrial organisation (particularly in the
mines). Also to be contended with were the dominant doctrines of
self-help and brotherly love which made up the Scottish democratic
Myth. Class representation could not precede industrial change and
the disintegration of the belief, peculiarly strong in Scotland, that class
interests were harmonious.

The first area where this 'harmony of interests' fell down was the
Highlands. Evictions and rack-renting during the 'Clearances' earlier
in the century produced much anti-landlord feeling among the crofters
and small farmers, and their 'gloomy memories' (the title of a book
on the Clearances by Donald Macleod) were revived in the agricultural
depression of the 1870s and 1880s (Hunter, 1976). Through land
reform organisations, such as the Highland Land League,[9] the
Highlands became politically active, and in the elections of 1885 and
1886 five independent Crofter MPs were returned, among them the
socialist Dr G. B. Clark (Caithness, 1885–1900). Clark, who became
the leader of the parliamentary group, is one of the most curious
figures in Scottish political history. A Marxist and a member of the
Communist International in London in the 1870s, he was also Agent-
General for the Transvaal, editor of the Temperance journal, the
*Good Templar*, and a medical doctor. His Scottish connections
included a Glasgow upbringing, but his link with the Highlands is
more obscure. Although a founder-member of the Scottish Parliamentary Labour Party in 1888, he was later expelled for continuing
to stand as a Crofter, and after 1895 was considered to be the official
Liberal candidate.

Nearly all the other Crofter MPs were Highland-born, but many
had moved to England for work, and a great deal of the support
for land reform was provided from outside the Highlands by exiles,
Irish Land Leaguers, and even by the American land reformer Henry

George, who toured the Highlands propagating his 'inflammatory' doctrines. While the Crofters Party was a rural Labour Party, it had strong connections with a similar land reform organisation in Glasgow, the Scottish Land Restoration League, which also contested seats in 1885 but without success. Land reform was the link between the Labour movement in the Highlands and the trade union movement in the Lowlands, where Keir Hardie, William Small, Chisholm Robertson and Robert Smillie led the miners.

The successes of the crofters, which included the Crofters Act of 1886 and subsequent Highland inquiries and legislation, were not paralleled in industrial politics. No industrial Labour candidate was returned to Parliament, and no labour legislation was forced on the major parties by a ginger group similar to the Crofters Party. Keir Hardie unsuccessfully contested the Mid-Lanark by-election in 1888 as a Labour candidate, and would have accepted the Liberal nomination had it been offered. Similarly, the Scottish Parliamentary Labour Party, founded at the same time, tried to negotiate a pact with the Liberals, but the local Liberal activists would not agree to support Labour candidates. This rejection by the Liberals embittered the Labour men such as Hardie and drove them further away from Liberalism towards socialism. One important factor which weakened the Labour movement in Scotland was the hostility of the Roman Catholics. As long as Home Rule depended on the Liberals, the Catholics voted for them and the Labour Party was deprived of much of its potential working-class vote. Socialists such as John Wheatley tried after 1900 to form a Catholic Socialist Society, but the priests were opposed both to a weakening of the Home Rule vote and to the 'atheist materialism' which seemed associated with Labour. The Protestant–Catholic split also entered the industrial wing of the movement, for the trade unions could not be effective when cheap labour in the form of Irish Catholic immigrants was readily available.

This feuding was of course strongest in the Glasgow and west of Scotland area, while in the east, particularly in Aberdeen, Dundee and the Fifeshire coalfield, there was a more united Labour movement and better industrial relations. Despite this, the Labour politicians were not content to fight only their opponents. They also engaged in internecine warfare, and before 1914 several 'Labour Parties' competed in Scotland, depending on the organisations which supported them and to a lesser extent on their respective doctrines. From 1900 to 1909 a Scottish Workers Representation Committee rivalled the (British) Labour Representation Committee in sponsoring candidates. The former body was set up by the Scottish Trades Union Congress, the latter by the (British) Trades Union Congress. It was not until 1909 that the Labour Party as we know it today gained full control of the political wing of the movement in Scotland, although it had secured the election of the only two Scottish Labour MPs in 1906.

The strength and significance of the pre-1914 Scottish Labour movement is difficult to assess accurately. It threw up some of the most important socialist leaders in Britain, such as Keir Hardie, Robert Smillie, Ramsay MacDonald (mostly in exile) and Bruce Glasier, but the Scottish people as a whole distrusted it as cranky and alien to their individualism. Labour espoused many planks of the Scottish Liberal and radical programme such as Temperance, Home Rule and the Eight-Hours Day for miners, but any distinctively socialist policies were bones of contention, even within the movement. Many of the leaders were forced to go to England and Wales, where the local Liberals gave them the chance to be elected to Parliament by not opposing their candidatures. Thus Alexander Macdonald in 1874 and Keir Hardie in 1892 became English, not Scottish MPs, as did other Scots (such as Smillie and Ramsay MacDonald) in later years, even without Liberal support.

By the end of 1910 there were three Labour MPs in Scotland out of a Labour total of forty in Parliament, hardly an indication that the Scots were in any sense 'red'. Yet five years later this was the epithet which came to be applied to the politics of the Glasgow area, and the reputation of extreme socialism in Scotland remained throughout the 1920s and 1930s. It all began during the First World War, when industrial conditions on the Clyde underwent severe strain. As a centre of prime importance for the manufacture of munitions, with its metal industries and shipyards, the area was subject to constant pressure to increase production. Overtime, the 'dilution' of skilled labour with unskilled men and women, a deterioration in housing conditions as a result of the influx of labour from outside: all these contributed to a militant protest movement organised by the Clyde Workers Committee of shop stewards. Its aim was: 'To organise the workers upon a class basis and to maintain the class struggle until the overthrow of the wages system, the freedom of the workers, and the establishment of industrial democracy have been obtained' (Middlemas, 1965, p. 61). This was something new in Scottish politics, and quite alien to its previous history. Even Labour leaders had rarely introduced such Marxism, and Keir Hardie, Robert Smillie and Ramsay MacDonald had always stressed the poetry of Robert Burns, with its 'brotherhood of man', or the Bible as the basis of the Labour creed.

Although only a small minority were converted to the aims of the Clyde Workers Committee, there was great unrest, culminating in strikes, violence and imprisonment. Lloyd George, the Prime Minister, travelled to Glasgow in 1915 to use his charm with the people, but the Scots were having none of it and his meeting ended in uproar. The alternative for the government was coercion, and, by a series of arrests, the militant section of the protest movement was silenced within the confines of the Calton Jail, Edinburgh. On the Clyde, conditions were eased somewhat, and work resumed.

But the stimulus to the Labour movement remained, to reappear after the war in the form of a group of Independent Labour Party (ILP) MPs, known as the 'Clydesiders'. Most of these men had participated in the wartime protests on the Clyde, and several had languished in jail for a number of months. In 1918 they emerged as parliamentary candidates and, although only two of the group were returned in that year, the total voting figures showed a marked improvement on the scattered prewar Labour candidatures. By the next election, in 1922, the Labour movement had gained from the disruption of the Liberals, the independence of Ireland (freeing Catholic votes for Labour) and the failure of Lloyd George's postwar utopia. The ILP group won ten out of the fifteen Glasgow seats and a total of twenty in Scotland in this election. There were also nine other Scottish Labour MPs elected who had been nominated by the trade unions. Since the total of Labour MPs in Parliament was 142, the Scottish contingent of 29 made a proportionately higher contribution to the party than those from England (but not as high as the Welsh).

Scotland's contribution to Labour was also greater in terms of the publicity it attracted. The Clydeside MPs were determined to shake the complacency of the House of Commons and to reject the gentlemanly conventions which prevailed there. The most famous occasion occurred on 27 June 1923 when James Maxton (Glasgow, Bridgeton, 1922–46), aroused by cuts in the Scottish Health Estimates, called the government and its supporters 'murderers'. As such usage was impermissible in the House, but was nevertheless taken up by other Clydesiders, several were expelled by force of the Serjeant at Arms. Similar scenes became familiar in the Parliaments of the 1920s, and were perhaps as much an embarrassment to the 'respectable' leaders of the Labour Party such as Ramsay MacDonald as they were to Labour's opponents. Modern assessments of the Clydeside group tend to disparage their antics and to concentrate on the intellectual abilities of John Wheatley, the only one of them to reach Cabinet office at the time (Minister of Health, 1924). It is true that Wheatley's ideas on housing reform were influential in shaping Labour policy, but the colourful members of the group, such as Maxton with his long hair, and Emmanuel Shinwell, the strike leader, captured the popular imagination and swelled the Labour vote in Scotland.

Even when the ILP split from the rest of the Labour Party in 1932, much of their support remained firm in Scotland. Despite official Labour opposition, they returned four of their eleven candidates in 1935 and all three in 1945.[10] But gradually the rebels returned to the fold, or attained respectability outside party politics. Thomas Johnston, as we have seen, served under Churchill in the Second World War, David Kirkwood became a peer, George Buchanan became chairman of the National Assistance Board, Shinwell took office under Attlee, and the others virtually fizzled out.

The Labour Party in Scotland is now a staid, socially-conservative and rather dull body. Its keynote is stability, since it is assured of a large number of safe seats, and in local government it has held the citadel of Glasgow almost continuously since 1933. Today's Scottish Labour MPs are no wild men, but ex-councillors and trade unionists, with a few safe teachers and professional men. In October 1974 their average age was 50, compared to 43 for the Conservatives, 46 for the Liberals, and 39 for the SNP. It would be unrealistic and undesirable to expect the conditions of the 1920s to continue, but no doubt the boredom which is undoubtedly felt by anti-Conservatives in Scotland about 'two-party politics' comes largely from the lack of emotion in left-wing campaigning. The Labour Party sometimes takes its support for granted in Scotland, and disaffected radicals, who wish for a more emotional or revolutionary approach, turn to the Liberals, or to the Scottish Nationalists, as the best expression of their 'protest' vote. Their attack is now aimed at a new Establishment: the vested interest of Labour in trade union and town hall, which has replaced some of the privilege of the past.

No significant contribution to the Labour Party's policy has been made by the party in Scotland in recent years. Its freedom to make a separate policy is severely restricted by the fact that the constitution and programme of the Scottish organisation must be 'within the lines laid down from time to time by the British National Conference of the Party'. This body directs the affairs of the party as a whole, and delegates attend from Scotland on the same basis as the rest. Despite this, the party leadership felt obliged in 1974 to get the sanction of the Scottish conference for its policy of devolution, which had previously been rejected by the Scottish Executive of the party. And it was not until 1976 that the Labour Party Conference voted in favour of devolution, by which time the government was committed to legislation.

This commitment did not satisfy all in the Labour Party, however, and two Labour MPs, James Sillars and John Robertson, joined a new 'Scottish Labour Party', which held its inaugural meeting in January 1976. The new party had a strong following of left-wing intellectuals and journalists, and at first it seemed a grave threat to the Labour Party in Scotland. Its aims were a socialist Scotland through strong Home Rule or even independence, and representation for Scotland in the European Community. It soon suffered splits, and was unable to appeal successfully to the Scottish electorate

(Drucker, 1978). Nevertheless, it offered a potentially powerful combination of socialism and nationalism, which was unavailable to the SNP, since the latter eschewed 'class politics'. A purely Scottish Labour Party could become more relevant if devolution were established.

The present Labour MPs in Scotland are to the left in their party on foreign and economic matters, but more conservative on 'moral issues' such as abortion, homosexuality and Sunday Observance. In these, of course, the influence of the Roman Catholic Church and the Church of Scotland is evident. Many MPs have inherited the puritanism which was so noticeable in the make-up of the early Scottish Labour leaders and which is part of Scottish life generally. Unfortunately, they cannot always be said to have maintained the pioneers' disdain for the *status quo*, since they are so much part of it themselves.

## THE COMMUNIST PARTY

Disdain for existing society there is in plenty among the Communists. Scottish Communists have played a prominent part in their party, and two, William Gallacher and John Gollan, became top officials with great influence on the movement. Since 1922, Communists have stood in every general election in Scotland, and their candidates were elected in Motherwell (J. T. Newbold, 1922–3) and in West Fife (W. Gallacher, 1935–50), half the total of Communists who have been returned to Parliament. However, their percentage of the vote has never been high, and reached its peak in 1923 at 2·6 per cent. In recent elections, it has averaged 0·5 per cent.

Extreme left-wing socialist organisations have existed in Scotland since the 1880s, especially those associated with William Morris (Socialist League) and H. M. Hyndman (Social Democratic Federation). Most of the modern Communists were associated with the latter, which was renamed the British Socialist Party at the time of the First World War. One of these was John Maclean, a Glasgow teacher, who lectured to crowded evening classes on economics, with a Marxist interpretation, and helped to found the Scottish Labour College. Willie Gallacher also emerged at this time as a militant trade unionist, and interviewed Lenin at the 1920 Communist International in Moscow as the representative of the Scottish Workers Committee (successor of the Clyde Workers Committee) (Gallacher, 1936, 1966). Gallacher did much to enforce Lenin's commands for unity on the squabbling British Communists, and in Scotland he helped to make many converts to communism among the miners, especially in Fife. They started a communist trade union, the United Mineworkers of Scotland (1929), which lasted until 1936 when it merged with the

National Union of Scottish Mineworkers. The Communists were strong in this body also, and a Communist, Abe Moffat, was elected president in 1942. When it became the Scottish Area of the National Union of Mineworkers in 1945, Moffat continued as president, and his influence was seen in the rebukes delivered by the Area to the Labour government over its 'weakness' on the terms for nationalisation of the mines, and its support for America in the Korean War. Laurence Daly and Mick McGahey have continued this tradition. Despite this, the Union has supported the Labour Party financially, through sponsored candidates and contributions to funds (Moffat, 1965).

With 7,500 members, out of a British total of around 25,000, the Scottish section of the Communist Party is a relatively strong one. But its political influence in Scotland is negligible, with no MPs and only a few local councillors. Even its industrial influence, once strong, seems no greater now than in other parts of Britain. The only well-known intellectual among its members was Hugh MacDiarmid, the poet, who was at one time expelled from the party for his Scottish Nationalism.

## THE SCOTTISH NATIONAL PARTY (SNP)

Scottish nationalism in its modern form began in the 1920s. Before that time, the Liberal Party, by its support for a Scottish parliament within the British state, had been able to restrain the ever-present discontent in Scotland with the Union and assuage the Scots' feelings of subordination to England. The nationalist movement of the 1880s gained wide support, culminating, as we have seen, in the establishment of the Scottish Office in 1885. This was not enough for some, and a Scottish Home Rule Association was formed in 1886 to demand 'Home-Rule-all-Round'. By 1894, the Liberal majority in the House of Commons was supporting a Scottish parliament, and they renewed their affirmative in 1913, passing the Second Reading of a Scottish Home Rule Bill by 204 votes to 159 (Scottish MPs 45 to 8) (Coupland, 1954, p. 306). Then came war, and united effort by all Britons. The proposal for a Scottish parliament seemed irrelevant to most in the reconstruction period of the 1920s, and a Speaker's Conference recommendation in 1920 that some watered-down devolutionary scheme be tried was ignored by the government. As the Liberal Party was shattered, no action was taken on the 1913 Bill, and it now seemed that Labour was the most nationalist of the major parties. The failure of George Buchanan's Home Rule Bill in 1924 and Barr's in 1926 soon showed that the Labour leaders were not interested, and in April 1928 a new National Party of Scotland was formed. It became the Scottish National Party in 1934.

This party was composed mostly of intellectuals: students and writers whose aim was to revive Scottish culture on lines distinct from elsewhere in Britain. This was to be the Scottish 'Renaissance', and a condition of its success was political independence for Scotland. The founders were Cunninghame Graham, the Scottish Labour pioneer, R. E. Muirhead and J. M. MacCormick, and its prominent supporters included Hugh MacDiarmid, the poet, Compton Mackenzie, the novelist, and the Duke of Montrose. Almost every shade of political opinion was represented, from communist to ultra-Conservative.

The successes of the movement, however, were not at first political. While a new 'Scottish' national consciousness took root in the universities and in cultural media, the voters remained obstinately loyal to the British parties. Only at a by-election in April 1945 was a Scottish Nationalist returned to the House of Commons for a brief three-month spell before the July general election. After 1945 there was another wave of Scottish nationalism, with the spectacular 'success' of the Scottish Covenant and its 2 million signatures, demanding a Scottish parliament. The Coronation Stone of Destiny was 'returned to Scotland' from Westminster by Scottish students in 1950, and in 1953 post-boxes with the inscription EIIR were blown up by militants (MacCormick, 1955, p. 165). This was all good newspaper copy, but the practical result was nil as long as no votes were being affected. Moreover, the Nationalists themselves were torn by schisms, reminiscent of bygone Presbyterian conflicts, and were generally regarded as cranks.

In the early 1960s, a change came over the movement. Respectable, sober-minded businessmen and teachers started to join, and the fratricidal activities died down. The SNP organised a membership drive, and branches were set up all over the country with activities which were often as much social as they were political. SNP membership rose from under 2,000 in 1962 to over 80,000 in 1967.

Votes also rose, at first in parliamentary by-elections and local elections, and then at general elections. There were 128,000 Nationalist votes in 1966 (5 per cent of the total), although the party put up only 23 candidates in the 71 Scottish constituencies. Then in November 1967 the first Nationalist MP since 1945 was returned for Hamilton at a by-election. This was Mrs Winifred Ewing, and she turned a Labour majority of 16,576 into an SNP majority of 1,799.

By now both the major parties were alarmed at the advance of the SNP. The Conservatives, not yet as threatened as Labour, were studying devolution, and in May 1968 the Conservative leader, Edward Heath, came out in favour. This was confirmed by a Conservative 'Constitutional Committee' Report, under Sir Alec Douglas-Home, and by the Scottish Conservative Conference in 1970. The Labour government responded to the SNP by setting up the Royal Commission on the Constitution ('Kilbrandon Commission'), which, however, did not report until late 1973. By this time, Scottish nationalism had gone through a period of decline, and the Commission's support for devolution was not at first taken up by the government.

The general election of February 1974, however, brought the SNP back on the scene with a vengeance. Seven seats were won, with a total of 22 per cent of the Scottish votes (633,180). This was taken by most people to be a vote in favour of devolution, and indeed, opinion polls indicated that about two-thirds of the Scottish electorate would support the establishment of a Scottish Assembly. The same polls showed that different forms of Assembly appealed to different people, and that no one constitutional solution commanded majority support. Total independence for Scotland usually obtained about 20 per cent support, with 'no change' about the same.

The October 1974 election increased the representation of the SNP to eleven seats, with 30 per cent of the vote (839,628). By now, Labour was committed to establishing an Assembly, but the legislation (the Scotland Act) was not finally passed until July 1978. Even then, it was subject to a Referendum of the Scottish electorate, against the government's wishes, and Parliament amended the Act so that at least 40 per cent of the total electorate should vote Yes for the Act to come into operation. The Referendum was held on 1 March 1979, and the result was as shown in Table 9.2. This was clearly well below

Table 9.2   *Result of the referendum, 1 March 1979*

| | YES | | | NO | | Turnout |
|---|---|---|---|---|---|---|
| | *% of* | *% of* | | *% of* | *% of* | |
| *Votes* | *votes cast* | *electorate* | *Votes* | *votes cast* | *electorate* | |
| 1,230,937 | 51·6 | 32·9 | 1,153,502 | 48·4 | 30·8 | 63·6 |

the 40 per cent requirement, although it was a Yes majority. In the circumstances, the Referendum was the death-knell for the Scotland Act.

That devolution should have been halted by a vote of the Scottish people is at first sight surprising. Opinion in Scotland had for years been consistently in favour of a Scottish parliament, and it seemed that the government was responding to a demand from Scotland when it introduced the devolution legislation. However, as we have seen, while Scots supported devolution in principle, they were divided as to what form it should take, and the Scotland Act was not always supported wholeheartedly even by strong devolutionists. Many saw the lack of taxation powers and powers over the economy as a flaw. Others, however, were afraid that powers over these matters would be divisive and lead to the break-up of the United Kingdom.

There were also short-term factors militating against a strong Yes vote. The Labour government was unpopular, after a winter of industrial strife, and a vote for devolution was for some a vote for the government generally. The Conservative Party was stronger in Scotland than for many years, and was virtually united under Margaret Thatcher in opposing the Scotland Act. Labour, on the other hand, was split, with a vigorous 'Labour Vote No' campaign. The SNP backed devolution wholeheartedly, but this worried supporters in the other parties, and in any case the SNP was at a low ebb in its electoral fortunes.

More generally, one might say that expectations in Scotland were less buoyant than they had been a few years back. Scotland had been humiliated in the football World Cup competition in Argentina in 1978; North Sea oil did not now appear the 'bonanza' for Scotland that it did in 1974; the prospect of an 'extra layer of government' in Edinburgh, with the cost and bureaucracy which that involved, was uninviting when both central government and the reorganised local government system were blamed for many of the current ills. The BBC's attempt at Home Rule, Radio Scotland, introduced in 1978, was unpopular, and seemed to point to yet another failure when Scots were left to 'manage their own affairs'.

In short, Scottish nationalism was at a low point of support in its 'cycle', having now passed two 'highs' in 1967–8 and 1974–7. This was confirmed by the results of the general election in May 1979. The SNP lost nine seats, retaining only the Western Isles and Dundee East. Its share of the total Scottish vote slumped from 30 per cent to 17 per cent. There were twenty-nine lost deposits, including all the Edinburgh seats and eight of the thirteen Glasgow seats. On the other hand, in some rural seats the SNP did well, and in a few cases actually increased their vote, while losing to the Conservatives on an increased turnout.

Viewed as a long-term development in the history of Scotland since 1870, Scottish nationalism appears as a succession of 'waves', affecting at first different generations, but more lately the same generation at different points in its lifetime. Each successive wave seems to take Scottish national consciousness and the SNP to a higher point than before, and young people are more nationalist than older people. Thus, it might appear that the SNP has a bright future, despite temporary set-backs.

It is these set-backs, however, which cause problems for the party. It is difficult to retain faith in long-term prospects when the immediate prospect is failure. Yet the party has been remarkably successful in doing just that, and its organisation has provided the essential element of continuity to reap the benefit of the successive waves of nationalism, when they come.

It is impossible to do justice to the complex history of Scottish nationalism in this work. For that, readers are referred to the now vast literature on the subject (the best are Webb, 1978; Brand, 1978; Bogdanor, 1979). Various academic theories have been propounded to explain the nationalist 'phenomenon'. These range from 'uneven capitalist development' to a 'protest vote'.

What is clear is that Scots are very ambivalent about their national identity and their national political aims. While most identify themselves as Scots, and are proud of their nationality, the great majority also wish to be 'British', and to participate fully in the British state. They would like a form of devolution which satisfied their Scottish aspirations, while posing no threat to their British ambitions and to the unity of the United Kingdom. Moreover, they are deeply afraid of too much change and uncertainty, perhaps even of taking on responsibilities for their own government. Quite often they distrust each other as much as they distrust the outsider. In this climate, it is clear that Scotland will not lurch violently towards a form of nationalism which entails drastic change. The kind of nationalism Scots support is much more an affirmation of traditional 'Scottish values' and well-tried ways of doing things. Thus the SNP is faced with a big problem: it must appeal to Scots to do something which is perhaps alien to their character – to embark on a kind of 'revolution', national independence. It is paradoxical that the Scottish National Party should find its main obstacle to be the Scottish people themselves, and not the 'hostile' English.

## PRESSURE GROUPS

No British government, and no British political party, can ignore the pressure groups in Scotland. They ensure that Scottish interests are directly consulted in the making of policy, and they do not suffer from the inhibition and relative impotence of the Scottish MPs, who are restrained by party discipline and largely ignored when policies are being formulated. Some groups are entirely 'Scottish' and speak for interests peculiar to Scotland. These include the Churches, the legal profession, the teachers, the Convention of Scottish Local Authorities and the Crofters' Union. While they may have counterparts in England, their history and organisation has been distinctively Scottish, and they argue for discriminatory treatment which will preserve their Scottish identity and their 'advantages'. To a lesser extent this is true of other interest groups which resemble those in England but which wish to preserve a Scottish organisation, separate representative machinery and separate terms of employment for Scottish members. Many trade unions, employers', traders' and professional associations operate in this way, some being specifically

Scottish, like the Educational Institute of Scotland, while others are linked to British bodies, like the Scottish Area of the National Union of Mineworkers.

A Scottish Trade Union Congress (STUC) has functioned since 1897, consisting of delegates from unions in Scotland, along with Trades' Councils' representatives. These Councils (excluded from the British Trade Union Congress) were formed in the large towns in the nineteenth century and played a special role in the Scottish Labour movement, establishing their own independent Labour Party in 1892 and putting forward candidates in the election of that year (Fraser, 1967). Most trade unions in Scotland are affiliated to the British TUC as well as to the STUC, and over the years top-level industrial negotiations have increasingly been undertaken by the British unions on behalf of Scottish members. The number of Scottish unions has diminished, as more merge in the British organisations.[11] In this way, separate negotiations for Scottish members get fewer, as the unions generally demand an equality of treatment for all their members. The London-based bodies naturally concentrate their pressure on Whitehall, leaving Edinburgh to implement the general policy agreed on for the whole country.

Similarly, employers' and traders' associations, even when purely Scottish, are closely concerned with the actions taken by their British counterparts. The Confederation of British Industry (CBI) has a Scottish Council and Secretary, and issues an annual report on economic trends in Scotland. A wide range of trading interests are organised on purely Scottish lines, from the Scottish Daily Newspaper Society to the Scottish Bookmakers' Protection Association. There is even a Scottish Football Referees' Association. Scottish trade and professional journals are published: for example, the *Scottish Farmer, Scottish Educational Journal, Scottish Licensed Trade News* and *Scottish Drapery Journal.*

Promotional groups of importance in Scotland are the Lord's Day Observance Society (a British body), the Scottish Temperance Alliance, the Scottish Society for the Prevention of Cruelty to Animals (English 'Royal Society'), the Royal Scottish Society for the Prevention of Cruelty to Children (English 'National Society'), the Saltire Society (cultural nationalism) and the National Trust for Scotland. With the exception of the first mentioned, these are all purely Scottish organisations, but their functions are identical to corresponding bodies in England.

While there is a continuous tendency for the groups representing economic interests to merge in larger, British bodies, the process is by no means complete. Scottish teachers, local government officers and electricians have had special disputes of their own with the government over pay claims, on account of their separate negotiating machinery, and many feel that a co-ordinated British wages and incomes policy must eliminate the Scottish 'anomalies'. As against this, the teachers reply that, since their qualifications and training are separate from those in England, so should be their salary scales. And Scottish interests as a whole combine to press for discrimination in favour of Scotland. The STUC sends frequent delegations to Edinburgh and London, and the Scottish Council, as we have seen, operates virtually within the Scottish Office itself on behalf of nearly all the groups.

All government advisory councils and committees in Scotland are composed of representatives of Scottish interests, and these amount to a separate network of such bodies, covering the entire activities of the central administration. No government action is taken in Scotland without at least formal consultation on the specifically Scottish aspects of a policy.

## IS BRITAIN POLITICALLY HOMOGENEOUS?

Most writers on British politics until the 1970s assumed that there was one British political system whose unity was not seriously disturbed by regional differences. People throughout Great Britain (that is, not including Northern Ireland) were considered to be subject to the same political institutions, and in their voting behaviour they nearly all preferred British to nationalist parties. When the reasons for party choice were examined, such factors as social class, age and economic opportunity were as important in Scotland as in England, and whether the voter was Scottish or not did not seem to matter.

Even before the Nationalists scored their successes in the late 1960s this view was being challenged, as for example in Budge and Urwin's *Scottish Political Behaviour* (1966). They found that voting behaviour patterns in Scotland were sufficiently distinctive to call in question the notion of British political homogeneity, and this, when taken along with Scotland's political institutions, made Scotland a 'political region' within Britain.

The use of the word 'region' for Scotland fell out of favour with the rise of the SNP, and the Kilbrandon Commission on the Constitution was left in little doubt that Scots perceived Scotland as a nation. Scottish voting behaviour now moved sharply away from the 'two-party system', so that in 1974 and afterwards the SNP sometimes drew as much support from the voters as Labour or Conservative. Now the commentators swung to the other extreme of analysing Scottish politics almost entirely in terms of nationalism and the differences between Scotland and England (Harvie, 1977; Brand, 1978).

The referendum and election results in 1979 gave a severe check to this interpretation, for they apparently reasserted the 'British' side to Scottish politics. Scots were returning to the major parties once more, and were seen as rejecting a further 'Scottish' dimension in devolution to their politics (although in fact a majority voted for the Scotland Act).

It is clear that neither homogeneity nor nationalism on its own does justice to the position of Scotland within the United Kingdom. There are strong features of both in Scottish politics. Nor is it possible to say in general which predominates, for as we have seen there are cycles or waves of nationalism, interspersed with periods of quiescence or relative homogeneity. Thus it is necessary to take account of both dimensions of Scottish politics, and to assess their importance in any period of Scottish history.

## NOTES

1 The North-East Industrial and Development Association is probably the most influential, and dates from the early 1960s. Similar private groups promoting regional interests in England are found in the north-west and south-west. The Eastern Borders Development Association includes interests from both Scotland and England (Northumberland).

2 The sixteen Scottish representative peers in the House of Lords were also identifiable, until the 1963 Peerages Act allowed all Scottish peers the right to sit in the House. Before then, the representative peers were elected by the Scottish peers from among themselves at each general election. For their history, see Sir James Fergusson, *The Sixteen Peers of Scotland* (Oxford: Clarendon Press, 1960).

3 The decision as to whether a Bill relates exclusively to Scotland or not is taken by the Speaker of the House of Commons.

4 This was a rare example of a veto by over ten MPs.

5 There was no Conservative Scottish Whip until 1911.

6 These were Aberdeen, Paisley and the Burgh Districts of Dumfries, Elgin, Kirkcaldy, Leith, Montrose and Stirling. Dundee was also Liberal throughout, except that one of its two seats was Labour from 1906 to 1914. Hawick Burghs was Liberal throughout its existence, 1868–1918.

7 Liberal county seats from 1832 to 1914 were Clackmannan and Kinross, Fifeshire (including one Labour seat after 1910), Caithness (including Crofter, 1885–95). Banffshire was Liberal from 1837 to 1914. No county was totally Conservative from 1832 to 1914.

8 A Scottish National Constitutional Association was formed in 1867, and the National Union of Scottish Conservative Associations in 1882. These amalgamated in 1885.

9 The name 'Highland Land League' was adopted in 1887 with the union of Highland Land Law Reform Associations dating from 1882. The League disintegrated in the 1890s, was revived in 1909, and co-operated with the Labour Party in promoting candidates at the election of 1918. In the 1920s it disappeared from view.

10 In 1945, however, two were unopposed by the Labour Party.

11 The expansion of the STUC may be summarised: 1897, 55 organisations, 41,000 members; 1924, 227 unions, 536,432 members (90

Scottish unions, 213,460 members); 1978, 74 unions and 45 Trades Councils, 1,033,896 members (9 Scottish unions, 62,957 members). The largest Scottish unions are the Educational Institute of Scotland (45,998), the Scottish Colliery, Enginemen, etc. (5,500) and the Scottish Carpet Workers' Union (4,570).

FURTHER READING

Brand, J., *The National Movement in Scotland* (1978).
As seen by a Nationalist.
Brown, G. (ed), *The Red Paper on Scotland* (1975).
Socialist views on modern Scotland.
Harvie, C., *Scotland and Nationalism: Scottish Society and Politics, 1707–1977* (1977).
An interesting interpretation of Scottish history, unfortunately let down in places by the passage of events.

# Chapter 10

# Some Economic Trends

## IS THERE A SCOTTISH ECONOMY?

So far in this examination of Scotland since 1870 it has been possible
to consider that country as a separate social and political entity within
the United Kingdom. This is because the laws, institutions and
culture of Scotland demand such a treatment, even when much of
Scottish life is interwoven with that of its neighbours. An attempt to
isolate for discussion the Scottish economy is not so easily realised
or perhaps so fruitful. In economic terms, the Union was a complete
one. No permanent economic rights were retained by Scotland, and
the aim of the Treaty was the eventual assimilation of trading conditions throughout Great Britain. In the nineteenth century, Scotland
and England benefited equally from British tariffs (or their absence),
and the wealth from colonial and overseas trade sustained the economy
of Glasgow, Dundee and Edinburgh, as it did that of Bristol,
Manchester and Liverpool. The demand for Scottish textiles, coal,
iron and ships was as great as for English, and the industrialisation of
both countries was based on it.

Until 1918, there was little evidence that Scotland was in any
way a 'depressed' economy, although during the British economic
depression of 1873–96 arguments were sometimes heard that government contracts for coal and ships were not placed often enough with
Scottish firms. This seems to have been put right in the 1890s and
later, for the Scottish heavy industries provided much of the naval
rearmament programme as well as many passenger and cargo ships
and railway locomotives of worldwide renown.

Few people in those days talked of the Scottish economy, either
of its virtues or of its failings. But there was one aspect of Scottish
economic life which was always considered to be unique: the crofting
problem. It was inevitable that, wherever land was involved, Scotland
would have peculiar problems. The feudal system with its vested

rights infuriated the tenant-farmer, and the lack of a formal tenure of any kind before 1886 placed the crofter and cottar at the mercy of the laird. Both groups combined in the 1880s to wrest concessions from the landowners and the government: the former through the repeal of the more oppressive Game Laws (1880) and the establishment of compensation for improvements (1883), and the latter through the revolutionary Crofters Act, 1886, which gave security of tenure and fair rents throughout the seven crofting counties.

Since 1886, the Highlands have been treated as an economy apart. Special government programmes and grants were immediately inaugurated, including state purchase of land by the Congested Districts Board (1897–1911) and Scottish Board of Agriculture (1911–28). (The Congested Districts Board operated in fifty-six 'congested' parishes and its main duty was to create new holdings, which had not been possible under the Crofters Act. Unfortunately, it was starved of finance, and was not allowed to assist crofters to stock their holdings. Moreover, most crofters did not wish to purchase holdings, since they feared paying owners' rates. This discovery paralysed the Board's activities, as it could not sell its land: Day, 1918, pp. 207–12). While the Crofters War of 1882–8, with its gunboats, deer raids and skirmishes, was not repeated, squatters seized land for crofts in 1906 and 1920 in several Highland areas, and the problem of overpopulation of the scanty agricultural land was never solved. Despite the 'Deer Forests' Commission Report of 1895 (C 7668, C 7681) and the Liberal Scottish Land Enquiry Committee's Report of 1914 (*Scottish Land*), both of which pointed to the abuse of agricultural land for sport, there was little change in the relative acreages for deer, sheep and arable land. Arable land had decreased by 101,734 hectares from 1882 to 1911, while deer forests rose from 700,000 to 1,200,000 hectares. State purchases of land continued, until the government became the largest landowner in the Highlands, but much of its property was devoted to forestry, which required few men.

A certain amount of industrialisation did take place in isolated pockets of the Highlands. Aluminium works powered by hydro-electricity operated in Foyers, Inverness-shire from 1896 to 1967, and larger developments of the same industry were opened in Kinlochleven, Argyll, and Fort William, Inverness-shire. But these are not in the principal crofting areas, and when Lord Leverhulme, the English soap millionaire, attempted to industrialise the crofting islands of Harris and Lewis in the early 1920s, his efforts met with little success. The crofters returning home from the war demanded land, not jobs in a factory, and their attitude to material profit was diametrically opposed to that of the English boss (Nicolson, 1960). This attitude was (and is) generally one of passivity, or lack of ambition, which leaves time for 'contemplation'. All subsequent attempts at industrialisation on the west coast have had to cope with such an outlook on life, and the successful ventures, such as atomic energy research stations or pulp mills, usually employ a large contingent of outsiders. On the east coast, a harder philosophy prevails, and the Highland firm of Duncan Logan of Muir of Ord (Ross-shire) built the Tay road bridge in the 1960s and many other large construction works in the Lowlands as well as in the north.

The relative failure of plans to develop the Highlands has resulted in emigration on a large scale, and the population of the crofting counties dropped from 341,535 in 1911 to 276,303 in 1966. A second Crofters Commission Report in 1954 (Cmnd 9091) (the first was in 1884) recommended the introduction of new blood into the Highlands by breaking the hereditary succession to crofts, a principle established in 1886. However, this meant some form of 'market economy' and selling to the highest bidder. Here, bitter memories of the past came to the fore, since prior to 1886 sheep farmers and sportsmen had ousted the crofters by offering to pay higher rents, which the crofters could not match. The Crofters Act of 1886 had defined fair rents as those which the crofter, and not the speculator, could pay, and this victory has always been cherished in the Highlands. Thus the dilemma remains: how to be just to the crofters and at the same time revitalise the crofting economy. Most crofters are ageing and are 'non-commercial' farmers. Quite often crofts are inherited by strangers to the area, who leave them empty for much of the year. But the social justification for the system is still pressed, and the crofters' privileged tenure remains virtually as it was in 1886. Since 1911 it has also been shared by small tenants throughout Scotland, with farms of under 20·2 hectares.

The Crofting Reform (Scotland) Act 1976 gave crofters the right to become the owners of their crofts, and to share with the landowner in the development value of the land if it is sold by him. This value has risen considerably in recent years, with the advent of North Sea oil and the increase in holiday houses and other forms of tourism. The reform has not been entirely welcomed, however, by those who seek to preserve the crofting way of life from commercial pressures. They see it as the thin end of a wedge which will introduce more outside control of Highland land, and an end to the distinctive culture of the region. While these fears are no doubt exaggerated, by the late 1970s Dutchmen, Arabs and Swiss were buying up estates and crofts, often for speculative gain rather than for agriculture or industry, and the subject of Highland land had again become political (Hunter in Drucker and Drucker, 1978, pp. 48–60).

At the centre of the Highland economy is the Highlands and Islands Development Board, established in 1965. Operating from Inverness, the Board has to tackle both the land question and the development of industry in the crofting counties. With regard to the former, it has so far played a marginal role. This is largely because its powers are limited to compulsory purchase of land for specific projects, and not of large tracts of land under private ownership where the problem is under-use or mismanagement. The Board has been conscious of its deficiencies here and since 1976 has sought wider land use and land purchase powers. These proposals have been resisted by landowners and farmers, and have had little response from central government.

On the industrial side (including agriculture and fishing), the Board has from the start been placed in something of a dilemma: how to square up the promotion of new industry with the preservation of the 'Highland way of life'. This has sometimes resolved itself into an east–west confrontation. Industrial plants such as aluminium smelters, oil refineries, oil rig and platform construction yards are naturally placed on the east coast, where they draw labour away from the west, and contribute to the further run-down of the Gaelic areas. They also introduce many non-Highlanders into the area. But there is no real alternative to such developments if employment prospects are to be improved and 'growth points' established. Once North Sea oil came on the scene in the 1970s, the Board was largely a spectator to much of the industrial expansion, which did not need a development agency to attract it. This was most noticeable in Orkney and Shetland, where the local councils themselves took on powers of controlling developments through private Acts of Parliament passed in 1974. They also gained a considerable 'private' income from the oil companies through 'disturbance payments', 'oil barrelage levies', and so on.

It can be seen that the picture in the Highlands is now much more complex than it has been in previous decades. In one sense, the old problems remain: landlordism, emigration from rural areas, high unemployment on the west coast. But in another sense this is a new era. The Highlands Board has given the area a strong voice in government, and practical assistance to Highlanders and others in a multitude of ways, which has contributed to the health of the economy. This has also contributed to a new confidence, and an inflow of population, which the oil boom has greatly speeded up. How much of this confidence and prosperity can outlast the oil era remains to be seen, and outside Orkney and Shetland there is little 'in the bank for a rainy day'.

If the Highland economy is agreed to be special and suitable for analysis on its own, what of the rest of the Scottish economy? Scottish economists have certainly not shirked the task, despite the difficulties. Cairncross, writing in 1954 in *The Scottish Economy*, summarises the view which is most widely accepted:

> The Scottish economy is an integral part of the British economy, sharing the same currency, supplying a common market, subject to identical rates of tax . . . Whatever other significance the Border may have, it is not a barrier between two separate economic systems but a line between two segments of a single economy.
>
> Yet the segment lying north of the Border is a distinct society with a unity and cohesion of its own . . . There is also a sufficient degree of segregation from the rest of the economy, and a sufficient diversity within Scotland, to allow one to speak of a Scottish economy, functioning as a unity and with an independent momentum; and there is a sufficient amount of statistical information about this economy to enable one to describe and analyse it. (Cairncross, 1954, p. 1)

Around the same time, official and semi-official reports set the seal of government approval on the concept of a Scottish economy. The Toothill *Report on the Scottish Economy*, 1961, examined Scottish industry, manpower, environment and regional development measures, and the five-year plan outlined in the Command paper, *The Scottish Economy, 1965 to 1970: A Plan for Expansion*, aimed at achieving 'a more balanced and progressively expanding economy in Scotland' through direct government action. The Scottish Council (Development and Industry) has conducted its own inquiries into emigration and Scottish exports, and is committed to promoting the health of the Scottish economy by attracting trade and industry from all parts of the world. If a Scottish economy does not in reality exist, then the illusion of it is firmly established.

### FROM PROSPERITY TO DEPRESSION

The major task facing the Scottish economic historian is to reveal the causes of the transformation of the Scottish economy from its pre-1914 buoyancy to its present state of ill-health or, at best, convalescence. Once these causes have been analysed, the economic planner can act the physician and use his science, and his art, to produce a cure – unless, of course, the disease is incurable.

In the Victorian and Edwardian period few Scottish businessmen were pessimistic about Scotland's economic health. While depressions occurred, as in England, progress was the keynote, and industrial Scotland was a land of opportunity. Immigrants flocked there,[1] and many Scots of humble origins made fortunes as 'lords' of tobacco, coal, iron or ships. Scotland was well able to support and direct its own Industrial Revolution, for it possessed a strong educational system, a 'Calvinist' outlook on material advancement which equated success with virtue, an earlier joint-stock company and limited liability system than in England (Campbell in Payne, 1967), and the natural resources of coal and iron to translate such advantages into action. The men who 'built the Clyde' were nearly all Scots, and Scotland's contribution to the technology of the world was remarkable for such a small population. Here were the road-builders Thomas Telford and John Macadam; Henry Bell, the first European steamship builder; Clerk Maxwell and Kelvin, pioneer scientists of electricity; James 'Paraffin' Young; and Neilson, whose 'hot-blast' made possible a vastly increased output of iron. These men of science were matched by the entrepreneurs of Scottish industry: businessmen who saw the relevance of new methods and technical inventions. Steel was used extensively on the Clyde for shipbuilding before it was accepted in England, and many innovations in marine engineering were promoted by William Denny of Dumbarton (1847–87). Scottish industrialists of this period had a worldwide reputation, and their names are still famous commercially: David Colville, James Lithgow, Sir William Arrol, J. and P. Coats, James Templeton, and Barr and Stroud.

Scotland also had its own banks, and in the eighteenth and nineteenth centuries they were renowned for the stimulus and help which they gave to small businesses through the 'cash-credit' system. But financial assistance on a larger scale, and for longer terms, seems to have been lacking. A conservative lending policy, with high rates of interest, was characteristic of the Edinburgh banks who dominated Scottish banking, and the more adventurous Western and City of Glasgow banks were forced into liquidation in 1857 and 1878 respectively. With these exceptions, Scottish banks have proved reliable and Scots have been better provided with bank branches in rural areas than the English. A considerable amount of Scottish investment went abroad in the second half of the nineteenth century, but much was poured into Scotland's own industries, which maintained most of their independence from outside control.

This independence did not survive the First World War. Not only did many of the banks come under English control, but takeovers of Scottish firms from England became common. In the case of the banks, a Scottish identity was preserved, complete with Scottish banknotes,[2] but the five Scottish railway companies[3] merged in the LNER and LMS in 1923, and industrial activities became subject more and more to priorities decided outside Scotland. Thus in times of depression and retrenchment, the Scottish branches of British firms were often sacrificed as the most expendable.

Why does the First World War mark the great dividing line in modern Scottish economic history? Several explanations have been produced, and they involve a subtle evaluation of the relative importance of 'human' and 'impersonal' influences on the economy. The 'human' factor includes the apparent change in the enterprise and drive of the Scots after 1918: a marked deterioration in Scottish inventive activities, and in the willingness of entrepreneurs to change to new products and techniques. Also in the human category belong the actions or inaction of the politicians, civil servants and economists when faced with Scottish economic problems. Clearly, this line of analysis is bound to be largely subjective, and it involves the dangerous assumption that 'it could have been different if only . . .' But there are interesting pointers which can be at least the basis of argument. Scotland's position in the world of science and technology, and its application of science to industry, have diminished greatly in importance since 1870, according to one study (Clement and Robertson, 1961). As an indication of this, the proportion of Scottish Fellows of the Royal Society dropped from a peak of 17 per cent in 1875 to 3 per cent in 1950 and 6 per cent in 1955. Of course, there have been famous Scottish scientists in the twentieth century, such as Fleming (penicillin), Baird (television) and Boyd Orr (nutrition), but the contribution of Scots to higher science does not seem as great as it once was. In applied science, too, the evidence suggests decline. Patents taken out by residents in Scotland have grown relatively fewer since 1850, although this does not include Scottish inventors who moved to England. Firms in Scotland rarely employ research scientists to the same extent as those in England, so that most science graduates of Scottish universities and colleges must take jobs in the south. Although Scotland has several important science research establishments, the strength has been in agriculture and fisheries rather than in technology. This is largely the result of the disinclination of Scottish firms to subsidise such research, and the hope that the state will do so instead.

The book on Scottish scientists which has been referred to attributes the major cause in the 'decline of Scottish genius' to the excessive emigration of the more gifted and highly trained citizens. However, this does not explain the causes of such emigration, which must be related to the prevailing economic conditions. Of relevance here is another human factor: the contribution of entrepreneurs. They too have been judged to be not the men they once were, and to have failed to provide the energy, vision and courage to meet changing circumstances. After 1870, the Scottish magnates of the heavy industries (other than shipbuilding and parts of steel and engineering) 'lacked enterprise, and this was in marked contrast to the earlier years of the century. Faced with a situation of depleted ores, competition from England and abroad, and rising wage costs (except in coal), Scottish entrepreneurs were inadequate in their response (Byres, in Payne, 1967, p. 289). Some were indolent, having inherited wealth from their parents who had built up the businesses, or turned to politics or sport. However, there seems no easy formula here, for others, such as Sir James Lithgow and William Denny in shipbuilding, kept up the pace set by their fathers.

The failure to change from the predominant heavy industries to new engineering and electronics projects has been repeatedly named as a root cause of Scotland's economic decline after 1918. It has been implied that the industrialists ought to have seen the way the wind was blowing in time, and to have altered course. In fact, some did, and motor engineering works were among the new industries established in Scotland before the First World War (Campbell, 1965, p. 245). Scottish motor-cars, such as the Albion and the Argyll, were well known at the time, and so was (and remained) the Acme wringer. But many of these new ventures disappeared, and they made little impact on the distribution of types of industry in Scotland. After the First World War, Scotland still depended for its prosperity almost entirely on the 'heavies', in particular shipbuilding and coal, and on agriculture, and these were hit severely by international competition. Not enough is known about the contribution of Scottish entrepreneurs between the wars to assess accurately the praise or blame which is their due. As some owners of Scottish industry were English or American in this period, the Scots cannot be accounted entirely responsible for the direction taken by the industries of the country. But stagnation there undoubtedly was, and very little visible sign of industrial initiative.

In agriculture, a parallel specialisation made Scotland more dependent on livestock production, which was badly hit by foreign competition. Argentine frozen beef and Australian lamb displaced many Scottish products in the British markets and it was difficult for Scottish farmers to change to alternative types of farming. Most Scottish farms were efficient and yields per hectare were high, but there was only a small amount of mechanisation. The number of horses on farms was 136,000 in 1918 and 105,000 in 1938, and it took the Second World War to increase the number of tractors from 6,250 in 1939 to 19,000 in 1945 (Symon, 1959, pp. 250–1).

Since 1945, the non-Scottish entrepreneur has been increasingly important. Most of Scotland was made a Development Area benefiting from special government industrial subsidies, and this encouraged outsiders to set up factories. Americans in particular found Scotland a suitable point from which to assail the European markets. From 1958 Scotland nearly monopolised the inflow of American companies to Britain, and received more English companies than any other subsidised area in Britain (Cameron and Reid, 1966, p. 61). Since that date, however, the extent of subsidised areas has been increased and Scotland is not so favoured as before.

With such a large sector of Scottish industry in 'foreign' hands today, it becomes even more difficult to talk of a purely Scottish entrepreneurial contribution to the economy. However, the prevailing impression is that go-ahead, experimental enterprise is less associated with the old Scottish firms than with the new factories managed by outsiders. Talbot (Chrysler), BL, and General Motors in motor engineering; Burroughs and IBM in business machines; Ferranti, Elliott Automation, Honeywell Controls in electronics; and BP in petro-chemicals: these are the leaders in Scotland's new industries, and they are all non-Scottish. The traditional Scottish industrial activities are not as secure, with the exception of whisky-distilling. Shipbuilding is tottering, and has only recently attempted modernisation in methods and management, with a 'new deal' at Upper Clyde Shipbuilders. Coal and steel are shaky, and textiles survive only in special lines (for example, carpets, vinyl-linoleum and tweeds).

Why the Scots themselves have not revitalised their industries remains a mystery to which no answer is provided here. As with the 'incentive' human factor, the managerial reservoir of talent was drained away by emigration, leaving a remnant of less adventurous and smaller men. The confidence shown in Scotland by outsiders ought to have been shared by its natives. The old Scots motto 'Wha daur meddle wi' me?' grows ever more inappropriate.

The final human factor concerns the role of the state in its economic and industrial policies. Here it must be remembered that, apart from fiscal controls, little direct economic planning was undertaken before 1945, and even less regional economic planning. An area such as Scotland, even when languishing under the weight of almost 30 per cent unemployed, could not expect to be rescued by state action. All that could be hoped for was an improvement through tariff protection, a certain number of agricultural subsidies, and the eventual self-adjustment of the world economy. Some slight relief could come from increased government contracts to Scottish firms; but then, were not the north-east of England and Wales just as depressed?

Arguments will no doubt be heard for years about whether Scotland received 'fair' treatment at this time (cf. Gollan, 1948), and perhaps more could have been done, even within the prevailing economic philosophy, to alleviate unemployment and aid the ailing Scottish economy. For example, Scottish agriculture suffered from an inappropriate system of subsidies to wheat and not oats and barley, the main crops in Scotland (Campbell, 1965, p. 291). The growth of the building industry, which was a prominent feature in the economic recovery of England in the 1930s, was checked in Scotland by the government's insistence on promoting private, not local authority, housing schemes; yet in the special circumstances of Scottish housing conditions, only state housing could meet the problem (Bowley, 1945, pp. 261–8). On the other hand, the jute industry was heavily protected by tariffs after the 1930s, and is still largely dependent on state support. The mid-1930s saw parts of Scotland designated as 'distressed', 'special' or 'development' areas, and these qualified for government grants. Industrial estates were opened after 1937, and with rearmament a false prosperity was returning by 1939.

This buoyancy disappeared soon after the Second World War, and Scotland became once more a poor partner in the United Kingdom. Government policy was now much more positive in relation to the economy, and Scotland benefited especially, in certain respects. The farmers were maintained at the new high level of activity established during the war, through legislation giving them security of tenure and guaranteed prices and markets (1947–8). The other sectors of the economy were less encouraged: coal-mining, for example, although nationalised, was partly phased out, and shipbuilding was left largely unprotected. Most of the Central Lowlands (except Edinburgh) along with Inverness became the Scottish Development Area and additional industrial grants and estate projects (including New Towns) were initiated. The efforts of the Scottish Council (Development and Industry) to advertise Scotland paid off, and by 1960 five-sixths of the floor-space in industrial estates was occupied by non-Scottish firms (Campbell, 1965, p. 323). In that year, aid was made available to any area of high unemployment, and grants on plant and machinery were paid in virtually the whole of Scotland.

But this fact alone shows the failure up to then of the economic policies for Scotland. Despite the new industries, the Scottish economy still relied on the health of the heavy industries, and these were not able to maintain consistent progress. The policy of subsidising all areas of unemployment came increasingly under attack, and in 1963 an alternative strategy of promoting 'growth areas' was announced in the Central Scotland Plan (Cmnd 2188). But the government soon changed its position on 'growth areas', and reverted to the earlier blanket subsidy for areas of high unemployment. This left the New Towns as the principal growth areas in Scotland.

The Plan for *The Scottish Economy, 1965 to 1970* (Cmnd 2864) included a system of regional planning bodies, and promised 50,000 new jobs by 1970. But it was quickly overtaken by events, in the shape of a sterling crisis and cut-backs in public expenditure. Although there was a substantial increase of manufacturing jobs between 1964 and 1973, the net loss of jobs in manufacturing industry between 1964 and 1976 was 86,000. In the same period, the primary sector lost 65,000 jobs, and construction 5,000 jobs. But there was a net gain of 139,000 in services, and that sector had 1,179,000 employees in 1976 compared with 844,000 in manufacturing and production industries. Other important changes in the employment situation were the decline in male employment (down 129,000, 1964–76), the rise in female employment (up 79,000), and the increasing imbalance between the west of Scotland and the east. Strathclyde's 9·3 per cent unemployment rate in May 1978 compared unfavourably with Lothian's 6·3 per cent and Grampian's 4·1 per cent (figures from *Scottish Economic Bulletins*). In the latter region, of course, North Sea oil employment was considerable, and it is to such optimistic features of the Scottish economy that we now turn.

SIGNS OF RECOVERY

There is a mood of qualified optimism today about the prospects for the growth of the Scottish economy. Many feel that the worst days of depression and high unemployment are past, and that there are now signs of a recovery sufficient to restore Scotland to a position of prosperity similar to that which it enjoyed before 1920.

Is there any real evidence for this belief? First, economic growth: Gavin McCrone's analysis of the Scottish gross domestic product between 1951 and 1960 showed a decline in its relative position, from 9·3 per cent of the United Kingdom total to 8·7 per cent (McCrone, 1965, p. 20). This was at a time when Wales was on average exceeding the British growth rate. Since 1960, however, there has been a more favourable trend, and an even more marked improvement from 1968 to 1976. In the former year, Scotland's GDP per head was 90·3 per cent of that of the UK, but in the latter it had risen to 97·3 per cent. Personal disposable income in Scotland rose from 92·1 per cent of the UK level in 1971 to 97·9 per cent in 1976, and this reflects the fact that earnings in Scotland had grown level with the UK average in the latter half of the 1970s.

This is in part a reflection of the changes in the industrial structure of Scotland. New industries, such as electrical engineering and vehicles, have partly counterbalanced the decline in the traditional heavy industries. In the 1970s, the development of North Sea oil has helped the Scottish economy: by 1978, around 60,000 jobs were oil-related, and they amounted to 12·4 per cent of all employment in Grampian Region, and 7·1 per cent in the Highlands and Islands (*Scottish Economic Bulletin*, No. 17, Spring 1979, pp. 9, 12). All this activity helped to cushion Scotland in the depression period of the mid-1970s, when the fall in Scottish industrial output was less than two-thirds of the UK fall.

Another indication of this improved position was that Scotland's unemployment rate grew nearer the British average, falling from about 75 per cent higher than average in the early 1970s to around 30 per cent higher in the later 1970s (see Figure 2.1, p. 22). In line with this was the drop in net migration, which in the 1970s was well below half what it had been in the 1960s.

Productivity is rising in Scotland faster than it is in the UK as a whole. Output in production industries in Scotland rose 6·9 per cent between 1970 and 1976, but only 2·2 per cent in the UK as a whole. Much of this was for export, and combined with Scotland's better position with regard to self-sufficiency in foodstuffs, this gives a favourable picture on the 'Scottish balance of payments'.

One of the paradoxical results of Scotland's higher productivity rate has been that the increased production has not been able to absorb the available labour force. Unemployment has continued at higher than the British rate, and there is still considerable emigration. But there are obvious signs of stabilisation in the industrial structure. The older industries have declined to a point where their impact on the overall trends in the Scottish economy has been neutral. A Central Statistical Office study of output growth in the UK regions between 1970 and 1975 stated that adverse structure had no effect on the relative performance of the Scottish economy (CSO, *Economic Trends*, November 1978). This shows that Scotland may have indeed turned the corner, and entered a new era of industrial expansion, based on North Sea oil and the new industrial base of fast-growing industries.

There are some drawbacks to this assessment, however. The old industries are still going through a painful retraction, and the problem of redundancies, 'ghost towns' and urban deprivation will be present for some time, while the restructuring of industry proceeds. This is particularly evident in the Strathclyde Region, where the steel, shipbuilding and other old industries are concentrated. North Sea oil employment, while buoyant in the 1970s, is expected to shrink drastically in the 1980s, as the production phase replaces exploration and construction. In any case, the benefits have proved highly localised. After 1980, the emphasis will be on oil revenues, and these go directly to the oil companies and the UK government, not to Scotland. The demand from some sections of Scottish opinion that oil revenues be earmarked for Scottish development has been met by a stern refusal in London. And it has not been widely pressed in Scotland, since it smacks of SNP opportunism and risks a 'break-up of the United Kingdom'.

Scots look well beyond Scotland for their economic salvation. For regional aid and general economic policy they look to the UK government in London. Since 1973, the UK has been a member of the European Community, and Scots have sought a special position in Brussels, through the presence of the Scottish Office in UK delegations, and through direct interest group representation. The National Farmers' Union of Scotland is established in the machinery of the EEC, and other pressure groups such as the Scottish Council (Development and Industry) and the STUC are heard there from time to time. Whether Scotland benefits from the European Connection is open to debate: as part of the 'periphery' it could suffer from the concentration of trade in the 'golden triangle' at the centre of the Community; but it also gains from the Community's pro-agriculture bias, and its new-found enthusiasm for regional policy. Some Scots see Europe as a new avenue of advancement, cutting out London. Thus there are good Europeans in the SNP, as well as in other parties. Beyond Europe, Scotland is closely linked to the United States. American companies now employ one in eight of all those working in manufacturing industry in Scotland, and their presence in the North Sea is predominant. It is obvious that these companies find Scotland attractive, but Scotland for its part is ambiguous in its welcome for Americans. There is a danger of a 'branch factory' status being established in Scottish industry, and the risk, realised in the Chrysler, Singer and Goodyear withdrawals from Strathclyde in the late 1970s, of insecurity of employment in American-owned companies.

But this is to put the blame on the 'foreigner'. There may be some truth in the observation that for many years the Scot has suffered from a national inferiority complex, showing itself in outbursts of aggressive self-pity. The periodic revivals of nationalism usually coincide with years of economic depression and high emigration, during which the traditional scapegoat, England, is held accountable and reviled. Perhaps it is enough to believe that an injustice has occurred to make it real, but it is hopeful that only a small minority of Scots are violently anti-English. The future may see the alteration of the national composition of Scotland's population through increased immigration, and of the structure of its industries through further diversification. What remains to be discovered is the effect this will have on the social and political institutions which Scotland has maintained and developed so independently since 1870.

NOTES

1  While this is true, it should be noted that there was always a net loss of population by migration at this time. Net loss by migration:

| | |
|---|---|
| 1871–81 | 93,238 |
| 1881–91 | 217,790 |
| 1891–1901 | 53,355 |
| 1901–11 | 254,092 |
| 1911–21 | 238,596 |
| 1921–31 | 391,903 |
| 1931–51 | 248,859 |
| 1951–61 | 254,701 |
| 1961–71 | 326,500 |

2  The note-issuing Scottish banks today are the Bank of Scotland, Royal Bank of Scotland and Clydesdale Bank. Of these the Bank of Scotland is 65 per cent Scottish; the Royal Bank owns two English banks, and the Clydesdale is English-owned.

3   These were the Caledonian Railway, North British Railway, Glasgow and South-Western Railway, Highland Railway and Great North of Scotland Railway.

FURTHER READING

Johnston, T. L., Buxton, N. K. and Mair, D., *Structure and Growth of the Scottish Economy* (1971).
Lenman, B., *An Economic History of Modern Scotland* (1977).
Hechter, M., *Internal Colonialism: The Celtic Fringe in British National Development, 1536–1966* (1975).
    Two orthodox accounts, and one controversial analysis, by Hechter, who sees Scotland as an exploited colony of England.

*Chapter 11*

# Culture in Scotland Since 1870

## by I. D. LLOYD-JONES

Culture is a complicated concept that essentially concerns the ways a people sees itself and creates things or forms of expression that are recognised as the outcome of its delights and enjoyments and its long-term ethical preoccupations. A culture involves both the grass-roots values and reactions of the people who form its various audiences, and the instruments of its expression, through professionals such as artists. These performers have been trained to use the tools transmitted by history and geography – whether their instruments are musical, artistic, architectural or verbal. In the broadest sense culture could be taken to include all those habits and behaviour patterns which a social anthropologist analyses to show the folkways of a people. In the narowest sense culture can be defined in terms of participation in the art, architecture, music, drama and literature of Western Europe. These prestigious forms of creativity have always been élitist and the degree of Scottish participation in them might be taken as a sign of integration into an international scientific and aesthetic tradition. Such relationships can be read either as an indication of the nation's subservience to values outside its own distinctive ways of life, or alternatively, as a mark of its civilization in producing people and works of European significance. But this is not a book about the influence of Scotsmen, such as Robert Adam, Adam Smith or Robert Louis Stevenson on European or English-speaking sensibilities. It is concerned to describe and analyse the situation within Scotland. The terms used to discuss culture are bound to have evaluative and hence political connotations; but the attempt to present an objective survey of culture here, in which neither international nor local values are preferred, entails focusing on institutions and describing how they relate to the various traditions or general attitudes that make up the cultural life of the nation.

Two prestigious traditions of thought and sensitivity were inherited which seemed to make Scottish culture valuable in the eyes of late 19th century educated people, because of their acknowledged effect on European perceptions. The first of these was the philosophical achievement of the Scottish Enlightenment, particularly the moral and sociological ideas of David Hume, and the more explicitly economic theories of Adam Smith. These scientific and philosophical attitudes were nurtured in the Scottish universities. The universities conserved such analytical values during the modern period, producing notable scientists or 'natural philosophers', such as Lord Kelvin; medical luminaries like Lister, and great engineers to create the momentum that made Glasgow the second city of the Empire. The boast of the four universities of Glasgow, Edinburgh, Aberdeen and St. Andrews was that they recruited a much higher proportion per head of the population to this culture than their English counterparts. This view of the Scots as a more scholarly people, respectful of learning, perhaps explains the degree of self-consciousness and seriousness with which a wide public applied itself to the written word. The establishment of free libraries, initially through the munificence of one classic example of a husbander of talents – Andrew Carnegie – helped to broaden public participation in this essentially literary culture. Its ideal was the rational individual examining the evidence, and his conscience, before acting sensibly and effectively.

The second great European tradition of sensibility was Romanticism. While Sir Walter Scott's novels were a seminal influence throughout Europe, the more vernacular poetry of Robert Burns nourished the links of the new urban middle classes with their peasant past. For if the Enlightenment tradition armed the intellect with weapons to subdue the changing world, Romanticism gave a people made mobile by industrialisation a vivid sense of their past, and hence an identity which helped them to relate themselves to the shocks of modernization in a coherent way. The picturesque popular view of history in terms of characters like Bruce and Wallace, Knox and Mary Queen of Scots, Bonnie Prince Charlie and Flora Macdonald, tended to extend into a similar dramatic mythology that simplified such phenomena as the Highland clearances or the problems of the urbanisation of the Clyde Valley. Thus at a popular level some of the horrors of slum life could be made more bearable by the 'couthy' characterisations of J. J. Bell and Neil Munro's stories. This creation of types and characters in literature enables a cultural community to illustrate its attitudes and values in relatively concrete forms related to – though far more subtle than – the stereotypes of political caricature. In thus placing, giving meaning to, and defining, people and events, the artistic activity of a society has the important function of reconciling, or alienating, or fusing, different groups who find themselves necessarily related by other economic or social factors. At its most popular level such a mythology is expressed in the performing arts of popular processions and sport. In the working class culture of a great city like Glasgow the May Day rallies and Orange Day parades, with their trade union banners and lodge insignia respectively, express dramatically different sets of priorities. Like the confrontations of the Protestant and Catholic football teams of Rangers and Celtic, they help to ritualise, and so to normalise, tensions which if not thus expressed might become more violent.

The predominant Scottish culture of our period takes its vocabulary and tone from the literary and musical traditions of Scottish romanticism. The 'Kailyard' concern with a small-town way of life, as seen in Barrie and Bridie, reflects the nearness of the urban middle classes to their pre-industrial culture both in generational and emotional terms. The tartan became a badge of identity. Paradoxically its designs became increasingly sophisticated, in terms of what to wear when and where, as its popularity spread in proportion to the actual disappearance of clans as significant social forces. The bagpipes sounded longer and louder in city drill halls than they ever had in the Highlands. Such very popular and long-lasting forms of cultural expression have become known as the ideology of 'Balmorality'. This is an apt term since the new-minted bourgeois monarchy gave the stamp of complete respectability to its characteristic manifestations. The popular and long-lived symbol of Queen Victoria's relationship with John Brown can be seen as a typically romantic myth expressing the desired reconciliation of traditional Highland ways and modern domestic virtues. Ghillies' balls, Scottish country-dancing and popular ballads, Highland gatherings and Burns suppers, may be deprecated as cultural forms by the coteries of the intelligentsia and cognoscenti. But when they unite the social spectrum in enjoyments, these activities provide a common idiom of communication and a powerfully reconciling set of attitudes. From the music halls of Sir Harry Lauder, through the 'white-heather' manifestations of contemporary television entertainment, to the slightly more vernacular celebration of proletarian Clyde culture by Billy Connolly, a living tradition of popular culture persists.

The links between such entertainments and the traditional Gaelic ceildh may be tenuous, but they are asserted. Institutionally supported by *An Comunn Gaidhealach* (founded in 1891) with its annual Mod concentrating on piping, singing and recitation, the Gaelic-speaking community is socially correlated with the crofting communities, still led by religious authorities. Gaeldom's distinctiveness means that rather than being an integral part of modern Scottish cultural expression, it operates through its prestige in the folk memory and thus continues to influence the mythology and forms of the majority's conscious cultural activity.

There are various other traditions, reacting to what they see either as the perversion of the original culture or as its subversion by anglicised and commercial interests. Such self-conscious protest movements are often linked closely with a radical political attitude. In so far as they become institutionalised it is often in conjunction with trade unions or political parties. Industrial radicalism thus found some cultural expression in the dramatic works staged by St. George's Co-operative players in Glasgow in the 1920s, and more permanently in the Glasgow Unity Theatre of the late 1930s and 40s, with its communist connections. Such groups were stimulated by the previous attempts to found a national theatre – the Glasgow Repertory Company (1909) and the Scottish National Players (1921), with their bourgeois and 'Kailyard' associations. This radical tradition has today been revived in the lively productions of the touring 7:84 Company.

Concern with community values in the city environment seems to lead to lively dramatic expression. In 1927 the Scottish Community Drama Association was founded and in 1943 James Bridie helped set up Glasgow's Citizens' Theatre in the Gorbals. It has not maintained an exclusively Scottish drama but has succeeded in focusing argument on what policy is proper for drama in Scotland. The Lyceum Theatre in Edinburgh has often taken a line opposite to that prevailing in Citizens' productions, so that a healthy spread of representative plays has been available to the public that supports these and the more ephemeral repertory groups. All draw part of their company from the students of the Royal Scottish Academy of Music and Drama. This had started as a mid-Victorian general 'Atheneum' but its school of music grew fast and by 1890 had a fine central building. Its academic standards were emphasised by a formal link with Glasgow University from 1928. In 1950 a college of dramatic art was added to the Academy that had been made 'Royal' in 1944, and from 1953 these two training grounds in the performing arts were recognised as an autonomous institution.

A similar concern with the mix between class-consciousness and national consciousness marks the main work of the Scottish literary revival that began in the late 1920s and is associated particularly with Grassic Gibbon the novelist, and the poets Edwin Muir and Hugh MacDiarmid. United with the radical left in their dislike of the conquering capitalist ideology, these nationalists re-affirmed the validity of the romantic tradition by attempting to revive the languages and community structures of pre-industrial Scotland without reverting to the sentimentalism of the Kailyard ethos. But the reconstruction of Lallans as a literary language creates another sub-culture, more esoteric than the living Gaelic tongue even if more accessible to the critics and teachers of literature. Radical, utopian views that constitute a sort of counter-culture to popular attitudes have maintained a more or less continuous expression and reached as wide a public as cared to be concerned, thanks to such institutions as the circuit of literary societies spreading from the universities and the numerous literary magazines like the contemporary *New Edinburgh Review*. These have come and gone as have many theatrical groups, with individual enthusiasms and the phases of fashion; but as an institutional structure they can be seen as an offshoot of the strong publishing tradition, based on Edinburgh and Dundee. As the home of many internationally famous publishers and printers for nearly two centuries, Edinburgh has engendered an important substratum of administrators and purveyors of culture. As commercial considerations made publishing firms such as Nelson's, Constable's, Blackwoods, and Chambers look to London and New York for their main business activity, their parent houses in Edinburgh could turn their talents to the congenial activities of maintaining the wider forms of native Scottish culture. But in Glasgow, Blackie's and Collins were able to retain their original printing and publishing plants. The continued success of Collins is partly due to its religious output, which aligns it with the achievement of the Drummond Tract Depository in Stirling in the nineteenth century and the St. Andrews Press of the Church of Scotland today. The D. C. Thomson press at Dundee has been the mainstay of the popular culture. Its journals and comics sustain the gentile conservative values of the majority, and the pawky humour that is the characteristic means for the working classes to come to terms with their fate.

The genuine popularity, in terms of sales figures, of such papers as the *Daily Record* will be regarded by their proprietors as sufficient riposte to the criticisms of the radical counter-culture minorities that such pabulum is designed to be an opiate. In so far as these popular forms of expression are owned and controlled by an international or alien cartel there is substance to such objections on behalf of Scottish culture. With the growth of international conglomerate companies since the Second World War, the share of the newsprint media owned, controlled and printed in Scotland has declined fast, but still nearly one-third of the market is controlled by D. C. Thomson and Scottish Universal Investments. 84 per cent of all daily newspapers and 74 per cent of the Sunday papers purchased in Scotland are printed north of the border. They may determine the types of bourgeois culture assimilated by the masses; but it is hard to deny that these are nevertheless valid expressions of a Scottish experience and perception. Correctives to their homogenous ethic have been expressed in vigorous but small-scale prints, such as the *West Highland Free Press*, and by local community newspapers.

The continuing coherence and power of the sense of Scottish community and nationhood, despite the universalising forces of commercialism and modern communication, is due to the strength of the institutions that traditionally transmitted a culture. The church, the law, the educational system, such bases of a culture, are examined in detail elsewhere in this book. Here it is only necessary to stress their function in integrating and maintaining an established pattern of cultural values that is similar to its English partner's, yet separately administered and distinguished by its own inflections. The Saltire Society (established in 1936), the National Trust for Scotland and the Scottish Arts Council (made independent of the English section in the mid-1960s) may be taken to represent the determination of the powerful native administrative establishment to formulate a policy for Scottish patronage within the general UK structures for the encouragement of culture. The distinguished museums of Edinburgh and Glasgow, which owe so much to the initiative and enterprise of the old aristocracy and nineteenth century industrialists, naturally lead the groups of smaller institutions in other towns in an association recently formed to concert exhibition policy and the allocation of resources, if not their funding by municipal and national authorities.

Architecture is the 'hardware' and most immediately obvious manifestation of a cultural climate. The character of the nineteenth century churches: the domestic enclaves of the professional classes, whether the New Town in Edinburgh or the substantial tenements and terraces of Glasgow's west end; the school board styles and the vast council estates of pre- and post-war period; imaginatively planned new towns like Cumbernauld; these are necessarily related to an international vocabulary of styles, but they are marked by a very distinctive local genius. The hand of Adam is to be discerned in the style of Edinburgh University, and the professional classes of the capital have preserved the rational aspect of an eighteenth century city that encompasses and sets off the gothic centre of castle, church assembly and palace along the 'royal mile' as gems of national history. Indeed, Enlightenment and romanticism are so explicitly celebrated in Edinburgh's architecture that its centrality to the nation's life has never been challenged, despite Glasgow's economic dominance and its role as an innovator in cultural as well as industrial spheres.

The burghers of Glasgow encouraged the massive simplicity of 'Greek' Thomson in the mid-nineteenth century, and constructed their magnificent commercial centre in a style appropriately reminiscent of the city-states of the Italian renaissance. In the utilitarian but impressive tenement system they devised an urban way of life whose density and vitality – until the vast demolitions of the last decades – made Glasgow more like nineteenth century continental cities than any other in Britain. In the countryside the recreation of a fantasy past with modern conveniences is symbolised by Balmoral. Some more sensitive examples of the relation of modern needs and technology to the indigenous fortified houses of the fifteenth century were created by architects inspired by the international arts and crafts movement at the turn of the century. Lorimer was encouraged by the patronage of the traditional landed gentry and the urge of newly enriched entrepreneurs to emulate them. C. R. Mackintosh's large surburban houses were commissioned, characteristically, by the noteworthy publisher Blackie and by an enlightened businessman. His Glasgow School of Art was so revolutionary as to make him a pioneer of the modern movement. He was more honoured in Vienna and Germany than in Scotland or England until very recently, when the general interest in Art Nouveau brought the realisation that the Scots had engendered a very distinctive Celtic variation of this stylistic attempt to recreate forms. The furniture, decors and decorative work of this group very consciously set about constructing an elegant response to the urban, industrial present by re-interpreting the forms and mythology of the Celtic twilight times. Contemporary Irish nationalism shared this vocabulary, which in Scotland found its most coherent manifesto in the works of Patrick Geddes, editor, sociologist, town-planner and professor of botany.

In painting, nothing so novel appeared – perhaps because of the strength of the Royal Scottish Academy which had been founded in 1826 on the approved model of similar European institutions. It ensured high standards of artistry and a market for genre, landscape and portraiture. Again the innovative work of the 'Glasgow Boys' in the 1880s and the reforms of Guthrie as President of the RSA in the first decade of the twentieth century, show the valuable relationship of competition and rivalry between the two types of culture – professional and traditional in Edinburgh, commercial and experimental in Glasgow. The relationship between Scotland and France – known to popular culture as the 'auld alliance' – is perhaps largely a myth designed to hearten the Scots in the face of the proximity of the English. But in painting, it operated to make the Scots more receptive than their English contemporaries to experiments in France and Holland (the other ancient commercial connection, between the East coast and Europe). A Glasgow dealer like Alexander Reid, operating primarily on behalf of the newly wealthy, such as the shipping magnate Sir William Burrell, helped to put the Glasgow Boys in touch with such revolutionaries as Gauguin and Van Gogh. The second generation of innovators, the Scottish Colourists, led by J. D. Ferguson, thus in the early decades of this century gravitated naturally to France; whereas more traditional painters found riches and honours through the network of British academic institutions.

The 'symphonic' character of music, combined with its more cumbersome equipment ensure that institutions have an even more central role in its support than they have in literature, painting or even drama. The European corpus of music has been well sustained by the Royal Scottish Academy of Music and Drama, the Scottish National Orchestra, and more recently Scottish Opera and Ballet. These companies are based on Glasgow but tour the large cities regularly. The genuine popularity of music, and the centrality of song in Gaelic culture, accounts for the largest centre of population – with its substantial Celtic inheritance – acting host in this sphere. The Glasgow Orpheus Choir, founded in 1905, became a symbol of the participation of amateur and professional talents; and it is from such relationships that the durable musical institutions of the Clyde Valley have emerged. The capital has re-asserted its presige by supporting the International Festival of Music and Drama since 1947 with typically professional organisation and high standards. But Glaswegians and the 'media' taunt the Edinburgh bourgeoisie for apparent indifference to this annual babel, and argue that the most creative aspect of the festival – its 'fringe' – has not been notably Scottish.

All culture is communicative, so it is apt in such a survey as this to conclude with a few remarks on 'the media'. Mention has been made of the distinctive organisation and sustaining role of the publishing tradition which conditioned the character of consciously cultural works. It aimed at an international English-speaking market and was able, out of its global profits to support some of the minority voices and views of a more radical, or more parochial, Scottish national culture. But film-making developed after Britain had lost its entrepreneurial lead, and in Scotland – even more than in England – it has been stunted by lack of capital to support work of a specifically native character. Film-makers such as Norman McLaren and John Grierson have profited from the close Scottish cultural connections with Canada. But the few film-makers who subsist on Scottish soil – such as Murray Grigor's imaginative productions – have to concentrate on promotion films for Scottish industry or tourism, with the help of their professional organisation, Films of Scotland (established in 1955). Broadcasting and television are distinctive media in that they are equally available to the whole population, irrespective of class or other conditioning factors, except the linguistic barrier of Gaelic. Given the potential of these media as cultural forces, it is not surprising that debate is primarily centred on who controls and funds them. But whereas this debate in England is now much concerned with the rights and opportunities of various cultural minorities to make their distinctive messages generally available, in Scotland the debate is primarily about the degree of autonomy of its media from England. Scottish Broadcasting House (BBC) was opened in Glasgow in 1938 and the amount of time it commands and the degree of independence it exercises has gradually, but continuously, increased. This tendency has been augmented by independent Scottish television and local radio developments. The various cultural traditions sketched in this chapter have found expression through the statutory duty of these bodies to present a balanced representation of views. As to what the fair proportions should be in such a balance, between the most popular manifestations of an international urban and industrial culture and the more esoteric voices claiming to be distinctively Scottish, there can be no definitive decision. But the lively debate about this eminently political decision as to the allocation of resources must itself be a valuable contribution to the sustenance of a developing, because vital, culture.

*Chapter 12*

# Conclusion

Since the 1960s, Scottish nationalism has been at the fore of Scottish life and the old questions have been raised regarding the place of Scotland within the United Kingdom. Is Scottish society essentially different from that in England? Is Scotland oppressed by England? Do Scots wish to dissolve or alter the terms of the Union of 1707?

This book has been largely concerned with the first question, and evidence has been put forward of marked contrasts between the two countries in social and economic structure, religion, education, law and administration. These differences are not just the dividing lines between regions of the same nation, but the divisions between separate nations. No two regions of England can be identified and compared on the basis of such a wealth of variables.

These tangible differences between Scotland and England are matched by the less determinate distinctions in national character, temperament and habits, which are often the subject of popular observation. While there is usually more than a grain of truth in these subjective assessments of nationality, they are also full of pitfalls and, on the whole, have been avoided in this text. For it is all too easy to disprove them by pointing to wide variations in national character within Scotland (for example, between Lowlander and Highlander, and between middle class and working class), and to similar group characteristics between Scotland and England (for example, northern Englishman and Lowland Scot). However, it is not so easy to disprove the separate identity of Scottish society, even after 270 years of Union with England. Unlike the different patterns of society which are found in the several regions of England, Scottish society is especially distinguished by the strength of its institutions. These cover a wide range of the life of the community and, despite the pressures of assimilation with England, seem today to be as vital as they have ever been.

It must come as something of a surprise to the social historian to find within the confines of one small island two distinct sets of social institutions, especially as the population is divided between the two in the ratio of nine to one. Why then has the larger not absorbed the smaller?

The answer comes in two complementary parts. First, at the time of the Union between Scotland and England the culture of Scotland was inherently strong, and had not been absorbed or greatly influenced by England, as had much of the culture of Wales and Ireland. Kirk, school and law court were thriving institutions, popularly supported, and on the whole well suited to the special needs and attitudes of the Scots, who were relatively poor but egalitarian and ambitious to succeed in life. This culture proved resilient throughout the succeeding years of the Union, when the forces of assimilation with England were naturally very strong.

The second reason is that England never attempted to colonise Scotland, as it had colonised Wales, Ireland and much of the world, nor did it try to impose an alien culture on the Scots. There were, indeed, English landlords (and anglicised Scottish landlords) in Scotland, and in the Highlands they wielded great territorial power, if not social influence. Yet even there the basic fabric of the native social life was untouched, and in the rest of Scotland Scots were firmly in charge of their own affairs. The English have always shown a great ignorance of, and indifference towards, Scotland, a fact which is illustrated by the enduring lack of interest in Scottish debates in the House of Commons. While this occasionally offends the Scots, who wish to be known and admired, it is in fact their guarantee of independence. They are left to solve their own problems and to live their lives as they wish.

Why then is there the continual undercurrent of nationalism and resentment against English domination? Unfortunately for those in Scotland who desire to remain different from England, being left alone is not enough. '*Laissez-faire*' may have served the interests of mid-Victorian Scotland, and have harmonised with the prevailing Liberal thought and the paramount role of the Church in society, but since the late nineteenth century positive state action has been demanded over a wide area of social and economic life. During the interwar period this became particularly necessary in the case of Scotland, where unemployment and housing deficiencies were particularly acute. Today, the state is probably more active in Scotland than in England in housing and in educating the populace, and in promoting economic development through formal planning.

But state action means power to the central government, and more 'remote control' from London. Although there has been increased decentralisation of administration in Scotland, the decision-making bodies, government and Parliament, are still in London, where the Scots are always in a minority. Thus, when there is discontent in Scotland, the 'English' government can be saddled with the blame. It should be noted that only very rarely does this discontent take on a cultural-nationalist form, for England has never overtly threatened Scottish culture, and there is no need for the Scots to proclaim, as the Welsh do, the virtues of being anti-English. In fact, no one prevents the Scots from being as Scottish as they care to be, nor indeed does anyone in Scotland prevent the English from donning the kilt and competing in Highland Games. Such trivia rarely affect the sensibility of the Scot, who, after all, may himself object strongly to the kilt and to many of the other fancies of Scottish nationhood.

What does worry the Scot is that in the Union of Scotland with England, Scotland may be the poor partner. Such features of Scottish life as low wage rates, shocking housing, high unemployment and emigration seem to be the result of government negligence and a lack of concern for peculiar Scottish conditions. Once more positive state action is demanded and, if necessary, discrimination in favour of Scotland. Scotland needs more industries, more roads, more subsidies and contracts, and the state must pay.

While most Scots would be happy to remain within the British state and to let it pay, a growing minority confidently claim that if Scotland were independent it would be better off financially and economically than it is at present. Unfortunately, no evidence can be produced to prove this argument, and the figures which are available show that Scotland receives more per head of population than England in a wide range of government expenditure. Another alternative is proposed of reconstituting the United Kingdom on a federal basis, giving Scotland, England, Wales and Northern Ireland 'home rule'. The main problem in the working-out of this scheme is the difficulty of counterbalancing 'the predominant partner' – England – with the other federal units, and fixing the division of powers between the central and regional governments in relation to taxation and the regulation of the economy. The devolution solution proposed in the Scotland Act 1978 was no less unsatisfactory, for very similar reasons, and proved to be unpopular with the people of Scotland in the Referendum of March 1979. The meaning of that vote will be discussed for some time, and there were both short-term and long-term factors at work to explain the mood of the electorate on that day. But it showed a clear division in Scotland, of long standing, between those who espouse what might be called a 'Little Scotland' philosophy, and those who value the escape channel to England. The historian Christopher Harvie has called this a division between 'black Scots' and 'red Scots' (Harvie, 1977, p. 17). Scottish politicians of the old school and most businessmen are unlikely to be content with a horizon of power restricted to Scotland, but a new political generation is rising which looks to Scotland as its arena of activity.

Undoubtedly, in many important respects, the destinies of Scotland and England have been well and truly linked together since the Union, so that undoing the bonds seems now almost impossible. It is not just that in the wars which Britain has fought Scots have shown themselves completely loyal and patriotic to the state, although this is significant. It is also that for centuries there has been an intermixing of Scots and English through marriage, migration and cultural influence which has profoundly affected the history of Britain. This cross-fertilisation of men and ideas has strengthened both Scotland and England, and it is essential to see the development of these countries, not in terms of a narrow nationalism, but as a process in which each has complemented the other. While Scotland gained from its entry to the imperial 'common market', England benefited from the influx of skilled and hardy pioneers to the colonies. In the Industrial Revolution of the late eighteenth and early nineteenth centuries, the technological strength of the Scottish educational system provided many of the inventors and scientists whose brains helped English (and Scottish) enterprise to capture the world's markets.

This was not the only contribution made by Scottish schools and universities to Britain. The Scottish ideal of widespread popular education was by no means accepted in England at the time of the Union, and the ancient English universities remained until the mid-nineteenth century part of the Anglican Establishment. English dissenters therefore came to Scotland, where the universities placed no religious barriers on entry. So too did many other Englishmen, such as Lord Melbourne, Lord Palmerston, Lord Brougham and Lord John Russell, pillars of the Whig Establishment of the Reform Bill era. The influence of Scottish ideas was great in this period: Adam Smith's free trade doctrines, and James Mill's and Joseph Hume's political radicalism. Much of the inspiration for British Liberalism in the nineteenth century came from Scotland, where an egalitarian society was further advanced. The example of the Scottish parish school system led Whitbread to demand a similar system for England in 1807, without success, and Jeremy Bentham, Joseph Hume and George Birkbeck were able to imitate the Scottish universities with the establishment in London in the 1820s of University College and Birkbeck College. From this time, other universities were established in England which adhered much more closely to the Scottish model than to Oxford and Cambridge; and more and more students at Scottish universities came from England, so that graduates from these universities made up a high proportion of the total for the country. A particularly high contribution has always been made by Scotland in the fields of medicine and science.

England's influence on Scotland is equally impressive. Scotland before the Union had been poor, unstable and dominated by religious feuds. After 1707, a new outlet for its energies was found in commerce, science and philosophy, and the civilising influence of a wealthy and well-governed neighbour soon penetrated to the north. At last, in 1745, the barbaric Highlands came within the political framework of the rest of the country, and the threat of civil war disappeared from Britain. Although England has not always taken kindly to Scottish immigrants (nor Scots to English), by the Victorian period Scots were firmly entrenched in English commerce and professions, and English capital was helping to finance Scottish development.

England has not influenced in any way the Presbyterian character of the Scottish Church, nor has Scotland ceased to be a much more church-minded country than England. However, intercommunication (if not intercommunion), especially in the twentieth century through mass media, has softened many of the rigours of the Scottish Sabbath and brought a more easy-going and secular atmosphere to Scottish life. Christmas, until recently virtually ignored, is now observed in Scotland, and many congregations in the Church of Scotland have adopted Anglican styles of ceremonial and choral responses. In education, the English tendency for specialisation at an early age has found some admirers in Scottish schools, but even more in the universities, where Honours degree courses are gradually replacing the general Ordinary degree courses. But Scottish education, like the Kirk, has proved resilient to attacks made on it, and there are still substantial differences between Scotland and England, both in the structure of the educational system and in the character of the teaching provided.

The Scottish legal system retains many of its distinctive features, but law as a whole is not the important influence on society that it was before the era of large-scale state intervention in the lives of the people. The welfare state and the controlled economy have increased the sphere of British law relative to that of Scots law, which is essentially concerned with private rather than with public law. While English legal reformers are now looking to Scots law for ideas, this has hardly ever happened in the past, for the law of Scotland has usually been treated in cavalier fashion by English legislators and judges, when they could get their hands on it. Scots lawyers often become quite nationalistic when discussing the virtues of 'their' system, but Scots as a whole are largely unaware of their legal birthright.

Finally, it may be that in government the example of Scotland will be used to establish a system of regional governments or administrations throughout England. This will probably not reach the heights of a federal system, but will attempt to match the (apparently) successful application of local knowledge and administration to local needs which has for years been the basis of Scottish government. It is too early to say how well this can operate within regions as ill-defined as those of England, which are not nations or even communities; but given the prevailing mood of widespread distrust of distant 'London' government, especially in the north and west of England, such a system may become a political imperative.

Scotland is physically further away from London than any region of England, and in other respects also it is less conscious of the metropolis, and has less feeling of inferiority towards it. This is partly because distance itself has allowed a distinct society, with its own life and its own capital city, to operate under its own momentum. While not completely self-contained, Scotland nevertheless has its communications media and social institutions to reinforce its national consciousness.

But is there not a national malaise in Scotland today? The emigration rates show deep dissatisfaction with the quality of life available in Scotland, and have contributed to the recent rise in nationalism, and the demand for devolution. Yet no one can be sure about the future of the Scottish National Party or devolution, for the reasons for voting Nationalist and supporting devolution are complex, and fluctuate dramatically. Even so, the desire to see more decisions taken in Scotland increases in proportion to the growth of 'big government'. This may not mean that Scots want to be distinct from the English: quite often it means the reverse, that they wish they were more the same, in economic opportunities, living standards and general cultural climate. Indeed, the process of assimilation within all modern societies seems likely to advance rapidly by popular demand.

Yet the history of Scotland since 1870 shows that this assimilation will probably show itself in some forms more than in others. For example, there has been a greater coming together in social habits than in social institutions. This is probably the clue to the future – the underlying structure of Scottish society will continue to alter in the direction of uniformity with Britain as a whole, but the formal symbols of Scottish nationhood, and the national consciousness of the Scottish people, will remain, and perhaps grow even stronger.

# References

Allen. 'Allen Report'. *Impact of Rates on Households,* Cmnd 2582 (London: HMSO, 1965).

Argyll. 'Argyll Commission'. *Schools in Scotland: Reports of Royal Commission,* First Report, HC Vol. 1865 XVII [3483]; Second Report, HC Vol. 1867 XXV [3845]; Third Report, HC Vol. 1867–8 XXIX [4011] (London: HMSO).

Arnold, M., *Arnold's Report to the English Schools Inquiry Commission,* HC Vol. 1867–8 XXVIII pt v [3966-v] (London: HMSO).

Balfour. 'Balfour Report'. *Scottish Affairs: Report of Royal Commission,* Cmnd 9212 (Edinburgh: HMSO, 1954).

Bogdanor, V., *Devolution* (Oxford: OUP, 1979).

Bowley, M., *Housing and the State, 1919–1944* (London: Allen & Unwin, 1945).

Brand, J., *The National Movement in Scotland* (London: Routledge & Kegan Paul, 1978).

Buckle, H. T., *History of Civilisation in England,* 1st edn, 1861, Vol. III (London: World's Classics, 1904).

Budge, I. and Urwin, D. W., *Scottish Political Behaviour* (London: Longmans, 1966).

Burleigh, J. H. S., *A Church History of Scotland* (London: OUP, 1960).

Burns, J. H., 'The Scottish Committees of the House of Commons, 1948–59', *Political Studies,* vol. 8 (1960), pp. 272–96.

Cairncross, A. K. (ed.), *The Scottish Economy* (Cambridge: CUP, 1954).

Cameron, G. C., and Reid, G. L., *Scottish Economic Planning and the Attraction of Industry* (Edinburgh: Oliver & Boyd, 1966).

Campbell, R. H., *Scotland since 1707* (Oxford: Blackwell, 1965).

Camperdown. 'Camperdown Report'. *Parliamentary and Municipal Elections: Report from Select Committee of the House of Commons,* HC Vol. 1870 VI [115] (London: HMSO).

Clement, A. G., and Robertson, R. H. S., *Scotland's Scientific Heritage* (Edinburgh: Oliver & Boyd, 1961).

Cooper, Lord, *The Scottish Legal Tradition,* Saltire Pamphlets no. 7 (Edinburgh: Oliver & Boyd, 1949); 4th edn, Saltire Pamphlet no. 1 (Glasgow: Clark, 1977).

Coupland, Sir R., *Welsh and Scottish Nationalism* (London: Collins, 1954).

Cox, J. T., *Practice and Procedure in the Church of Scotland* (Edinburgh: Church of Scotland, 1964; 6th edn, 1976).

Crapster, B., 'Scotland and the Conservative Party in 1876', *Journal of Modern History,* vol. 29 (1957), pp. 355–60.

Crewe, Marquess of, *Lord Rosebery*, 2 vols (London: Murray, 1931).
CSO. Central Statistical Office, *Economic Trends. Regional Statistics* (London: HMSO).
DAFS. Department of Agriculture and Fisheries for Scotland, *Types of Farming in Scotland* (Edinburgh: HMSO, 1952).
Davie, G. E., *The Democratic Intellect* (Edinburgh: University of Edinburgh Press, 1961).
Day, J. P., *Public Administration in the Highlands and Islands of Scotland* (London: University of London Press, 1918).
Department of the Environment, *Census Indicators of Urban Deprivation* (London: HMSO, 1975).
Donaldson, G., *The Scots Overseas* (London: Hale, 1966).
Drucker, H. M., *Breakaway: The Scottish Labour Party* (Edinburgh: EUSPB, 1978).
Drucker, N. and Drucker, H. M., *The Scottish Government Yearbook 1979* (Edinburgh: Harris, 1978).
Edwards, G. E., 'The Scottish Grand Committee, 1958 to 1970', *Parliamentary Affairs*, vol. XXV (1972), pp. 303–25.
Fearon, D. F., *Report for the English Schools Inquiry*, HC Vol. 1867–8 XXVIII [3966-v] (London: HMSO, 1868).
Ferguson, W., *Scotland: 1689 to the Present* (Edinburgh: Oliver & Boyd, 1968).
Ferris, P., *The Church of England* (London: Gollancz, 1962).
Fleming, J. R., *The Church in Scotland*, Vol. I, *1843–74*; Vol. II, *1875–1929* (Edinburgh: Clark, 1927, 1933).
Fraser, W. H., 'Scottish trades councils in the nineteenth century', *Bulletin of the Society for the Study of Labour History*, no. 14 (Spring 1967), p. 11.
Gallacher, W., *Revolt on the Clyde* (London: Lawrence & Wishart, 1936).
Gallacher, W., *Last Memoirs* (London: Lawrence & Wishart, 1966).
Gibb, A. D., *Scottish Empire* (London: Maclehose, 1937).
Gibson, A. H., *Stipend in the Church of Scotland* (Edinburgh: Blackwood, 1961).
Gilmour. 'Gilmour Report'. *Scottish Administration: Report of Committee appointed by the Secretary of State for Scotland*, Cmd 5563 (Edinburgh: HMSO, 1937).
Gollan, J., *Scottish Prospect* (Glasgow: Caledonian Books, 1948).
Haddow, W. M., *My Seventy Years* (Glasgow: Gibson, 1943).
Hanham, H. J., *Elections and Party Management: Politics in the time of Disraeli and Gladstone* (London: Longmans, 1959).
Hanham, H. J., 'The creation of the Scottish Office', *Juridical Review*, 1965, pp. 25–44.
Hanham, H. J., *Scottish Nationalism* (London: Faber, 1969).
Harvie, C., *Scotland and Nationalism: Scottish Society and Politics, 1707–1977* (London: Allen & Unwin, 1977).
Hechter, M., *Internal Colonialism: The Celtic Fringe in British National Development, 1536–1966* (London: Routledge & Kegan Paul, 1975).
Highet, J., *The Scottish Churches* (London: Skeffington, 1960).

Howie, R., *The Churches and the Churchless in Scotland* (Glasgow: Bryce, 1893).

Hughes, E., *Parliament and Mumbo-Jumbo* (London: Allen & Unwin, 1966).

Hunter, J., *The Making of the Crofting Community* (Edinburgh: Donald, 1976).

Hutchison, D. and McPherson, A. F., 'Competing inequalities: the sex and social class structure of the first year Scottish university student population, 1962–72', *Sociology*, vol. 10 (1976), pp. 111–16.

Jennings, Sir I., *Parliament*, 2nd edn (Cambridge: CUP, 1957).

Johnston, T., *Memories* (London and Glasgow: Collins, 1952).

Johnston, T. L., Buxton, N. K. and Mair, D., *Structure and Growth of the Scottish Economy* (London and Glasgow: Collins, 1971).

Kellas, J. G., 'The Liberal Party and the Scottish Church disestablishment crisis', *English Historical Review*, vol. 79 (1964), pp. 31–46.

Kellas, J. G., 'The Liberal Party in Scotland, 1876–96', *Scottish Historical Review*, vol. 45 (1965a), pp. 1–16.

Kellas, J. G., 'The Mid-Lanark by-election (1888) and the Scottish Labour Party (1888–94)', *Parliamentary Affairs*, vol. 18 (1965b), pp. 318–29.

Kellas, J. G., *The Scottish Political System*, 2nd ed. (Cambridge: CUP, 1975).

Kelsall, R. K., *Applications for Admission to Universities* (London: Association of Universities of the British Commonwealth, 1957).

Knox, H. M., *Two Hundred and Fifty Years of Scottish Education, 1696–1946* (Edinburgh: Oliver & Boyd, 1953).

Lenman, B., *An Economic History of Modern Scotland* (London: Batsford, 1977).

MacCormick, J. M., *The Flag in the Wind: The Story of the National Movement in Scotland* (London: Gollancz, 1955).

McCrone, G., *Scotland's Economic Progress, 1951–60* (London: Allen & Unwin, 1965).

McDonald, I. J., 'Educational opportunity at university level in Scotland', unpublished B.Ed. thesis, Glasgow University, 1964.

MacKay, D. I. (ed.), *Scotland: The Framework for Change* (Edinburgh: Harris, 1979).

Mackintosh, J. P., 'Regional administration: has it worked in Scotland?', *Public Administration*, vol. 42 (1964), pp. 253–75.

MacLaren, A. A., *Religion and Social Class: The Disruption Years in Aberdeen* (London and Boston: Routledge & Kegan Paul, 1974).

McLean, I. S., *Keir Hardie* (Harmondsworth: Allen Lane, 1975).

Maxwell, Sir H., *Evening Memories* (London: Maclehose, 1932).

Middlemas, R. K., *The Clydesiders* (London: Hutchinson, 1965).

Milne, Sir D., *The Scottish Office, and other Scottish Government Departments* (London: Allen & Unwin, 1957).

Mitchell, J. D. B., *Constitutional Law* (Edinburgh: Green, 1964).

Moffat, A., *My Life with the Miners* (London: Lawrence & Wishart, 1965).

Muir, A., *John White* (London: Hodder & Stoughton, 1958).

Muir, E., *Scott and Scotland: The Predicament of the Scottish Writer* (London: Routledge, 1936).

Nairn, T., 'The Festival of the Dead', *New Statesman*, vol. 74, 1 September 1967, pp. 265–6.

Nicolson, N., *Lord of the Isles* (London: Weidenfeld and Nicolson, 1960).

Norris, G., *Poverty in Scotland: An Analysis of Official Statistics* (Glasgow: University of Glasgow Department of Social and Economic Research Discussion Paper no. 17, 1977).

Omond, G. W. T., *The Lord Advocates of Scotland, 2nd series, 1834–1880* (London: Melrose, 1914).

Osborne, G. S., *Scottish and English Schools* (London: Longmans, 1966).

Payne, P. L. (ed.), *Studies in Scottish Business History* (London: Cass, 1967).

Pottinger, G., *The Secretaries of State for Scotland, 1926–76* (Edinburgh: Scottish Academic Press, 1979).

Reid, A. (ed.), *Why I am a Liberal* (London: Cassell, 1885).

Robbins. 'Robbins Report'. *Higher Education. Report of Committee, with Appendices*, Cmnd 2154 (London: HMSO, 1963).

Simpson, I. J., *Education in Aberdeenshire before 1872* (London: University of London Press, 1947).

Simpson, P. C., *Life of Principal Rainy*, Popular edn (London: Hodder & Stoughton, 1909).

Smith, T. B., *British Justice: The Scottish Contribution* (London: Stevens, 1961).

Smith, T. B., *Scotland: The Development of its Laws and Constitution* (London: Stevens, 1962).

Stuart, J. (Viscount), *Within the Fringe* (London: Bodley Head, 1967).

Symon, J. A., *Scottish Farming* (Edinburgh: Oliver & Boyd, 1959).

Toothill, J. N. (Chairman), *Report of the Committee of Inquiry into the Scottish Economy, 1960–1* (Edinburgh: Scottish Council (Development and Industry), 1961).

Urwin, D. W., 'The development of the Conservative Party organisation in Scotland until 1912', *Scottish Historical Review*, vol. 44 (1965), pp. 89–111.

Urwin, D. W., 'Scottish conservation: a party organisation in transition', *Political Studies*, vol. 14 (1966), pp. 145–62.

Wade, E. C. S. and Phillips, G. G., *Constitutional Law*, 6th edn cited (London: Longmans, 1960); 9th edn, 1977.

Walker, D. M., *The Scottish Legal System*, 2nd edn cited (Edinburgh: Green, 1963); 4th edn, 1976.

Webb, K., *The Growth of Nationalism in Scotland* (Glasgow: Molendinar Press, 1977; Harmondsworth: Penguin, 1978).

Willson, F. M. G., 'The organisation of British central government, January 1962–October 1964', *Public Administration*, vol. 44 (1966), pp. 73–101.

# Index

(Note: Major references in the principal entries are printed in **bold** type.)